# Kant's Dog

A volume in the SUNY series in
Latin American and Iberian Thought and Culture

---

Jorge J. E. Gracia and Rosemary Geisdorfer Feal, editors

# Kant's Dog

## On Borges, Philosophy, and the Time of Translation

DAVID E. JOHNSON

SUNY
PRESS

Cover art courtesy of Felipe Cooper. Boceto for "Aporia de un gesto" (watercolor and Chinese ink on paper), 12 × 16, 2011.

Published by State University of New York Press, Albany



Printed in the United States of America



For information, contact State University of New York Press, Albany, NY
www.sunypress.edu

Production by Diane Ganeles
Marketing by Michael Campochiaro

**Library of Congress Cataloging-in-Publication Data**

Johnson, David E., 1959–
Kant's dog : on Borges, philosophy, and the time of translation / David E. Johnson.
p. cm. — (SUNY series in Latin American and Iberian thought and culture)
Includes bibliographical references (p. ) and index.
ISBN 978-1-4384-4265-5 (hdbk : alk. paper) 978-1-4384-4264-8 (pbk. : alk. paper)
1. Borges, Jorge Luis, 1899-1986—Philosophy. 2. Kant, Immanuel, 1724–1804—Criticism and interpretation. 3. Philosophy in literature. 4. Translating and interpreting. 5. Argentine literature—20th century—History and criticism. I. Title.

PQ7797.B635Z73736 2012
868'.6209—dc23 2011031097

10 9 8 7 6 5 4 3 2 1

*for*

*Paula Cucurella Lavín*

*and*

*Thomas Simms Haydon, Jr.*
*30 July 1938 to 7 March 2007*

# Contents

# Acknowledgments

For more than a decade the Department of Comparative Literature at the University at Buffalo has been my intellectual and social home. I owe a tremendous debt of gratitude to Henry Sussman for making possible my move into Comparative Literature and for doing so with a grace and charm that are uniquely his.

Three people and one group deserve much of the credit (and bear none of the responsibility) for the book that follows.

I began to learn to read philosophy in the seminars of Rodolphe Gasché, whose teaching is exemplary not only for its clarity, rigor, and humor, but also for its insistent rejection of all discipleship. More importantly, for the last decade Rodolphe has demonstrated what it means to be a colleague and a friend. Without his and Bronia Karst's steady and delightful friendship, life in Buffalo would be poorer indeed.

I have no better or more loyal friend and interlocutor than Martin Hägglund, whose influence is legible in nearly every sentence of this book and, somewhat less obviously, in those he kept me from writing. The notes to and citations from his work are a minor indication of the importance of his thinking for my own. Since first drafting the entire manuscript, Martin has read and reread its pages. What I owe Martin could never be acquitted in a few words of acknowledgment; quite the contrary, my debt to him remains always before me.

For too short a time in Buffalo, Bill Egginton and I had an ongoing conversation about philosophy and literature—in particular about Borges, Kant, Heidegger, and Derrida—over beer, coffee, and wine, in his garden and my kitchen. We agree about very little except the importance of reading philosophy, taking Borges seriously, and laughing a great deal while doing so.

The University at Buffalo's Philosophical Reading Group nurtures the philopolemics that I most value in the academy. The PRG provides the space, if not for a nondisciplinary, at least for a nonauthoritarian reading of philosophy.

Earlier versions of chapters of this book were given as lectures at Cleveland State University; Duke University; The Johns Hopkins University; Cornell University; Universidad de Chile; and at the on-going Seminario Central de Investigación jointly organized by the Instituto de Arte, Pontificia Universidad Católica de Valparaíso, and the Doctorado en Filosofía con mención en Estética y Teoría del Arte of the Universidad de Chile. I thank those institutions and the faculty and students who attended the lectures for their kind hospitality. Most especially, I thank the friends who invited me: Stephen D. Gingerich, Alberto Moreiras, Bill Egginton, Richard Klein, Juan Manuel Garrido, Pablo Oyarzún, and Bruno Cuneo. I owe especial thanks to Juan and Pablo. During month-long stays in Santiago in July 2008 and June 2009, Juan welcomed me into his home and opened to me an entirely new world at the other end of the globe. The encounters I have had in Santiago haunt me still. No one is more committed to and takes more delight in friendship than Juan Manuel. The opportunity to present drafts of three of this book's chapters in Santiago provided the impetus to rethink and revise the entire project. I owe Pablo not only for giving me those opportunities but also for participating in them. Andrés Claro read the second chapter and made the kind of comments one hopes to receive.

Parts of this book have been published previously. Shorter and different versions of the introduction, and Chapters 1 and 3, have appeared under the following titles and in the following publications: "Introduction: Borges and the Letter of Philosophy" in *Thinking With Borges*, William Egginton and David E. Johnson, editors (Aurora, CO: The Davies Group Publishers, 2009), 1–17; "Time: For Borges" in *CR: The New Centennial Review* 9.1 (2009): 209–225; and "Kant's Dog" in *Diacritics* 34.1 (2004): 19–39. I thank the respective editors and publishers—the Davies Group Publishers, Michigan State University Press, and The Johns Hopkins University Press—for permission to reprint this material here.

For several years I shared my office and often my lunch with my son Isaac, from whom I have learned much about film, to be sure, but also about being a father and then a friend to a son. He is also a wonderful squash partner. Much of this book was first drafted one hot summer while my daughter Elena did math problems in the room next to my study. Over the course of that summer she kept me awake by forcing me to get up to make sure that she had not fallen asleep. I owe her for that, as well as for the incalculable joy she brings to my life. My son Christopher suggested that I gather into a book various texts I had written on Borges. It took far longer than either he or I imagined it would and, in fact, this is not that book, but writing it would not have occurred to me without his suggestion. I thank him for the idea as much as for his good company, and his delight in the Yankees, Kansas basketball, and red meat. If not for a phone call from my brother Tom late one night in September 1983, telling me to read Paul de Man, Jacques Derrida, and Michel Foucault, in all likelihood I would not do the work I do today.

I could not have asked for three more professional editors than Amanda Lanne, Beth Bouloukos and Diane Ganeles. Two anonymous readers for SUNY Press helped make *Kant's Dog* a better book. On very short notice, Felipe Cooper distilled a handful of concepts (writing, translation, repetition, *borrón*) into the painting that is reproduced on the cover of this book. I thank him for his contribution to the project and only hope the book lives up to his painting.

*Kant's Dog* is dedicated to two people.

To Paula Cucurella Lavín, whom I met in Santiago de Chile in July 2008 when I thought this book was nearly finished. During the years of rewriting and revision, Paula's embrace—often from several thousand miles away—provided the warmth for my life.

To the memory of Thomas Simms Haydon, Jr., my uncle Tommy, with whom, over the course of some fifteen years, along with my parents, Bob and Pauline Johnson, I traveled to various cities—New York, Los Angeles, Chicago, Detroit, St. Louis, Lexington, and Louisville—to watch Kansas and Kentucky basketball, eat, drink, and talk.

Buffalo, New York

# Introduction

# Philosophy, Literature, and the Accidents of Translation

The attempt to marginalize Borges's philosophical investment is widespread and often buttressed by his own statements.[1] For instance, in *Unthinking Thinking: Jorge Luis Borges, Mathematics, and the New Physics*, Floyd Merrell quotes Borges as saying that he is "neither a thinker nor a moralist, but simply a man of letters who turns his own perplexities and that respected system of perplexities we call philosophy into the forms of literature" (1991, ix).[2] On another occasion, in response to María Esther Vázquez's observation that the literary critic Anderson Imbert had argued that Borges was "a nihilist with vast knowledge of all philosophical schools" and that "in each of his stories he had attempted a different philosophical direction without participating vitally in any of them," Borges simply remarks, "I am neither a philosopher nor a metaphysician; what I have done is to exploit [*explotar*: also 'explode'], or to explore—a more noble word—the literary possibilities of philosophy" (Vásquez 1977, 105; my translation).[3] Moreover, of the claim that he was an idealist, Borges observes, "if I have a share in that philosophy, it has been for the particular propositions of the story and while I was writing it" (105). On more than one occasion Daniel Balderston has followed Chilean philosopher Carla Cordua, who, Balderston affirms, "argues that Borges was not a metaphysician and, hence, that for him 'the philosophical element, first isolated from its context and then treated not as a concept but as a thing or as a singular existing situation, is thus removed from its medium, separated from the function it had in that medium, and converted into an opaque sign, suggestive but in the final analysis undecipherable' " (1993, 140n8).[4] More recently Balderston has relied on Cordua in order to assert that "Borges does neither philosophy nor theory, but his texts take philosophy and theory as an object" (Balderston 2000, 154). But Cordua goes further than Balderston when she writes that Borges's statements that he is not a philosopher prove to be "immediately convincing and, moreover, the study of Borges's work confirms that he does not do philosophy [*inmediatamente convincentes y, además, el estudio de la obra de Borges confirma que allí no se trata de filosofía*]" (Cordua 1997, 118; my translation). Indeed, Cordua notes, when it was time to decide about Borges's relation to philosophy, "The best critics adopted, as was logical, these declarations [*Los mejores críticos adoptaron, como era lógico, estas declaraciones*]" (118). But Borges's statements are not *immediately* convincing, if only because there remain a few holdouts: "Almost all of us, save for a few notorious divergent opinions, are in agreement on this [*Casi todos, salvo por algunas pocas y notorias opiniones divergentes, estamos de acuerdo en esto*]" (118–19).

Why is it important for literary scholars to save Borges *for* literature and *from* philosophy? What is the philosophical contaminant that threatens to ruin literature? Where does one draw the line between literature and philosophy? What is a philosopher if not someone who reads philosophy, thereby taking the philosophical text "as an object," as Cordua and Balderston claim Borges does? But it is not only literary critics and scholars who patrol the border between literature and philosophy and who want to keep Borges on literature's side. Cordua, for one, is an important South American philosopher, author of major works on Hegel, Husserl, and Heidegger. How does exploiting and exploring—but also exploding—the *literary* possibilities of philosophy *not* amount to *doing* philosophy? Is the "philosophical element," as Cordua calls it, so easily determined, so easily isolated from its context and *not* treated as a concept? What concept, finally, is *not* opaque, suggestive but finally indecipherable, untranslatable? What is so unsettling about Borges that so many feel compelled to take a stand on where he stands? It is possible that Borges belongs on the list of those whose work, as Paul de Man put it, "straddles the two activities of the human intellect that are both the closest and the most impenetrable to each other—literature and philosophy" (de Man 103).

In her introduction to *Literary Philosophers: Borges, Calvino, Eco*, Carolyn Korsmeyer points out that one achievement of philosophical discourse is precisely "a certain detachability of philosophical content from its textual vehicle" (Korsmeyer 4). It is on this basis that Jorge J. E. Gracia distinguishes literature from philosophy and ultimately denies the Borgesian text, *qua* literature, entry to philosophy: "My thesis about philosophy and literature in general is that literary works are distinguished from philosophical ones in that their conditions of identity include the texts through which they are expressed. Moreover, literary texts are distinguished from philosophical ones in that they express literary works" (Gracia 86).

This understanding of the difference between philosophy and literature ultimately turns on the problem of translation. According to Gracia, the difference between philosophy and literature depends on the indissociability of the literary work and text. "A literary work is distinguished from a philosophical one in that its conditions of identity include the text of which it is the meaning. This is to say that the signs of which the text is composed, the entities of which these signs are constituted, and the arrangements of the signs and the entities that constitute the signs are essential to the literary work" (91).[5] Because literariness is defined as a constitutive relation between text and work, the literary work is necessarily singular: it cannot be divorced from its articulation. As a consequence, literary works are, *stricto sensu*, untranslatable.

This is not the case, however, for philosophical works: "It should not really matter whether I read Kant's *Critique of Pure Reason* in German or English (in fact, many believe it is better to read it in English). What should matter is that I get the ideas. The work is not essentially related to German, whereas Shakespeare's *Hamlet* could have been written only in English and Cervantes' *Don Quixote* could have been written only in Spanish" (91). The border dividing philosophy and literature is translation. Gracia interprets Gustav Mahler's statement, in a letter to his wife, that what is "peculiar"—most proper, but also what is singular—to works of art is their defiance of "rationality and expression," as meaning "that works of art are not reducible to ideas and, therefore, cannot be effectively translated" (85). The peculiarity or idiosyncracy of works of art lies in their idiomaticity or their textuality. They are, therefore, untranslatable as such. Gracia stipulates that the difference between philosophy and art or literature hinges on the possibility of translation: "Whereas art is irreducible to ideas and defies translation, philosophy is reducible to ideas and can be translated" (85). It follows from this that for Gracia translation is fundamentally a question of the transference or communicability of ideas pure and simple. A work of art—literature, say—does not attain a level of ideality sufficient to transcend and thus to relieve itself of its textuality or materiality. Literature cannot separate itself from the idiom in which it will have been written. By definition, literature is too idiomatic, too idiosyncratic. Philosophy, however, is so thoroughly ideal that it will never have had any necessary attachment to the language of its articulation. There is nothing idiomatic about philosophy, nothing peculiar or singular. For this reason, philosophy is essentially translatable. That is, according to Gracia, language is accidental to philosophy's articulation. He contends that because Kant's *work* is essentially reducible to ideas, his *text* should be translatable into any language without any loss of meaning. Precisely this possibility establishes Kant's work as philosophy. Because Borges's work is art, thus irreducible to ideas, it is essentially related to the idiom—the material or vehicle—of its articulation. In fine, Borges's *obra* is properly untranslatable, hence it is legible *only* in Spanish.

We should be sensitive to the implications of Gracia's parenthetical claim that "many believe it is better to read [Kant's *Critique of Pure Reason*] in English," because this comment unwittingly problematizes Gracia's avowed position. Inasmuch as philosophy expresses the ideas that remain essentially separable from the idiom in which they are articulated, it should not in fact make any difference in which language these ideas are either written or read. In other words, that the *Critique of Pure Reason* would be *more* legible or that it would be *better* to read it in English than in German means that English expresses Kant's ideas *more* clearly than does the language in which Kant both conceived and wrote his philosophy. The upshot is that both English and German affect Kant's ideas, which in principle are separable from and translatable into any particular language. Accordingly, it will be impossible to read Kant—and by extension any philosophical work—without being affected, *at the level of the idea* and thus at the level of philosophy, by the text, by the idiom in which the text takes place. The idiom makes a difference, and it does not simply make a difference in the *text*, but in the *work* as well. On Gracia's account, however, this is the condition not of philosophy but of literature, which means it is impossible either *to read* or *to write* (philosophy as) anything other than literature.

Gracia is not the only one to assess the possibility of philosophy by making an example of Kant.[6] Borges does so as well. Although he considered German the language of philosophy, he confessed that Kant should be read in *any* language *but* German insofar as not even Germans were able to read him (Borges 1999, 44).[7] Borges claims that the *Critique of Pure Reason* "quizás hubiera dejado perplejo al mismo Kant en muchos casos [perhaps, in many cases, left Kant himself perplexed]" (Vázquez 1984, 46; my translation). When applied to the criteria Gracia uses to distinguish philosophy from literature, the irony of this assertion becomes unmistakable. If German is *the* philosophical language, but Kant's *Critique of Pure Reason* can only be read in any language but German, then it follows that Kant does not write philosophy. Or he writes philosophy but in a language that obviates the possibility of reading the text *as* philosophy, and thus of its being understood *as* philosophy. In its original German articulation, the *Critique of Pure Reason* is *not* philosophy. At best it is literature.

If we were to make Borges's assertions conform to Gracia's distinctions there would be two consequences for the possibility of reading the *Critique of Pure Reason* as literature or philosophy. *First*, if the *Critique of Pure Reason* can only be read as literature, then Borges's determination that it is best read in any language but German will be impossible in that, *qua* literature, it will be properly untranslatable. Thus, it will only be readable as literature in the German that perplexed Kant. *Second*, it will never be readable *as* philosophy because, unreadable in German, it can make no claim to the universality necessary for philosophy. In other words, for Borges, Kant is legible *neither* as literature *nor* as philosophy. Kant's text is not legible *as literature* because, on the one hand, it cannot be read in the singular language that determines its peculiarity as art; and, on the other hand, it ought to be read in—and thus translated into—any other language. Nor is it legible *as philosophy* because, although it can be translated into and read in any other language, so long as it remains illegible in German, it is not universally translatable. Because it remains unintelligible in the German in which it was written and cannot be read, its idea is not universally communicable.

Gracia's distinction between literature and philosophy turns on two distinct relations between work and text. On the one hand, the work of literature (or of art in general) cannot be "reduced" to ideas pure and simple because the relation between the work and the text is necessary. On the other hand, the work of philosophy can be "reduced" to ideas; therefore, the relation between work and text is accidental. Yet the text nonetheless makes a difference such that the accidental relation between the work and the text of philosophy is in fact necessary. The accident is necessary. This does not mean that philosophy *is* literature, however. It means that the *inscription* of philosophy is necessary to the *work* of philosophy. Such inscription, which is necessarily material, and therefore spatial-temporally determined, is literary. It is not the case that philosophical ideas remain uncorrupted by their articulation in a particular idiom. As Gracia's text (perhaps unwittingly) makes clear, the idiom affects the idea. And insofar as the idiom affects the idea, the idea is irreducibly idiomatic and, therefore, idiosyncratic. Consequently, at the level of its articulation or expression, philosophy is irreducible to ideas pure and simple. The accident corrupts the idea (the essentially philosophical) enabling philosophy to articulate itself in the first place. The accident is necessary, but it nonetheless remains accidental in its determination of philosophy in that, *qua* necessary to the articulation of philosophy, it instances philosophy *as literature*. The instance or the accident of philosophy is the necessity of literature.

Yet, despite its necessity, according to Gracia's claim that the work of art is essentially idiomatic and untranslatable, literature is impossible. The criterion that the work of art be "effectively untranslatable," as Gracia puts it, means that the singularity of literature is such that it is incommunicable. If we take seriously Borges's claim in "Las versiones homéricas [The Homeric Versions]," that translation not only occurs between two languages but also within a single language, a position shared by Martin Heidegger, then the impossibility of translation signals the end of language.[8] Where there is no translation, there can be no language. It goes without saying that where there is no language, there can be no literature.

If it is the case that the relation between the work of art and the text is necessary, thereby obviating any translation of literature, it is no less the case that if there is literature (or art more generally), there *must* be translation. The work of art—the singular, idiomatic, idiosyncratic work—must be translatable. The untranslatable must be translatable. The impossible possibility of such translation means that the necessary or essential relation between work and text must be accidental. The necessary becomes accidental. The irreducible work of art must become the reducible work of philosophy as the condition of possibility of the work of art. In order to articulate itself, which requires the possibility of translation, literature must become philosophy. The possibility of literature, then, is its impossibility. The necessity of literature is the accident of philosophy. The conclusions that must be drawn from the aporias of Gracia's attempt to distinguish philosophy and literature according to their respective translatability is that both philosophy and literature are impossible as their condition of possibility. There is no philosophy that does not become literature and there is no literature that does not become philosophy. By necessity *and* by accident. In sum, translation is essential *and* accidental, *con*substantial *and in*cidental, *at the same time.*

From the very beginning, the accident is excluded from the highest form of philosophical inquiry, namely, the study of being *qua* being, which entails, according to Aristotle in the *Metaphysics*, the determination of "what it [being] is and the attributes which belong to it *qua* being" (1984, 1026a31–32/1620). The attributes or "elements [*stoicheia*]" (1003a30/1584) of being *qua* being must be necessary or essential to being; hence such elements cannot be "kata sumbebekós," by accident (1003a30/1584).[9] Being, or *ousia*, is that which presences in itself; as such, it cannot be affected by what is not essential to it. Walter Brogan explains: "*ousia* is *to ti en einai*, that which is always already there . . . in contrast, *sumbebēkos* is that which just happens to be together with that which is and is not itself a lying-forth on its own" (51). Brogan affirms that "the contrast" in Aristotle "is between beings that are in themselves, and the nonbeing that 'is' as *sumbebēkos*. That which is in the first sense is necessary; that which merely appears along with what is is a kind of nonbeing, what 'happens to be' along with what is" (66). The accidental therefore "is merely present *along with* what is and thus can be otherwise than it is" (70). It can be otherwise than it is because it is not in itself and thus does not endure. Nonbeing is the essential attribute of the accidental. That accidents are not *kata to auto*, but rather are always predicated of another, of a subject (*ei aeì tò sumbebekòs kath' hupokeiménon*) (Aristotle 1984, 1007a35–1007b1/1590), means that accidents are always *accidents* of being, of substance or of the subject. Accidents, therefore, are not themselves of the order of being. On the contrary, although the accidental may *be*, because it may also *not be*, it is rather of the order of nonbeing and, as such, Aristotle excludes the accidental from philosophy: "Since 'being' has many meanings, we must say regarding the accidental [*peri tou katà sumbebekòs lektéon*], that there can be no scientific treatment of it" (1026b3–4/1620–1).[10]

*Metaphysics* VI takes up where the first Western philosophical lexicon, *Metaphysics* V (the last entry of which concerns the accidental) leaves off: "We call an accident that which attaches to something and can be truly asserted, but neither of necessity nor usually" (1025a14–15/2.1619). Hence, Aristotle repeats, whatever "does not happen of necessity nor usually" (1025a20/1619) is an accident. An accident is that for which "there is no definite cause . . . but a chance cause, i.e. an indefinite one" (1025a25–6/1619). The accident happens by chance, *here and now*; it is unpredictable, unanticipatable. It takes the subject, the *hupokeimenon*—which Brogan interprets as "the givenness, the thereness, of what has come forth" (51)—by surprise.

Aristotle's determination that philosophy concerns what happens necessarily or for the most part does not translate into an opposition between philosophy and literature. On the contrary, in the *Poetics* Aristotle defines poetry (epic, tragedy, comedy) according to philosophy: "the poet's function is to describe, not the thing that has happened, but a kind of thing that might happen, i.e. what is possible as being probable or necessary. The distinction between historian and poet is not in the one writing prose and the other verse—you might put the work of Herodotus into verse, and it would still be a species of history; it consists really in this, that the one describes the thing that has been, and the other a kind of thing that might be" (1984, 1451a37–1451b5/2322–2323). "Hence," he concludes, "poetry is something more philosophic and of graver import than history, since its statements are of the nature rather of universals, whereas those of history are singulars" (1451b5–6/2323). Poetry is philosophical because it does not take up the accidents of history. Because poetry concerns the possible understood as what either necessarily or probably happens, in principle it is not surprising. Poetry that surprises its audience is an accident.

That the accident takes being by surprise, and thus always arrives from an unpredictable future, relates accidentality to time and thus to unpredictable alterity and alteration. It is this relation that is most important for understanding the relation of philosophy to literature—that the one *always* takes the other by surprise, surprising itself in doing so—as well as for any reading of Borges, whose *ficciones* often turn on the implacability of time and the unpredictability of an accident.[11]

In Aristotle, both the accident and time are conceived as nonbeing, thus unessential to being, which means time is an accident of being. But the accidental also singularizes the subject and does so precisely by opening it to the future. Accidents attach to the subject *here and now* in the subject's presence to itself. Nevertheless, insofar as the accidental may always not be, accidents attach to the subject without being determined by the horizon of the subject's *here and now* or present. Otherwise they would be essential to the subject. That is, it is always possible that accidents will not be *here and now*. "Therefore since there are attributes and they attach to a subject [*hupokeimenon*], and some of them attach in a particular place and at a particular time, whatever attaches to a subject, *but not because it is a subject*, at this time or in this place, will be an accident" (1025a21–25/1619, emphasis added). Without being essential or necessary to the subject, to that which lies-forth in presencing from out of itself or according to its own principle (*arche*), the accidental nonetheless instances (inscribes, marks) the spatial-temporal singularization of the subject.

Just as he excludes the accidental from philosophy arguing that there can be no science of what does not happen always or for the most part, Aristotle also excludes the singular from philosophical consideration. On Aristotle's account, "sensible individual substances" have neither "definition [*horismo*]" nor "demonstration [*apodeixis*]," because "they are capable both of being and not being; for which reason all the individual instances of them are destructible" (1039b28–30/1641). Aristotle thus concludes, "For perishing things are obscure to those who have knowledge of them, when they have passed from our perception. . . . Therefore when one of those who aim at definition defines any individual, he must recognize that his definition may always be overthrown; for it is not possible to define such things" (1040a2–7/1641–1642). The appearing of whatever appears *each time* that it appears is singular and therefore beyond definition. The singular is temporal; it perishes; it may or may not be. Hence any determination of the essence of the singular is subject to being overthrown in that the singular, what appears, can always not appear or appear otherwise. The existence of the singular, then, is accidental; and the accidental, inasmuch as it is always spatially-temporally determined, is singular. And neither the singular nor the accidental is of the order of being. Yet, insofar as the subject appears, it must be affected by accidentality and singularity. The *here and now*, the present of the subject is always marked by the accidental, the singular. In other words, the self-presencing of being, the necessity of *phusis* or *ousia* must always be read off from the spatial-temporal—thus accidental and singular—appearance of beings. According to Aristotle, although no accident is necessary to being, nevertheless, whatever *is* does not appear without the unnecessary and singular appearance of accidents. Being *as such* never appears outside accidental—spatial-temporal—determinations.

But if being cannot appear to itself or in itself, if it cannot present or represent itself to itself, if it cannot give itself to itself without or outside the mediation of the accident of appearing, *here and now*, if being always and only shows up and shows itself *here and now*, then it is clear that being never shows itself *in itself*. Rather, being always presents or represents itself *as* another, *as* something else, that is, *as something*. Being does not appear: it appears *as what is*, which means being happens *along with* the accidental appearance of *beings*. "What is" is accidental insofar as it can either be or not be, insofar as it can be otherwise than it is. Appearing is always accidental.

Although Heidegger does not arrive at the conclusion that being is always only accidental and that therefore it is never simply in itself, nonetheless this is the furthest implication of his understanding of the as-structure of language, of thought, and of being *as logos*. According to Heidegger, the as-structure of interpretation—the fact that Dasein encounters what is in the world with it *as something*—is nothing less than "the *a priori* existential constitution of understanding" (1996a, 140/149). He makes clear that the interpretation of " 'something as something' lies before a thematic statement about it"; hence, the as-structure is the condition of possibility of encountering something in the world: " 'what is' encountered in the world is always already in a reference which is disclosed in the understanding of world, a reference which is made explicit by interpretation" (140/150). Further, "Things at hand are always already understood in terms of a totality of reference. This totality need not be explicitly grasped by a thematic interpretation" (140/150). Heidegger points out, however, that the lack of an explicit statement does not obviate the necessity of the as-structure. On the contrary, "the simple seeing of things nearest to us in our having to do with . . . contains the structure of interpretation . . ." (140/150). The totality of reference, which is the world in which Dasein exists, is disclosed or discovered in the understanding of Dasein. This understanding is an existential possibility of Dasein. Put simply, where there is Dasein, there is world, that is, there is the totality of reference, which means that whatever is in the world with Dasein—whether so-called inner-worldly beings or other beings-in-the-world—appears there *as something*. According to Heidegger, the appearance—the discovery or disclosedness—of something as something is *meaningful*: "we say that they have *meaning*" (142/151). Heidegger contends, however, that "Strictly speaking, what is understood is not the meaning, but beings, or being" (142/151). This is so because "meaning is an existential of Dasein, not a property which is attached to beings, which lies behind them or floats somewhere as a 'realm between.' Only Da-sein 'has' meaning in that the disclosedness of being-in-the-world can be 'fulfilled' through the being discoverable in it" (142/151).

The importance of this is difficult to overstate. Meaning is always my own, always Dasein's. Meaning is not a property, an attribute, of what is discovered in the world; rather it is the mode of its being discovered. In other words, when Dasein understands those beings in the world—whether inner-worldly beings or other beings-in-the-world—what Dasein in fact understands are not only beings, but being itself. Being, then, is discoverable in the world *as something*. But *as such*, being cannot be thought as enduring presencing, as presence in itself. Or, rather, it can only be thought *as* such. As something, being exists and whatever exists comes to be and passes away. And whatever comes to be and passes away is affected by another. That is, being *as such* is only *as if* it were.[12] Thus, being is an accident.

The as-structure is consubstantial to the possibility of being *qua ousia*, *qua logos*. It is impossible to posit being without recourse to the *as* that displaces it in order to locate it in the first place. The as-structure necessarily opens being, *logos*, to translation and therefore to accidentality. Pablo Oyarzún writes, "The 'as' is the thesis of a commensurability, placed—but with nothing more to prop it up than our obstinate and fragile zeal—there where only slippage rules" (2009, 258; my translation). The *as* (*como*) provides what Oyarzún calls "a limited confidence": "With the 'as' or 'like' we believe to have given a structure to translation, and perhaps to language: we persuade ourselves that the structure of translation, and perhaps of language itself, is comparative, analogical. The text that I read here . . . is like the text that is there in the distance of another language" (258). The *as* figures the limited confidence of translation even as it signals its fundamental insecurity, for the *as* (and therefore translation) takes place where only displacement (*desliz*: slippage) rules. If the *as* instances translation as essential displacement, which at the same time provides and undermines the place of whatever appears and of whatever is said, then translation, strictly speaking, does not take place. Translation *literally* never shows up. Oyarzún contends, correctly, "translating, we are always on one side or the other, but never in the passage" (258). Consequently, he notes: "There is no way to make a thesis of translation. It is, in essence, the no-position, pure arbitrariness" (250). There is translation, but translation is never *in itself* or *as such*. It has no being, no essence, no substance.

*On the one hand*, the absolute and universal demand for translation means that translation (the movement of the *as*) is necessary. No one and no thing is exempt from translation, which means translation does not depend upon the volition of the subject. *On the other hand*, because translation is not in itself, because it always comes from another, it happens arbitrarily, accidentally, by chance. It comes as a surprise. Thus, the absolute and universal demand for translation takes place, if it ever does, singularly, without precedent.

According to Gracia's distinction between philosophy and literature, the *taking place* of translation, the *accident* of translation, *qua* singular, names the taking place of literature. *As such*, the singular and accidental *taking place* of translation is untranslatable. The absolute and universal demand for translation demands the untranslatable.[13] Only the untranslatable is translatable. This is what is at stake in Oyarzún's proposal to call the *lapsus* between one language and another, which is the *no-place* of translation, "the *individual*: that which hides [*se hurta*] in language, the untranslatable" (259). *Hurtarse* means "to hide" or "to withdraw." In its nonreflexive, transitive form *hurtar* means "to steal," "to withdraw, deflect," but also "to plagiarize." Singularity thus instances an improper relation to the other, a theft, an unauthorized and unacknowledged, an illegitimate citation or repetition of the other. It is worth recalling that Borges once remarked that all his stories were plagiarized: "Yes, plagiarized, like all of mine [*Sí, plagiado, como todos los míos*]" (Vázquez 1984, 115).

Whenever and wherever one writes, one writes in translation. That is the law of inscription, the law of writing and the law of the letter. It is the letter of the law. In Spanish *letras* signifies not only literature (*belles lettres*), but also letters, alphabetic characters, the substance of writing. In the singular, *letra* also means handwriting. One writes in a language—in a character or hand—that is not one's own in order to write one's *own* language in the first place. One's own language is always cited, stolen, plagiarized from the other. What is most proper, what is most one's own, what is most idiosyncratic or peculiar, is also necessarily what is most foreign. This holds not only for language and letters, but also for the one who writes. The connection between letters (*letras*)—alphabetic script and literature—and the technicity of inscription (*letra*: handwriting) ought not to be dismissed. As handwriting or penmanship, *letra* refers to a technology or a mechanism of inscription and the production of identity. One is known by one's hand: the signature, the mark, is binding. And one always writes in another's hand; one always already trespasses the limit of one's own signature and does so as the condition of possibility of the signature. My signature is a forgery. There is no other way to sign my name.

In a witty turn in a text devoted to Borges's "Pierre Menard," Daniel Balderston draws attention to Menard's "suppressed" work: "The *Zeitgeist* did, however, preside over a publication by Menard that the author of the obituary saw fit to pass over in silence, *L'Ecriture et le subconscient: Psychanalyse et graphologie* [Writing and the Unconscious: Psychoanalysis and Graphology] (1931)" (1993, 35). Balderston's project in *Out of Context* is to historicize—albeit creatively—Borges's *ficciones*, thereby taking a stand against the dominant "irrealist" tendency in Borges criticism, a tendency that Balderston admittedly shared.[14] Balderston identifies the historical Pierre Menard, "a lesser disciple" (35) of Freud, as the fictional Pierre Menard, which means Balderston practices the literary-critical methodology suggested by the narrator at the end of "Pierre Menard": namely, anachronistic attribution, as if Pierre Menard were Pierre Menard. The importance of Balderston's account depends on its turn to graphology, to the science of handwriting, which is the science of the inscribed or written letter, the *letra.* Graphology is the science of the singular.[15]

Balderston points out that the author of *L'Ecriture et le subconscient* insists "on the importance of contingency in the study of personality: an individual does not have a single script, but instead the handwriting will vary to show the impact of circumstance" (1993, 37). Indeed, Balderston argues: "Menard's greatest insight is that everything matters in handwriting analysis" (38). He quotes from Menard's "suppressed" work: "Neither in graphology nor in psychoanalysis are there insignificant signs; all signs acquire importance depending on the manner in which one knows how to examine and interpret them and reconnect them to general causes" (Menard, *L'Ecriture* 142; quoted in Balderston 1993, 38). There are no insignificant signs, but their significance, both their importance and their meaning, depends on interpretation. The significance of the sign, of the letter, depends on its subordination to the "general cause." The singular inscription—the autograph, say, or the signature—becomes meaningful only insofar as it is comprehended under a category. According to Balderston, Menard "urges his readers to undertake the very exercise to which he devoted himself for so many years—copying: 'To fully be cognizant of all of the peculiarities of a script, a good method consists in tracing it and reproducing it with a pen. In this fashion, one sees the differences that exist between the original and the copy or reproduction' " (1993, 38; Balderston quotes Menard 49).

In his attempt to establish the historical reference of "Pierre Menard," Balderston seeks to secure the difference between the original and the copy, something that cannot be done on the basis of the letter alone. This is because the letter is never alone. The letter is never *in itself.* Because the letter—whether graphic sign, literature, or handwriting—depends on translation, which means the letter is always already in translation. The letter is always double, always already dubbed, foreign to itself, divided in itself. The inscription of the original marks out, erases the original. Tracing the original—copying it, plagiarizing it—*both* inscribes it as original *and* erases it.

On the one hand, the meaning of letters—of literature and of alphabetic signs, of the hand—depends on the general category, on the universalization that is only possible on condition of the subordination or forgetting of the letter's inscription, its singularity. On the other hand, singularity—the marking or tracing of the letter, of the hand—makes possible the self-identity of the letter, making possible its ideality and universalization by constituting the letter as divided in itself. There is no general category, thus no meaning, *before* inscription, *before* singularity. The letter makes meaning possible, but the law of the letter—namely that it is marked by translation and therefore never in itself—makes the letter *as such* impossible.

The fact that Borges always located philosophy or metaphysics within the genre of fantastic literature does not mean he did not take philosophy seriously. It means he did not conceive them as simply opposed to one another. In response to a question concerning the theme of identity, Borges notes, "It is another of the essential themes, which would comprehend the uncertainty and the bifurcations of identity" (Vázquez 1984, 145). In the context of his discussion of a pantheistic idea of identity promulgated in India and rationalized, he says, by Spinoza, Borges adds: "here we see how fantastic literature can become confused with philosophy and with religion, which are perhaps other forms of fantastic literature" (145). Elsewhere he observes that in an anthology of fantastic literature that he edited with Bioy Casares, they left out several of the major practitioners of the genre, including Kant and Hume. In "Tlön, Uqbar, Orbis Tertius," he claimed that in Tlön, "all philosophy is by definition a dialectical game, a *Philosophy of As If*" (1996, 1.436/CF 4). The "philosophy of as if" is the title of Hans Vaihinger's 1911 neo-Kantian treatise in which he argues that although we cannot know the external world, we nevertheless produce "as if" models of reality, illusions, which we then take for reality. Our relation to the world, therefore, is illusory, fictive. Although Vaihinger's reading of Kant is suspect, to say the least, nevertheless, as Derrida notes, the *as if* plays a "decisive and enigmatic role" in Kant's system (2005b, 168n52).

In Kant, the *as if* describes the operation of the regulative Ideas of reason, which provide for the unity of experience but which cannot be derived from experience. In other words, the cognition of nature or of experience provides an *empirical* manifold that cannot give the *transcendental* rule for its own unification and thus provides no principle of purposiveness in itself. Regulative Ideas posit the *telos* or finality of nature such that nature can be comprehended *as if* it were organized according to a finality or purposiveness inherent to it. The difficulty, according to Kant, arises when one thinks that such Ideas can be derived from experience and that they are thus the effect of the understanding. But if the Idea of the purposiveness of nature is not derived from concepts of the understanding, nor does it result from practical reason. Kant explains: "The purposiveness of nature is thus a special *a priori* concept that has its origin strictly in the reflecting power of judgment. For we cannot ascribe to the products of nature anything like a relation of nature in them to ends, but can only use this concept in order to reflect on the connection of appearances in nature that are given in accordance with empirical laws. This concept is also entirely distinct from that of practical purposiveness (of human art as well as of morals)" (2000, 68/5:181). Although the concept of the purposiveness or end (*telos*) of nature does not derive from a practical judgment (and thus from a concept of practical reason) it is nonetheless, Kant remarks, "certainly conceived of in terms of an analogy with that" (68/5:181). It is clear that the Idea in the Kantian sense is neither a determinate concept (a concept of experience) nor a practical one; "it is neither a *concept of nature* nor a *concept of freedom*" (Derrida 2001b, 211). This means that regulative Ideas are neither of the order of pure reason nor of practical reason; they derive neither from concepts of the understanding nor from the moral law. Thus, they cannot be said to originate in either sensibility (in which all cognitions of experience must be grounded) or intelligibility (where moral judgments originate without any sensible or pathological contamination). Indeed, Kantian Ideas trouble both these orders of decision. Derrida concludes that "although Kant does not say as much . . . this 'as if' would itself be something like an agent of deconstructive ferment, since it in some way exceeds and comes close to disqualifying the two orders that are so often distinguished and opposed, the order of nature and the order of freedom" (2001b, 211).

The *as if* ruins—even as it articulates and makes possible—the all-too-often opposed logics of structure (system) and decision (agency or singularity). It does so, moreover, by opening onto fantasy, that is, the imagination (*phantasía*). This is what is at stake in Borges's remark that all of his stories were plagiarized, copied, from another. They were, he confessed, "plagiarized from reality, which, in its turn, has plagiarized a story. One lives stealing. Stealing air in order to breathe. . . . All the time one is receiving foreign things. . . . One could not live even a minute if one were not receiving" (Vázquez 1984, 115). From Aristotle to Kant, the imagination mediates the sensible and the intelligible, the faculties of sense and the understanding, without belonging to either. The imagination is nothing but such mediation; it names the exposure to the other. We are always receiving, in short, from the other. Life is borrowed, stolen, plagiarized from the other. The other is before us: we always write in its name, under its auspices. We live always under a pseudonym, a pen name.

If the imagination is that which opens us to the other as the condition of possibility of life, it follows that life is fundamentally aesthetic, which gives a somewhat different sense to Borges's claim that he is interested in exploring the aesthetic possibilities of philosophy. The fantastic, therefore, is the only possible genre, not only of literature, but also of thought and of life. There is no writing, no thought, no experience, without the operation of *phantasía*, without the mediation of the imagination. Not only, then, is there no literature, no philosophy, but there is no auto-affection—no auto-biography—without the imagination's constitutive—absolute and universal—opening toward the other. Life, then, is symbolic. This is the upshot of Borges's understanding of the all-encompassing "genre" of the fantastic. It is the upshot as well of Derrida's contention that "[a]uto-affection is a universal structure of experience," and that "[a]ll living things are capable of auto-affecting" (1974, 165). Auto-affection is another name for symbolizing. If all living beings must be capable of auto-affection, that is, if "[a]uto-affection is the condition of an experience in general" (165), in that it makes possible exposure to an exteriority in general, then it follows that life is symbolic.

The imagination names inscription. It names the mediation that constitutes and ruins, at the same time and in the same stroke, the possibility of sense perception and cognition, of singularity and universality. This is what Borges means when he cites David Hume, who famously awakened Kant from his dogmatic slumber, as having said, "I am a philosopher when I write" (Vázquez 1977, 105–106). On the one hand, writing leaves the trace of singularity; on the other hand, it lays claim to a necessary ideality and universality. It provides for the possibility of identity. I am a philosopher (*only*) when I write: writing identifies me as a philosopher, makes me identifiable *as such* among others. The possibility of this identity is the determination of an ideality that permits the repetition necessary to the production of identity. Writing produces the possibility of abstraction, of universality, of ideality; writing holds together or collects Hume's "bundle" of perceptions into an identity (1978, 252; quoted in Borges 1996, 2.146/SNF 328). Insofar as it necessarily functions in the absence both of the one who writes and the one who reads, the graphic mark, the inscription, makes possible the endurance over time necessary for the possibility of identity. Only because the mark is not *in itself* is it possible for one mark to relate to another mark *as* to itself, *as if* it were the same, such that identity becomes possible.[16]

Yet, the graphic mark also and necessarily happens *here and now* for the first and last time, singularly. As the inscription of singularity, the graphic mark always happens by accident, by chance. The mark is necessarily fungible. It can be erased. It erases itself in its own inscription and in doing so it *necessarily and automatically* erases any relation either to the one who writes or to the one who reads the mark. At stake here is the singular, hence accidental, inscription of the philosopher and of philosophy and, at the same time and in the same place, the necessary universalization of such inscription. There is no inscription that does not bear the mark of this double gesture. Every letter inscribes singularity and universality, literature and philosophy, accident and necessity.

In order to spell out the aporetic structure of the mark, it is worth considering one of Borges's best-known fictions. "The Library of Babel" outlines the total library, which some call the universe. The library's physical organization of identical hexagons whose interiors are also uniform allows the narrator to discern certain incontrovertible principles of the library's structure. For instance, "*The Library is a sphere whose exact center is any hexagon and whose circumference is unattainable* [*inaccesible*]" (1996, 1.466/CF 113) and "The Library is endless [*interminable*]" (1.465/CF 113). This endlessness coupled with the internal structure of each hexagon—five shelves per wall, thirty-two books per shelf, four hundred pages per book, forty lines per page, eight letters per line—enables the narrator to *remember* certain axioms. The first is that the library "has existed *ab aeternitate* [*existe ab eterno*]" (1.466/CF 113). The second is that there are twenty-five orthographic symbols. The discovery of a book "containing almost two pages of homogeneous lines" and the insight of "a librarian of genius" (1.467/CF 114) made possible the discovery of "the fundamental law of the Library," namely, "that all books, however different from one another they may be, consist of identical elements: the space, the period, the comma, and the twenty-two letters of the alphabet" (1.467/CF 114). On the basis of the elemental identity of all books, the librarian "also posited a fact which all travelers have since confirmed: *In all the Library, there are no two identical books*" (1.467/CF 114–115). The librarian thus deduces "that the Library is 'total'—perfect, complete, and whole—and that its bookshelves contain all possible combinations of the twenty-two orthographic symbols (a number which, though unimaginably vast, is not infinite)—that is, all that is able to be expressed, in every language, *All*" (1.467/CF 115). Henry Sussman points out that the library's totality "result[s] . . . from the combinatory potential of the orthographic symbols," which means creativity is "automatic and accidental" (156). Creativity is automatic (or necessary) in that it does not depend on the volition of the individual (or even collective) author for its production and determination. Every book is an instance of a generative machine that cannot not produce every possible combination according to the logic of the book: the calculable distribution of the same variables. At the same time, however, insofar as the production of each singular text is random and without intention, it is arbitrary and accidental.

The upshot of the library's totality is that, by definition, the library is autonomous, self-contained, *in itself*. Its border or limit is absolute. The library has no outside.[17]

The library contains a single instance of all that it is possible (*dable*), which is to say *given* to express. There are no copies. There is no exact repetition. Every instance is singular. Whatever the library contains is absolutely singular despite the uniformity of its presentation. *Expresar* means to manifest something in words or gestures, by signs. The library's totality thus extends to all that it is possible, given, to express: to write, to say, to think. The narrator recognizes the problem this poses: "To speak is to commit [*incurrir en*] tautologies. This pointless, verbose epistle already exists in one of the thirty volumes of the five bookshelves in one of the countless hexagons—as does its refutation" (1.470/CF 117–118).

In the impossible possibility of repetition, of tautology, of citation, which is also and always plagiarism, the limit of the library shows itself. On the one hand, the library cannot be total unless it contains all that it is possible to express. The library is only closed, total, insofar as it contains everything, insofar as everything is given or present in it. Therefore, self-expression—the unpredictable, unanticipatable and accidental, the singular, articulation of one's *own* thoughts and of one's *own* self—must be possible or the library would not be total. It would rather be determined by the exclusion of such articulation. On the other hand, insofar as the library already contains all that is given to express, any self-expression necessarily repeats what the library already contains and therefore opens the library to citation or repetition, thus to an outside that effectively destroys the library. The possibility of the library's closure, the possibility of its totality or absolution, is therefore *structurally* impossible. The instant in which the library closes upon itself—this instant *here and now*—is the instant in which the library repeats or cites itself in the singularity of one's *own*—idiomatic—expression, and thus exposes itself to what it is not. Repetition constitutes and conserves the library at the same time that it destroys it by exposing it to what cannot be contained in it. Every expression articulates—inscribes and erases—the limit, the border, of the library. And this articulation is always both *necessary* and *accidental* to the library. It is *both* the structural possibility of the library *as* universal *and* the accidental articulation of the library *as* particular or singular.

In the epiloque to the *Obras completas* version of *Otras inquisiciones* Borges writes that one of the tendencies he discovered while correcting the proofs of the "miscellaneous works of this volume" was "to esteem religious and philosophical ideas for their aesthetic value and even for what they contain of the singular and the marvelous." This, he says, is perhaps the index (*indicio*) "of an essential skepticism" (2.153). It would be a mistake to dismiss too quickly Borges's investment in religious (or theological) and philosophical ideas on account of his interest in their aesthetic value. At issue in this investment in the aesthetic is the singular and the marvelous. The aesthetic signals the *sensible* inscription of the philosophical and theological idea. As sensible, the inscription is singular, marvelous. A marvel is precisely *extraordinary*, that which is both unexpected, *more than* or *beyond* the ordinary (a marvel always comes as a surprise); and that which is *extra* ordinary, *more* ordinary than the ordinary. At stake, then, is the extraordinary inscription of the idea: Philosophy's inscription as the *extra*ordinary and as the extra*ordinary*. There is no philosophy, no idea, without such inscription; no philosophy without singularity and marvel.

But nor is there the ordinary without marvel, without singularity. The ordinary, the everyday, is also singular, marvelous. The ordinary, insofar as it comes to pass, is extraordinary, hence surprising, unexpected, incalculable, without precedent. Whatever happens, if anything happens, comes as a surprise. But because whatever happens is surprising, singular and marvelous, it also indicates an essential skepticism because the ordinary, the everyday, no longer has any determinate ground. The extraordinariness of the ordinary, the singularity and marvelousness of the everyday, means that whatever happens does so always without anticipation. In other words, whatever happens, whatever comes, the ordinary extraordinary or the extraordinary ordinary, does so by accident, by chance, in every case singularly, marvelously. The most ordinary is marvelous, singular. It is the *inscription*—the singularization—of being.

*Kant's Dog* teases out the implications of the accidents of translation. It remarks the impossible relation between the singular or the accidental and the universal or the necessary. Chapter 1, "Time: For Borges," takes its point of departure from Borges's consistent position that the fundamental problem "for us" is time or what he calls the contradiction between the identity that endures and the time that passes away. The chapter pursues Borges's determination of time in order to demonstrate that in his most explicit statements about time, Borges often repeats its most classical philosophical definition. And yet in every case the Borgesian text also provides the resources for thinking against the philosophical or metaphysical understanding of time. Chapter 1 establishes the temporal logic that organizes the interpretations of Borges and philosophy throughout the remainder of *Kant's Dog*. After describing the logic of temporality that explains the apparent contradiction between identity and temporality, "Time: For Borges" elaborates the logics of impossibility, the promise, and survival, all of which follow from the structure of time and each of which plays an important role in the chapters that follow. Indeed, the ensuing chapters demonstrate that Borges consistently deploys the logic of temporality that follows ineluctably from his understanding of the intractable contradiction of temporal succession and identity in order to re-mark—to respond to, to trace, to reinscribe—classic philosophical problems. For instance, Chapter 2, "Belief, in Translation," rethinks the stakes and logic of translation in order to reconsider the relation of translation and original. Through readings of "Las versiones homéricas [The Homeric Versions]" and "Pierre Menard, Author of the *Quixote*," the chapter problematizes the conditions of identity and authority. Central to this chapter is an analysis of time in Hume's *A Treatise of Human Nature*, in which it becomes clear that Hume's empiricism ineluctably grounds itself in something other than experience, namely, in the enigmatic translating operation of the imagination. Chapter 3, "Kant's Dog," takes up in detail the relation of sensibility and the understanding to temporal synthesis by reading in "Funes el memorioso [Funes the Memorious]" an oblique reference to Kant's description of the synthesis of time in the operation of transcendental schematism. Taken together Chapters 2 and 3 offer a sustained assessment of the limits of empiricism and transcendentalism. At stake in Chapter 2 is the impossibility in Hume, but also in Borges's "Pierre Menard," of constituting the empirical impression—which for Hume is the ground of all possible experience—without recourse to the figure of a necessarily nonempirical belief. In Chapter 3, in Kant, but also in Borges's "Funes," the issue is the discernment of the necessarily empirical inscription of the operation of transcendental schematism. In short, the logic of temporality implicitly at work in the Borgesian text challenges the limits of the transcendental and the empirical.

The first three chapters of *Kant's Dog* argue that the time of translation, which informs at the same time the universal demand for translation and its singular impossibility, structures the entire Borgesian archive and, as well, corrupts the distinction between necessity and accidentality, transcendental and empirical, philosophy and literature. Chapters 4 and 5 spell out the implications of the logic of translation for the possibility of decision (hospitality, justice) and the name of God. The Afterword pursues the aporetic logic of translation toward the question of the secret and the possibility of culture.

Chapter 4, "Decisions of Hospitality," begins with a consideration of the problem of the temporality of metaphor in Borges and Aristotle. Following a suggestion of Borges, the chapter turns to the metaphor of hospitality and to the temporal structure of decision in order to establish the parameters for an interpretation of "The Garden of Forking Paths" and its determination of the time of the possible. Chapter 5, "Idiocy, the Name of God," reads across Borges's interest in the religions of the book (Christianity, Islam, Judaism) in order to think through his investment in the name of God and to rethink the limits of the idiom and the *idios*. Finally, the Afterword, "The Secret of Culture," expounds the logic of the secret in order to argue that Borges proposes a relation to the other that—in the figure of the secret, despite all necessary calculations and precautions—remains singular, incalculable, and in jeopardy.

*Kant's Dog* is not simply expository. On the contrary, it pursues a reading strategy that might best be characterized as accidental. Every chapter opens onto the singular, the contingent, following a minor detail, an arbitrary reference, in order to read in—and at the constitutive limit of—the Borgesian archive, its philosophical, hence its *fantastic*, interlocutors. If it is true that metaphysics belongs to the genre of fantastic literature, then the Borgesian text must of necessity be inscribed within the horizon of metaphysics. It is this double inscription of literature and philosophy—each inscribed at the limit of the other—that *Kant's Dog* seeks both to demonstrate and to perform. It does so by translating literature *into* and *as* philosophy, philosophy *into* and *as* literature. As if there were literature, as if there were philosophy—the traces of each remaining *in* and *as* the other.

# 1

# Time: For Borges

In the Prologue to the *Obras completas* version of *El otro, el mismo* (The Other, the Same), Borges ascribed his preference for this collection of verse to the fact that it encompassed all of his literary obsessions: "There, likewise, are my habits: Buenos Aires, the cult of the elders, Germanic studies [*la germanística*], the contradiction of time that passes and the identity that endures, my stupor at the fact that time, our substance, can be shared" (1996, 2.235). The items in this list might be generalized in the following terms: space (Buenos Aires), the archive of cultural secrets ("the cult of the elders"), philosophy (Germanic studies), time, identity, and the possibility of community. That these are Borges's principal concerns is undeniable, but he does not accord each of these obsessions equal importance.

Borges underscores the importance of the problem of time and identity by repeatedly insisting that time is the fundamental problem of metaphysics. At the University of Belgrade in 1978, in a lecture entitled "Time [El tiempo]," he concluded: "time is an essential problem. I mean that we cannot do without time. Our consciousness is continually passing from one state to another, and that is time: succession" (4.199). Moreover, he suggests that were we to have only one sense, that of hearing, for example, and were we to imagine our perception of the world on the basis of this sense alone, although we would be unable to perceive space, "[i]n that world, nevertheless, we would always have time. Because time is succession" (4.198).

The privileging of time over space means that the "congenital idealism" of the inhabitants of Tlön is *our* idealism: "For the people of Tlön, the world is not an amalgam of *objects* in space; it is a heterogeneous series of independent *acts*—the world is successive, temporal, but not spatial. There are no nouns in the conjectural *Ursprache* of Tlön [*El mundo para ellos no es un concurso de objetos en el espacio; es una serie heterogénea de actos independientes. Es sucesiva, temporal, no espacial. No hay sustantivos en la conjectural Ursprache de Tlön*]" (1.435/CF 72–73). Temporal succession makes the self-identity of the substantive—that is, substance—possible. However ironically presented, the critique of the doctrine of materialism, which depends on identity over time and thus on spatiality, spells out the consequences of idealism's necessary privileging of temporal succession over spatial perdurance (1.435/CF 75). In "A New Refutation of Time," however, without attempting to establish the priority of space, Borges nonetheless challenges both Berkeley's and Hume's assertion that according to their respective temporal logics, neither could support the thought of identity.

The distinction between space and time can be read in an anecdote Borges related to Carlos Peralta: "an Argentine philosopher and I were talking about time, and the philosopher said: 'We have made a lot of progress in that in the last years.' And I thought that if I had asked him about space surely he would have answered: 'We have made a lot of progress in that in the last blocks'" (Irby 108, my translation).[1] In both cases the philosopher measures progress according to the particular intuition of sense under discussion, as if the measurement of space and time were absolutely discrete, as if it were possible to progress over the last few years without a spacing of time; or, alternatively, as if it were possible to progress through the last few blocks without a temporalization of space.

Although the joke is on the philosopher, Borges in fact does not object to the logic that conceives space and time as distinct from one another. A few years earlier, during a "conversation" at New York University, he observed, "I tend to be always thinking of time, not of space. When I hear the words 'time' and 'space' used together, I feel as Nietzsche felt when he heard people talking about Goethe and Schiller—a kind of blasphemy. I think that the central riddle, the central problem of metaphysics—let us call it thinking—is time, not space. Space is one of the many things to be found inside of time—as you find, for example, color or shapes or sizes or feelings" (Christ 400–1). In the same vein, in the lecture on time Borges argues that it is possible "to do without space, but not time, in our thought" (1996, 4.198). The privileging of time over space corresponds to Kant's argument that as time is the *a priori* form of inner sense there can be no sensibility, thus no experience whatsoever, including the experience of space, that is not temporally determined.

Despite the consistency of his remarks, it would be a mistake to think that over the course of some forty years of literary and critical production Borges developed a coherent solution to the problem of time and identity. On the contrary, he suggested that the problem of time and identity could not be solved: "I believe Henri Bergson said that time is the capital problem of metaphysics. If that problem were resolved, everything would be resolved. Happily, I do not believe there is any danger of it being resolved" (4.199). Thus, Borges remarks, "the problem of time touches us more than the other metaphysical problems, because the others are abstract. The problem of time is our problem" (4.205). No doubt because the problem of time is *our* problem, Borges figures it as a problem of identity: "Who am I? Who is each one of us? Who are we?" (4.205). The problem of time touches us where we can no longer *simply* locate ourselves. As our problem or limit, time both provides the horizon for any possible identity and divides us from ourselves. It follows, therefore, that the joint problem of time and identity is no less a problem of space.

Given Borges's avowed privileging of time over space, the question of identity haunts him. If our substance is time and if time ceaselessly passes, how is it possible to account for identity, which requires duration or permanence over time? As Borges recognizes, the determination of time itself requires the possibility of identity.[2] In "Historia de la eternidad [History of Eternity]," he writes that "successive time" is "inconceivable" (1.364) without the possibility of identity. Without a synthesis of time, temporal succession would not be unknowable; it simply would not happen. Yet, if we are essentially temporal, thus mortal, as Borges avows, then there can be no possibility of an atemporal or eternal consciousness or mind that would ground the synthesis of time. Borges makes just this argument against both Berkeley and Hume in "A New Refutation of Time."[3]

The outline of the problem is clear. On the one hand, Borges not only supports the distinction between time and space, but he privileges time over space, succession over simultaneity. On the other hand, he recognizes that a synthesis of time, hence a certain identity, is necessary for the cognition of time. These two positions result in the intractable problem that Borges calls the contradiction of time that passes and the identity that endures (2.235). The question is how to synthesize succession in order to provide for the possibility of identity over time without, however, positing an atemporal instant, which would have the effect of making identity depend upon eternity or immortality?

The first sentence of the Prologue in which Borges indicates his preference for *El otro, el mismo* suggests the solution to the irresolvable contradiction between temporal succession and identity. Borges writes: "Of the many books of verse that my resignation, my negligence [*descuido*], and at times my passion scrawled over the years [*fueron borroneando*], *The Other, the Same* is the one I prefer" (2.235). The verb *borronear* means not only scrawled or scribbled, but also erased. Inscription, writing, is *at the same time* and *in the same gesture*, erasure. A *borrón* is an ink blot, a smudge, a mark. It is a ruin or trace not of what is no longer, but of what never was in that the inscription *at the same time* and *in the same place* erases in order to leave a mark in the first place. In short, *at the same time* and *in the same place* that Borges writes—however carelessly, negligently, or distractedly—he erases, but such erasure leaves a mark, a smudge, a blot. It leaves a trace. Thus Borges writes with two hands. His is a double marking or a marking-out that outlines (another meaning of *borronear*) and blots at the same time and in the same gesture. Whatever Borges writes appears only under erasure; it appears *as* erased.

It is necessary to stress the "at the same time" and "in the same gesture." It is not the case that *first* Borges writes and *then* he erases. The constitution of time as succession argues against this possibility. The classical—but also the common or exoteric—definition of time states that time is composed of the *no longer* and the *not yet* and that no part of time *is* or *exists*. This definition of time, which Aristotle states at the outset of his discussion of time in *Physics* IV, recognizes, albeit implicitly at this junction, the problematic status of the *now*. *On the one hand*, insofar as time is divided between the *no longer* and the *not yet*, there must be a limit at which they are distinguished. The *now* names the limit. There is no time where the *now* does not mediate or limit the *no longer* and the *not yet*. The *now* marks the site of succession. Time is thus composed at the *now*. Hence the *now* is necessary to time. *On the other hand*, as Aristotle points out, the *now* is not a part of time. This must be so and for more than one reason. First, because the part provides a measure of the whole, but since no part of time *is*, it must be impossible for the *now* to take the measure of time. Second, a limit is never *simply* a part of what it limits. If time is defined as the *no longer* and the *not yet*, the *now*, which limits them such that time can be composed, cannot simply be a part of time. Aristotle is clear that no part of time *is*; yet the *now* is thought to be. If the *now* is not a part of time, then it is *accidental* to time. The *now*, then, is both necessary to time and accidental to time—*at the same time.*[4]

It is the "at the same time" that jeopardizes Aristotle's conception of identity, which hinges on the self-sameness of the *now*, its presence in and to itself. As what is *no longer* and *not yet* and as that of which no part *is*, time cannot provide the ground for identity conceived on the basis of self-presence. This includes the impossibility of time's self-identity. The definition of identity as presence in itself derives from the principle of noncontradiction, which in the *Metaphysics* Aristotle calls the most certain principle and which states that "the same attribute cannot at the same time belong and not belong to the same subject" (1005b19–20/2.1588). According to the principle of noncontradiction, time cannot be self-identical because it is *not.* What has identity must be present in itself and self-presence depends on the possibility of self-sameness over time, which means what is identical to itself cannot *at the same time* both be and not be. At the *now*, however, time is *not* at the same time that it *is*, because insofar as the *now* marks the limit (*peras*) of time in order to measure motion, it is necessarily divided in itself, for, as Aristotle remarks in *Physics* IV, "no determinate divisible thing has a single termination" (218a23/1.370).[5] And the *now* is a "termination" or "time limit": *tò dè nun pèras esti.* Consequently, the *now* is infinitely divisible between the *no longer* and the *not yet* at the same time that it marks their limit. The *now*, then, neither is nor is not; hence time, which is determined at the *now*, neither is nor is not.

The relation of the *now* to time—that it is both accidental to time and necessary to time—disarticulates the principle of noncontradiction. The *now* is necessary to time in that it marks or inscribes the limit between the *no longer* and the *not yet.* This limit takes the measure of time. But as a limit, the *now* is divided in itself, hence it is already ruined in its appearing. Because the *now* is divided in its appearing, it is not and is therefore accidental to time. There is no time without the *now*, but the now *as such* or *in itself* is impossible. Aristotle recognized that to understand the function of the *now* one had to think it by analogy with the spatial point, which he also acknowledged was impossible, because the *now*, *qua* temporal, is always different from itself. Unlike space, which affords the possibility of a pause such that one point could be considered as two, time does not hold still in order to posit the *now* twice. In order for the *now* to serve its double function as the *place* in which time is both made continuous and limited, it must be spatialized. The *no longer* must leave a mark for the *not yet*. This is what is at stake in Borges's understanding that to write (*escribir*) is to erase or to blot (*borronear*). In order for there to be identity, the *no longer* must leave a mark or trace, a smudge or *borrón*, for the *not yet*. Something must remain. Yet, the succession of time ruins or erases whatever remains in its inscription. The possibility of identity is its impossibility. This is the logic of impossibility, which Martin Hägglund generalizes as the following principle: "the spacing of time makes X possible while making it impossible for X to be in itself" (2008, 121).

It should be clear that this general principle, which is legible in Borges's determination that to write is to erase, does not suggest that the possible and the impossible are simply opposed to one another. On the contrary, as Derrida has argued, "the impossible is at the heart of the possible." Or, as Hägglund puts it, "the impossible is . . . what happens all the time" (122). This is the case because in order for something to happen (in French, *arriver*; in Spanish, *pasar*, *suceder*), it must be marked by temporal succession; it must arrive from the *not yet* (the future) and pass to the *no longer* (the past). But the movement of temporal succession must leave a mark or trace of what passes or arrives. This mark, however, is no less susceptible to temporal succession and is, therefore, *erased in its appearing*. Its arrival is ruined by temporal division. What is impossible—namely, that something *be* in itself or self-identical—*happens* all the time. Hägglund explains that the "impossibility of being in itself is not a privation, since *nothing could happen* if being were given in itself. Rather, the impossibility of being in itself opens the possibility of everything we desire and the peril of everything we fear" (122).

*At the same time* and *in the same gesture* what Hägglund calls "the trace structure of time" (4) makes possible both the best and the worst. The chance for the best is the risk of the worst. No desire, no decision, no act escapes the logic of the impossible. For this reason Derrida considers every act a promise. On Derrida's account, the promise is an "impossible act, therefore the only one worthy of its name" (Derrida 1989, 150). The promise is impossible because it always and only promises the future. A promise is not a promise if it is guaranteed. A calculable, predictable promise is not a promise. A promise is only a promise if it is open to the future, if it promises alteration. Because the promise is always a promise of time (Hägglund 2008, 137), it must be convertible. As Derrida writes, "A promise must be able not to be kept, it must risk not being kept or becoming a threat to be a promise" (Derrida 2002b, 362). This does not mean that the promise is threatened; it means that the promise is the threat; the chance of the promise is the threat of the promise.

According to Derrida, "The promise is the basic element of language" (2007a, 458). This is so because language is constitutively temporal or, as Borges puts it in "A New Refutation of Time," "All language is of a successive nature" (2.142/CF 324). The succession of language, that it happens or *passes* (*sucede*), inscribes language within the double bind of the promise. Language is no longer: as Borges claimed, "A language is a tradition, a way of feeling reality, not an arbitrary repertory of symbols [*Un idioma es una tradición, un modo de sentir la realidad, no un arbitrario repertorio de símbolos*]" (2.459). As a tradition, language is always already past, *no longer*; it is what we must inherit. To speak is to promise to remember that there is language and that there is a shared heritage or community. Hence, language is to come. It is *not yet.* It is always possible that there will not be language, that there will not be community or communication. It is always possible, as Borges notes on more than one occasion, that one will not understand the language one speaks. It is always possible to lose language, to lose one's own or the other's. Thus to speak is to promise language, to promise community and communication. The promise of language, therefore, that there is and will be language and community, is the threat of and to language, that it will be no more, that it will result in the destruction of community, the expropriation of others, and of oneself as other. The promise—both chance and threat—of language takes place in Borges in the singular and marvelous articulation that repeats, always for the first time, that which the library always already contains. The constitutive repetition that Borges notes both is and is not tautological. The promise of language is legible every time Borges thematizes, however parenthetically, the impossibility of deciding, of knowing, in what language one speaks or writes, in what language one listens or reads.

The promise's relation to the future means that it "promises the coming of a future that in its turn will have the structure of a promise" (Hägglund 2008, 137). Insofar as the promise does not promise the consummation of time, but is rather marked by the exposure to the future as the condition of its possibility, it follows that the promise is always the promise of mortality.[6] An immortal being would be incapable of promising since such a being would never be at risk of alteration. Nothing happens to immortals. A promise is necessary and possible only because an undecidable future jeopardizes at the same time that it opens every possibility.

The temporal logic of the promise opens onto what Hägglund calls the logic of survival in that to survive "is to remain after a past that is no longer and to keep the memory of this past for a future that is not yet" (2008, 1). To promise or to survive thus means to be exposed to the time of life, to mortality, and accordingly to be at risk of being eradicated. In the context of the promise of language, then, it should be obvious that there are neither living nor dead languages; rather there are only surviving languages: all languages are at risk of being lost, destroyed, forgotten, but they are also open to the chance of their being used, remembered. And yet such use and remembrance is also their destruction in that every use necessarily alters the language. On the one hand, there is no survival without the possibility of the future; on the other hand, the future necessarily threatens the possibility of survival. To overcome the "radical finitude of survival" (1) is literally undesirable because the structure of desire, in that it depends on the possibility of alteration, affirms the temporal logic of survival. Desire, in short, is mortal, which means that the so-called desire for immortality merely dissembles the desire for survival: "The desire to *live on* after death is not a desire for immortality, since to live on is to remain subjected to temporal finitude. The desire for survival cannot aim at transcending time, since the given time is the only chance for survival" (2). According to Hägglund, the desire for immortality contradicts itself: "If one were not attached to mortal life, there would be no fear of death and no desire to live on. But for the same reason, immortality cannot even hypothetically appease the fear of death or satisfy the desire to live on. On the contrary, the state of immortality would annihilate every form of survival, since it would annihilate the time of mortal life" (2).[7]

The logic of survival and the so-called desire for immortality can be read in the conclusion of Borges's "History of Eternity," which repeats, *verbatim*, a text Borges published in *El idioma de los argentinos* (The Language of Argentines) in 1928. "Sentirse en muerte [Feeling in Death]," which presents Borges's "personal theory of eternity" (1.365), dramatizes one of Borges's most persistent claims, namely, that a single repetition is enough to destroy time. At the instant Borges articulates "the facile thought *I am in the 1800s*," that thought "ceased being so many approximate words and became [*se profundizó a*] reality" (1.366). "I felt dead, I felt myself an abstract perceiver of the world" (1.366). Borges does not, however, feel that he had arrived at the source ("las presuntivas aguas") of time. Rather, he suspected that he had become the owner (*poseedor*) "of the reticent or absent sense of the inconceivable word *eternity*" (1.366). *Feeling* oneself to be dead, then, is what it takes to possess the meaning of eternity. Yet, Borges admits that it takes time to define the "imagination" (1.366) of one's own death, and thus of eternity. "That pure representation of homogeneous acts . . . is not merely identical to what was there on that corner so many years ago; it is, without appearances or repetitions, the same. Time, if we can intuit that identity, is a delusion: the indifference and inseparability of a moment from its apparent yesterday and another from its apparent today, are enough to disintegrate it" (1.366). This passage succinctly illustrates what Borges identified as the contradiction between the time that passes and the identity that endures.

At stake is the tension between time as infinite succession and alteration, on the one hand, and identity as sameness over time, on the other hand. Borges remarks that if it were possible to intuit the identity of time, time would be revealed as a delusion, because in order for time to be identified *as such* it must remain the *same* over time; hence, for time to be known or identified *as* time, it must be *essentially* atemporal.

Despite this, in order for there to be identity and thus in order for there to be self-sameness or presence to self, there must be time, for identity is defined as sameness *over time*. Consequently, in order for there to be identity, synthesis is necessary. But a synthesis is possible and necessary only insofar as "[a]n interval . . . separate[s] the present from what it is not in order for the present to be itself"; yet, "this interval that constitutes it as present must, by the same token [*de même coup*: at the same time, in the same stroke] divide the present in and of itself" (Derrida 1982, 13). Derrida proposes to call "this constitution of the present, as an 'originary' and irreducibly nonsimple (and therefore, *stricto sensu* nonoriginary) synthesis of marks, or traces of retentions and protentions, . . . archi-writing, archi-trace, or *différance*" (13).[8] "This interval might also be called," Derrida notes, "*spacing*, the becoming-space of time or the becoming-time of space" (13). Spacing or *différance* inscribes difference and deferral within temporal succession as its possibility.[9]

Borges is thus correct that were it impossible to separate one instance from another, yesterday from today, *no longer* from *not yet*, there would be no time. But if it were impossible to separate one instance from another, it would be equally impossible to speak of repetition. Repetition is possible only insofar as one instance differs from and defers not only the next instance, but "itself," and this must be possible even if the instances of repetition are identical. The difference between them is spacing, and it is this interval that constitutes the identity of any single instance and ruins it at the same time. Because every instance is always already divided in itself, it is fundamentally impossible for any two instances of repetition to be the same. As will be seen in Chapter 2, it is this that allows for the determination of the visible and invisible work of Pierre Menard as well as the assertion of contextual difference.

Borges derives the following conclusion from his "experience" of feeling in death: "[L]ife is too poor for it not to be also immortal. But we do not even have the security of our poverty, in that time, which is easily refutable in the sensible realm [*lo sensitivo*], is not so [easily refutable] in the intellectual realm, whose essence seems inseparable from the concept of succession" (1.366). Although life is too poor not to be immortal, the poverty of life is nevertheless not proper to life such that life might be secure in it. On the contrary, life can never be secured *in itself*—even if that security were defined as impoverished and immortal—

because temporalization or spacing, which is the condition of possibility of life, destroys life. No life without the time of life, which means no matter how poor life may be it could never be immortal.

The determination that time *qua* succession is easily refutable at the level of sensibility follows from the value that metaphysics has placed on presence. In *De Anima*, Aristotle distinguishes sensibility from the imagination on the basis that sensation is always present whereas the imagination is not (428a5–12/680). On account of such enduring presence, sense perception is always true, according to Aristotle, while the imagination is for the most part false. The uninterrupted presence of sense perception also provides the necessary ground for the sense of existence.[10] This, in any case, is the argument for why time is refutable at the level of sensibility: because sense perception is always *both* present *and* of the present, it follows that we live in the present, that life is always present to itself. Everything thus *happens* (to us) in the present. Conceived this way, sense never passes. According to the logic of this argument, the present would be unscathed by either coming to be or passing away. But if nothing either comes to be or passes away, then *nothing happens*.

Borges thus argues that sensibility or perception is unmarked by temporal division; consequently, it is unmarked by the synthesis of time. Yet, the absence of temporal synthesis obviates *any* perception in that only a synthesis of time makes possible the relation to the future, to alterity and alteration, without which nothing happens. Therefore, without the synthesis of time, which is only possible if there is succession, Borges would not be able to *feel* in death; he would not be able to *feel* himself an abstract perceiver of the world, nor, for that matter, would he be able to discern the "pure representation of homogeneous acts." Without the synthesis of succession, nothing *happens*, nothing *arrives*, not even, as Borges writes, "in the confessed irresolution of this page, the true moment of ecstasy" (1.366). No ecstasy without the exposure to the future, *here and now*, as precisely that which constitutes the impossible possibility of the here and now.[11] In sum, to *feel* oneself in death is not an experience of immortality. On the contrary, because feeling is an effect of temporal finitude, it is mortal through and through.

In his lecture on time Borges appears to challenge the present and presence of feeling that he asserts in "Sentirse en muerte":

> How strange to think that of the three tenses into which we have divided time—the past, the present, the future—, the most difficult, the most inaccessible, would be the present! The present is as inaccessible as the point. Because if we imagine it without extension, it does not exist; we have to imagine that the apparent present would turn out to be [*vendría a ser*] a little of the past and a little of the future. In other words, we feel the passage of time. When I speak of the passage of time, I am speaking of something that all of you feel. If I speak of the present, I am speaking of an abstract entity. The present is not an immediate given of our consciousness." (1996, 4.204–5)

If sensation happens always and only in the present, then it does so, Borges suggests, only insofar as the present is divided between the past and the future. Only in this way can sensation be experienced or felt as the *passage*—the coming-to-being and passing-away—of time. The present is not immediately given to consciousness because the present is an effect of the synthesis of succession. The problem for Borges, however, is how to conceive the synthesis.

The insistence that the present is composed of a little of the past and a little of the future follows Augustine's discussion of time in *Confessions*. Borges turns to Augustine because he believes the concept of eternity solves the problem of the synthesis of succession. According to Borges, time is the "gift of eternity," and although he admits that Augustine "ignores the problem" of how eternity comes into being, he nonetheless sees in Augustine's text "something that allows for a solution: the elements of past and future that exist in every present" (1.364/SNF 136). Forty years later, in the lecture on time, Borges repeats this Augustinian solution: "The present moment is the moment that is composed of a little of the past and a little of the future" (4.202). And, again, "The present always has a particle of the past, a particle of the future. And it seems that this is necessary for time" (4.205). Despite his claim that "[t]he present in itself does not exist" (4.202), Borges's interpretation of Augustine's *distentio* re-imports the value of presence in that the present contains both a *part* or a *particle* of the past and a *part* or a *particle* of the future. In other words, whereas Aristotle claims that no *part* of time *is*, Borges interprets Augustine as arguing that the past and the future necessarily *are*, even if only *in* and *as* part of the present. Therefore, according to Borges's understanding of the Augustinian solution to the synthesis of succession, the present comprehends or encompasses the past and the future, because the past and the future can *be* only in the present.

Borges initially takes up Augustine's description of the distention or stretching-out of time because he sees in it a possible solution to the problem of eternity, but he ultimately dismisses the concept of distension on the grounds that it continues to rely upon succession (1.364/SNF 136). In other words, rather than deploying Augustine's conception of distention in order to disavow the idea of eternity, Borges rejects Augustine's temporalization of the present through the concept of distention. He does not explain, however, how succession contaminates or corrupts the distension or stretching-out of the present by dividing it incessantly.[12] Consequently, Borges retains the idea of a present that stretches or distends itself in order to comprehend both past and future without the negative effects of succession. This structure of time grounds the necessary synthesis of time in an atemporal instant. *Contra* Borges, however, Augustine agrees with Aristotle's conclusion that no part of time is: "If we can think of some bit of time that cannot be divided into even the smallest instantaneous moments, that alone is what we can call 'present.' And this time flies so quickly from future into past that it is an interval with no duration. If it has duration, it is divisible into past and future. But the present occupies no space" (1991, XI.15/232). The present, on Augustine's account, has *neither* duration *nor* extension. It is not.

In fairness to Borges, he is not alone in thinking that the present's comprehension of past and future solves the problem of temporal synthesis. In *Being and Time*, Heidegger finds the basis for his understanding of the temporality of Dasein in Augustine's understanding of time as *distentio*. "The making present that awaits and retains," Heidegger writes, "interprets a 'during' with a 'span,' only because in so doing it is disclosed to *itself* as being ecstatically *stretched along* in historical temporality, even though it does not know itself as this" (1996a, 376/409).[13] Earlier Heidegger explained, "The movement of existence is not the motion of something objectively present. It is determined from the stretching along of Da-sein. The specific movement of the *stretched out stretching itself along*, we call the *occurrence* of Da-sein" (344/375).

The determination that Dasein is "[e]cstatically *stretched along*" undoubtedly translates Augustine's *distentio*.[14] The figure of being "stretched out stretching itself along," which Heidegger also thinks as an "ecstatic unity" (314/342), conjures up the image of a rubber band or piece of elastic, fixed in the middle and stretched out or extended in either direction. Effectively, Heidegger's "ecstatic unity" functions more like an "elastic unity."[15] Heidegger's conception of authentic or primordial temporality establishes the present as the regulatory site of time. The present or the *Moment*, as Heidegger calls it, despite his claim that it temporalizes itself from the future (1996a, 391/426–427), nonetheless *extends itself* and in doing so occupies—takes over—the past and the future. If this were not the case, it would be inconceivable for Heidegger to speak of the *unity* of the three ecstasies of time, the future, the having-been, and the present (302/329).[16]

Borges's problematic relation to eternity and to time notwithstanding, the logic of survival—hence, the trace structure of time—is legible throughout his text. For instance, in the 1953 "Prologue" to *Historia de la eternidad* (History of Eternity),[17] Borges offered the following reflections on the structure and the stakes of that book and its investment in the idea of eternity:

> I will say a little about the singular 'history of eternity' that gives the name to these pages. In the beginning I speak of Platonic philosophy; in a work that aspired to chronological rigor, it would have been more reasonable to depart from the hexameters of Parmenides ('it has never been nor will be, because it is'). I do not know how I could compare Plato's Forms to 'immobile museum pieces' and how I did not understand, reading Schopenhauer and [Johannes Scotus] Erigena, that these are living, powerful and organic. Movement, occupation of different places at different instants, is inconceivable without time; likewise so too is immobility, occupation of the same place at different points of time. How could I not sense that eternity, lovingly longed for by so many poets, is a splendid artifice that frees us, even in a fleeting way, from the intolerable oppression of succession. (1996, 1.351)

Borges's recognition that eternity is a "splendid artifice," hence necessarily technical and temporal, does not mitigate his mistaken understanding of its effect. Because the liberation eternity ostensibly makes possible is *fleeting*, it must be conceded that eternity cannot liberate us from "the intolerable oppression of succession," for succession, however oppressive, is the condition of possibility for anything—including liberation—to *flee*. Further, the conception of liberation as fleeting ought not be understood as a derivative modality of freedom. Quite the contrary, liberation *must* be fleeting. Otherwise, it would not be emancipatory. An eternal or absolute freedom would, by definition, not be free in that it would obviate the possibility of the decisions constitutive of freedom, which would have to include the possibility either that one would abdicate one's freedom or that another would take it. Absolute freedom is absolute bondage. As a consequence, what Borges calls "the oppression of succession"—which the idea of eternity dissembles rather than suspends—provides the *only* possibility of liberation.

If eternity is merely a "splendid artifice" and if the logic of the Borgesian text demonstrates that eternity is in any case undesirable, then why invoke it at all? Borges does so because he believes only the concept of eternity and the permanence it promises answer "the contradiction of time that passes and the identity that endures." On this argument, the idea of eternity secures identity and memory against the ravages of time. Moreover, although he recognizes that desire necessarily relates to the future, he conceives the future of desire in terms of a *return* to eternity. Despite his suggestion that eternity guarantees memory, identity, desire, even time, the Borgesian text insistently articulates the logic of survival, that is, the logic of mortality. Indeed, even Borges's description of the origin of the concept of eternity is organized by the affirmation of survival.

In *Historia de la eternidad*, Borges notes that "remote men, bearded, mitred men conceived" of eternity, "ostensibly to confound heresies and defend the distinction of" the Trinity, "but secretly in order to staunch [*restañar*: to detain] in some way the flow of hours" (1.363/SNF 135). Thus eternity is conceived as a way to *put off* or *delay* the passage of time, for, as Borges quotes from George Santayana, "To live is to lose time; we can recover or keep nothing except under the form of eternity" (1.363/SNF 135). Borges emphasizes the desire to hold on to, or staunch the flow of time when he claims, "Archetypes and eternity—two words—promise firmer possessions [*posesiones más firmes*]. It is certain that succession is an intolerable misery and that magnanimous appetites desire [*codician*] all the minutes of time" (1.364/SNF 135–136). To desire or to be greedy for (*codiciar*) time means to hold onto—to detain or delay—the passage of time. According to Borges, however, to put off or delay is the very definition of time: "It is true that *time* . . . must be synonymous with delay [*demora*]" (1.361/SNF 132). By definition, then, *putting off* time *takes* time. To hold onto time, which is to delay the passage of time and thus to put off time, on the one hand, means to deny the condition of life, our constitutive temporality; on the other hand, it means to desire *more* time insofar as time is delay. At stake here is the logic of survival. The passage of time results in the desire to hold on to time, to delay its passage under the figure of eternity. In short, time is unconditionally affirmed,[18] which means the desire for eternity dissembles the desire for *more* time. Consequently, the desire for eternity is the desire for survival, the desire to live on, which desire is mortal.

The same logic informs Borges's conception of the relation of eternity to memory and identity. For instance, Borges writes: "Personal identity is known to reside in memory, and the annulment of that faculty is known to result in idiocy" (1.364/SNF 136). Without memory, we are idiots. The possibility of the "annulment" of memory indicates that the ostensible archive of personal identity is temporal and thus insecure. Because it is always possible for memory to be annulled and for us to forget ourselves, Borges suggests that memory must be protected by the idea of eternity: "Without the idea of eternity, without a sensitive, secret mirror of what passes through every soul, universal history is lost time, and along with it our personal history—which rather uncomfortably makes ghosts of us" (1.364/SNF 136). On this argument, eternity makes it possible for what "passes through every soul" not to be lost, but rather to remain present. If memory is secured by the idea of eternity, then what passes does not pass away. It persists, which means the "no longer" *is*. In Borges's calculation, without eternity and its "sensitive, secret mirror," what passes through every soul would pass incessantly, without halt or detention. Without eternity to hold onto time, identity would be impossible as there would be no synthesis of time. This is the argument in favor of the necessity of the idea of eternity. Following the logic of eternity, identity would only be possible for Borges if time were *not* to pass, if forgetting were impossible.

The possible loss of memory and with it the loss of identity haunts Borges and no doubt leads to the suggestion that memory is guaranteed by eternity. Without the idea of eternity, there is no identity because there is no memory, the loss of which, Borges suggests, "makes ghosts of us." It is this haunting—which instances the relation to an undetermined future—that gives the lie to the idea of eternity as necessary for the constitution of identity. In Borges, the ghost signals the absolute loss of identity, which means that for Borges identity is possible only in an indivisible or absolute present that is haunted by neither the *no longer* nor the *not yet*, by neither passing away nor coming to be.

This is a mistaken understanding of the ghost, however, because the ghost—which is virtual, an apparition, and thus not of the order of being—figures the impossible possibility of identity. Because it is always already no longer and not yet, the ghost or specter cannot be comprehended according to the logic of the present, which is itself the effect of the Aristotelian hierarchical opposition between *entelecheia* (actuality) and *dúnamis* (potentiality), where *entelecheia* names presence and *dúnamis* names absence *qua* the potentiality to be present. The ghost is neither present nor absent. It is rather the specter of what cannot be thought either as what has been or as what will be.[19] All identity is spectral; we have never been anything but *revenants*, ghosts. Identity, then, *is not*, as the condition of its possibility; for without the coming of the future, without the exposure to the other, to the *revenant* that we are, there could be no relation to the past as what haunts us, as what comes (back). There would be only an absolute resting in peace, without memory, without identification, without life.

Nevertheless, Borges not only suggests that the idea of eternity sustains and secures memory, but also that desire and time are effects of eternity. "The style of desire," Borges writes, "is eternity" (1.364/ SNF 136). In the lecture on time, Borges argues that "time is successive because, having left from eternity, it wants to return to eternity" (4.204). And he concludes, "time is the gift [*dádiva*] of eternity. Eternity permits us all those experiences of a successive nature [*todas esas experiencias de un modo sucesivo*]. We have days and nights, we have hours, we have minutes, we have memory, we have actual sensations, and then we have the future, a future whose form we do not even know but which we anticipate [*presentimos*] or fear" (4.200). Fear is a form of anticipation. It is impossible to see how eternity, which is characterized by its atemporal security, which means nothing comes to alter eternity, to threaten it, could give onto a future that remains undetermined and thus frightening. Eternity anticipates nothing.

In "Vindicación de la cábala [In Defense of Kabbalah]," published in *Discusión* in 1932, Borges had already acknowledged the tension between an undetermined future and its anticipation, when he admitted that he tried "to bear in mind that every object whose end is unknown to us is provisionally a monster" (1.210/SNF 84). Against what appears to be Borges's express intention, this early remark explains why time cannot be "the gift of eternity." Insofar as the idea of eternity corresponds to a desire that seeks to fulfill itself in an eternal present, it must not be susceptible to temporal division. As presence in itself, eternity must necessarily be absolutely determined. But if everything is absolutely determined, if everything is always already decided, then there can be neither giving nor receiving, neither gift nor return. Moreover, insofar as eternity is conceived as absolute presence in itself and thus as absolute being, eternity cannot give time, since time is not and therefore could never be generated out of being or presence. On the one hand, eternity lies in state, rests in peace, and, because it cannot give anything, it remains intestate, without will or bequest, without legacy. It is impossible to inherit from eternity, from the immortal and the immemorial. On the other hand, time incessantly comes. It is time, then, that gives. But what or who comes remains necessarily undetermined as the condition of its coming. Thus the gift of the future is a monster, a promise, and as such both a chance and a threat, which explains why we must both anticipate and fear the gift.

Borges retreats from the furthest implications of the understanding of the future as undetermined. In so doing, he re-imports the authority of the present in the figure of eternity. In effect, he follows the metaphysical strategy: because time is destructive, agonistic, metaphysics attempts to save us from time, but in order to do so it must also save us from life, for life is unconditionally temporal. In the lecture on time, Borges writes, "The idea of the future would turn out to justify [*vendría a justificar*] that ancient idea of Plato, that time is the mobile image of eternity. If time is the image of eternity, the future would turn out to be [*vendría a ser*] the movement of the soul toward the future. The future would be in turn [*a su vez*] the return to eternity. That is to say, our life is a continual agony" (4.205). That life or mortality is continual agony is the Augustinian position, but a future that returns to itself as eternity is not the future. It is not a monster, which is how Borges designated—however provisionally—the future that remains unknown and incalculable. On the contrary, an already determined future is the present, which, because it is not exposed to the chance and threat of the future, is inalterable.

Even here, however, in his attempt to think the future not as the monstrous to come but as the present, the logic of survival operates. The Borgesian text perhaps unwittingly but no less ineluctably exposes the ruse not only of eternity, but of the desire for eternity. It jeopardizes the figure of eternity in that a certain *turning*—a coming to be (*vendría a ser*)—*marks* the eternity it invokes. To turn and to return—to come (*venir*)—take time and a future that turns and turns again, that comes, necessarily turns away from—thus puts off, delays—itself in turning toward itself. In other words, a future that would come to be (*vendría a ser*) cannot be eternal. Eternity neither turns nor returns; eternity does not come. Further, Borges exposes temporality as the motive force driving desire in the first place in that the soul *moves* toward the future. This movement *toward* the future, here and now, as the figure of desire, is possible only if there is temporal division, only if the future comes, which is to say only if the coming of the future, here and now, puts off, delays, defers.

Borges's determination that eternity gives time and that only eternity can guarantee identity, memory, and desire, therefore must be wrong. Borges recurs to the figure of eternity in order to mitigate the deleterious effects of time, thus to hold on to or defer time. In order to save us from the passing of time, however, Borges necessarily subscribes to a prophylaxis that spells the end of us, since, as he argues, time is our substance. The upshot is that the possibility of identity, memory, and desire within the Borgesian schema would require that we be immortal. But an immortal being, because it would not be susceptible to alteration, would have neither the need nor the possibility of an identity, a memory, or desire. No identity, no memory, no desire, without temporalization or spacing, which means the possibility of identity, memory, and desire is their impossibility.

# 2

# Belief, in Translation

> This accident is all the more interesting since it touches on the idiom, precisely—on the untranslatable singularity at the very heart itself of translation.
>
> —Jacques Derrida, *On Touching—Jean-Luc Nancy*

> As soon as one makes a literal translation everything is changed.
>
> —Martin Heidegger, "Only a God Can Save Us Now"

> One can always act as if it made no difference.
>
> —Jacques Derrida, *Margins of Philosophy*

During a roundtable discussion devoted to the problem of translation, Derrida availed himself of Borges's "Pierre Menard, autor del *Quijote*" in order to respond to a series of comments posed by Patrick Mahoney. Mahoney prefaced his remarks and question with an anecdote. After noting that "The diagnosis of schizophrenia is much more frequent in America than it is in Europe," Mahoney observed: "if ever someone were to be diagnosed here as schizophrenic, then the cheapest cure would be quite simply for him to book passage on a transatlantic ship" (Derrida, et al. 1985, 94). He remarked that this would be "a case of translation curing translation" and then concluded, "But now, let's be serious" (94). Undoubtedly, Mahoney's desire to return to an appropriate seriousness indicates that the preceding has been intended more or less as a joke, but it also recalls Walter Benjamin's claim in "The Task of the Translator" that there can be no translation of translation, which makes impossible, therefore, translation's viability as a cure for translation. In short, translation is fatal, terminal. It is serious business and the possibility of the translation of translation as the cure for or of translation is no less so, not least because such restorative translation is impossible.

Mahoney's comments turn on the problem of singularity and repetition, on the return to the father. Derrida responds by invoking two examples. The first is the challenge Joyce's *Finnegan's Wake* poses for translation. The second is Borges's "Pierre Menard," which, Derrida writes, "gives the account of a Frenchman who has conceived the mad project of writing, for the first time, *Don Quixote*. That's all there is to it: He wants to write not a version, not a repetition or a parody, but *Don Quixote* itself" (99). Derrida goes on to point out that although "Borges's text is written in Spanish, . . . it is marked by the French atmosphere" (99), specifically, that "there are all sorts of resonances that led Borges to write this text in a Spanish tongue which is very subtly marked by a certain Frenchness" (99). This French accent accords to "Pierre Menard" its untranslatable singularity. Derrida explains: "Once, in a seminar on translation, I had a discussion with a Hispanist student who said about the text: 'In the end, the French translation is more faithful and thus better than the original.' Well, yes and no, because what is lost in translation in the French translation is this superimposed Frenchness or the Frenchness that inserts a slight division within the Spanish, all of which Borges wanted to mark in the original. Translation can do everything except mark this linguistic difference inscribed in the language, this difference of language systems inscribed in a single tongue" (99–100). In order for the French translation to be "more faithful" than the original, it would have to translate the story's "superimposed" Frenchness, which Borges marks by overdetermining *as foreign* the Spanish in which the story is told and which, therefore, constitutes the atmosphere of "Pierre Menard." To do so would require translating this foreignness into the French of the story's context. Such a translation would have to find a way to make the French of a French symbolist poet from Nîmes foreign to itself. The way to mark this would, perhaps, be to turn Pierre Menard into a Spaniard and to have him write, for the first time, France's most important early modern text. But this would no longer be a translation—in the strictest and most common sense—of "Pierre Menard." It would amount to a French rewriting of the story.

Derrida's anecdote draws attention not only to the impossible task of translation insofar as every language or linguistic system is contaminated by linguistic difference, but also to the role of faith, of belief, in the constitution of the original. The Hispanist's assertion that the translation would be *more faithful* than the original suggests that the original is not *faithful enough* either to itself or to its translation. Derrida does not simply reject this proposition. On the contrary, his "Well, yes and no" and his subsequent elaboration of a response make clear that translation—or what might be called translation effects—operates at the heart of every language, of every linguistic system, such that the essential loss constitutive of the translation (the fact that no translation could do justice to or capture the French accent of the original Spanish text) operates in the original. At stake in what follows is the operation of a belief that is neither subjectively nor objectively determined, which makes possible the institutional investment in the origin, the original, and the author. Indeed, such belief makes possible experience in the first place, but as such it also inscribes translation and the imagination at and as the origin, thereby displacing the origin and all that it organizes.

## *In the beginning, (there was) translation*

From the earliest beginning of his literary career, Borges occupied himself with translation. His first publication, at the age of nine, was a Spanish translation of Oscar Wilde's "The Happy Prince." Borges notes in his *Autobiografía*, "As the translation was signed simply 'Jorge Borges,' people supposed it was the work of my father [*Como la traducción estaba firmada simplemente 'Jorge Borges,' la gente supuso que era obra de mi padre*]" (Borges 1999, 30; my translation). The misattribution of translation haunts Borges from one end of his career to another. Writing of his mother, Leonor Acevedo de Borges, he claims that in the wake of his father's death, she turned to translation in order to learn once again how to concentrate on the printed page. Her translation of William Saroyan's

*The Human Comedy* was published. Later, she translated various short stories by Hawthorne as well as an art book by Herbert Read. Borges then confesses: "She also did some of the translations of Melville, Virginia Woolf and Faulkner that are attributed to me" (22). Although Borges's father was a writer—his novel, *El caudillo*, was published in Mallorca in 1921—and although Borges inherited the patronym, he acknowledges that although he was late in realizing it, it was his mother "who silently and efficaciously stimulated my literary career" (22). When the son signs his translation, he does so with and in the father's name. When the mother translates, she loses herself in the son's name, which both is and is not the name of the father. The mother's work, her translation, silently, as if it made no difference, stimulates the son's literary career and makes possible, according to Borges, the son's signature *as original*, as if it were not the father's, as if it were his own. The mother opens the space of "proper" attribution, of the son's proper name and signature. The mother signs (in) the name of the other. The possibility of the signature, of the son's signing in his father's name as if it were his own, the possibility of the son's literary propriety and originality depends on his mother's translation, on his mother's disappearance in the name of the other, in the name of the father and of the son. The patronym is an effect of maternal translation. From the beginning it is a question of attribution.

Borges's "mother" tongue comes from his father in and as translation. His paternal grandmother, Frances Haslam, was born in Staffordshire, England, and she taught her son, Jorge Guillermo Borges, the English in which he would later give classes at the Normal School of Living Languages (Escuela Normal de Lenguas Vivas). Borges's father taught his mother—who, Borges writes, "has always had a hospitable attitude" (21)—the English in which she would read for the rest of her life, from which she would translate, and which she would use to stimulate her son's literary career. In 1970, when Borges dictated his autobiography to Norman Thomas de Giovanni, he did so in English, in a mother tongue inherited from his father.

For Borges, then, translation is no simple matter. Rather, it has a relation to the original that cannot be explained or dismissed as secondary. Indeed, in 1932, at the beginning of a text devoted to the various translations of Homer, Borges attests: "No problem [is] as consubstantial to literature and its modest mystery as the one posed by translation

[*Ningún problema tan consustancial con las letras y con su modesto misterio como el que propone una traducción*]" (1.239/SNF 69).[1] Borges opened his preface to the 1932 Spanish translation of a collection of poems by Paul Valery, *El cementerio marino*, with the same sentence (1996, 4.151).[2] The importance of this sentence cannot be overestimated for understanding and conceptualizing the role of translation in the Borgesian text.

Nevertheless, it is no accident that translation can be forgotten. On the contrary, the forgetting of translation is perhaps a necessary effect of its operation. One can always act as if translation made no difference. "Las versiones homéricas [The Homeric Versions]," for example, begins by opposing the original to the translation along the lines of their respective relation to transparency, to visibility and invisibility. Borges claims that the original or "direct writings" (*escrituras directas*) are marked by a forgetfulness animated by vanity (*animado por la vanidad*) and the fear of confessing to mental processes that we guess (*adivinamos*) are dangerously common, but also by the desire "to maintain, central and intact, an incalculable reserve of obscurity [*una reserva incalculable de sombra*]" (1.239/SNF 69).[3] Accordingly, the original "is a visible text" that nonetheless maintains "an incalculable reserve of obscurity." On the one hand, direct writings, despite their visibility, harbor a secret. On the other hand, translation exposes everything in that "[t]he model to be imitated is a visible text, not an immeasurable labyrinth of former projects or a submission to the momentary temptation of fluency" (1.239/SNF 69). But translation models only what is *visible* of the original, that is, it is predicated upon the original *qua* phenomenon, which means, although it appears to reveal the very heart of the matter, it in fact leaves intact and untouched the secret—the shadow, *sombra*, and also the ghost—that the original ostensibly conceals. The original's incalculable reserve cannot be accounted for or measured in translation, because translation models itself on the original *qua* visible. This would be one way to posit the limit of translation.

But, in fact, Borges complicates the relation between original and translation when he claims that "A partial and precious document of the vicissitudes it suffers remain in its translations [*Un parcial y precioso documento de las vicisitudes que sufre queda en sus traducciones*]" (1.239). Eliot Weinberger's translation of this sentence, while elegant, ineluctably subordinates translation to original. Two things are at stake. *First*, the understanding that translations *document*, hence record and archive but also present or make visible, the changes that the original *suffers* means that the original is subject to time. The original is *pathetic*. Insofar as it suffers—and the transcription or record of such suffering is translation—it is *moved*. It is alterable. Translation takes the measure of the movement of the original. If the original is thought according to Bertrand Russell's notion of an external object that is a radiant circular system of impressions, then translation marks the time of its circularity, of its return to itself. Translation names the spacing of the end and beginning of the circle. There is no circle, no system, without such spacing, without the tracing of the circle such that it comes (back) to itself. The presence to itself of the original depends on the movement, the measure, that returns the original to itself. Nevertheless, the suffering—thus the passion—of the original manifests itself in and as its translations. Translations inscribe the impressions of the original and the vicisstudes it suffers. *Second*, the possibilities of the original, the impressions it radiates, do not exhaust its translations. Although translation documents—archives and makes visible—the changes the original suffers, these possibilities do not exhaust it. In short, a translation can never be reduced to the original, to the documentation of the changing attitudes toward the original. It is not simply a record of the reading of the original. The impressions the original radiates, that it leaves behind in and as its translations, displace the original, its privilege and authority, and do so precisely as the cost of institutionalizing the original. More exactly, (the) translation takes the place of the original: the original becomes the original in the taking place of (the) translation. The singularity of the taking place of (the) translation, an event that cannot be predicted, calculated, anticipated, makes possible the institution of the original insofar as it makes the original *visible*. The original *takes place*, *happens*, in and through the *movement* or *measure* of translation. But this movement also makes possible the taking place of the translation *as* the original. Borges makes this clear when he invites "the mere South American reader . . . to immerse himself in the fifth strophe of the Spanish text, until he feels that the original verse by Néstor Ibarra . . . is inaccessible, and that its imitation by Valéry . . . does not accurately return the entirety of its Latin flavor [*al mero lector sudamericano . . . a saturarse de la estrofa quinta en el texto español, hasta sentir que el verso original de Néstor Ibarra . . . es inaccesible, y que su imitación por Valéry . . . no acierta a devolver íntegramente todo el sabor latino*]" (4.152).[4] The displacement of the original in and as the singular appearing of the translation is legible in both "The Homeric Versions" and "The Translators of the 1001 Nights" in that in both these texts Borges compares translations to translations without reference to the originals. It is as if the original made no difference.

At issue is the singular taking place of the original in and as (the) translation. If this is the case, then the original can no longer be said to determine (the) translation. Translation takes place according to the logic of an impossible *fidelity* to that which it institutionalizes, to that which takes place only through it. (The) translation leaves behind the original. And this, according to Borges in "The Homeric Versions," does not require translation between two languages. On the contrary, translation happens within any single language: "(There is no essential necessity to change languages; this intentional *game of attention* [emphasis added—DEJ] is not impossible within a single literature [*de una misma literatura*])" (1.239/SNF 69). The consubstantiality of translation and letters means there is never a moment in which there is literature (*letras*) without the constitutive possibility of translation. Consequently, at the moment translation within any *one* language or literature becomes possible—and this would be the very beginning of the possibility of literature and language—*one* language or literature becomes at least *two*, which means every language, every literature, has the structure $n+1$ languages, $n+1$ literatures.[5]

The problem translation proposes to letters does not supervene upon letters as a foreign pathogen or contagion that comes from a simple outside. Translation is not *simply* exogenous to the constitution of letters as such. Rather, their consubstantiality means that the relation between translation and letters is irreducible.

Translation thus poses a problem—*the* problem—for literature and letters. A problem is a limit.[6] This means that translation poses or instances, in a word, posits the limit of letters. But if translation posits the limit of letters, it also trespasses or oversteps that limit in that translation means crossing over—and thus crossing out—the limit or border. Translation crosses over and crosses out, transgresses, the problem or limit that it poses or posits. It does so, however, as the problem, by proposing *itself* as the limit of literature and letters. Thus, not only does translation pose an infinite task to literature, as the condition of literature's possibility, but it never shows up *in* or *as* itself. This is the case because translation is nothing *in itself* but the limit of letters and, like every determinate limit, it is necessarily divided in itself, trespassed in the instant of its being-posited. As the problem of letters, translation transgresses itself—crosses itself out—in order that letters and literature appear in the first place. Accordingly, translation names the secret of letters. It constitutes literature's, letters', "modest mystery," but does so by disturbing the presumption of the substantiality or being—the presence—of letters and literature.

In the same text in which Borges establishes the necessity of translation for the possibility of literature and letters and thus undermines the authority of the original, he also suggests the conditions for the *belief* in the original's privilege and authority. "The superstition about the inferiority of translations," Borges writes, "is the result of absentmindedness [*una distraída experiencia*]. There is no good text that does not seem invariable and definitive if we have turned to it a sufficient number of times. Hume identified the habitual idea of causality with that of temporal succession. Thus a good film, seen a second time, seems even better; we tend to take as necessity that which is no more than repetition" (1.239/SNF 69).[7] Absentmindedness, *una distraída experiencia*, which results in mistaking mere repetition for necessity, produces the belief, the superstition, but also the impression that the translation is inferior to the original. In other words, the authority of the original depends on the failure to pay attention, on distraction and forgetting, on a certain irresolution. It would be a mistake, however, to posit such distraction as an empirical modification of the subject; indeed, it may be a mistake to attribute it to the subject at all.

Along with Berkeley, William James, Bertrand Russell, and Arthur Schopenhauer, David Hume is one of Borges's favorite philosophical referents[8]; and it is in Hume that he finds the theory of causality that governs translation's relation to the original. Borges's remark that Hume's understanding of causality depends on temporal succession is of interest in that temporal succession not only makes possible causation (and thus necessity) in Hume, but also exposes such "natural" association to the vagaries of time, in short, to accidents, to contingency. The reference to Hume's understanding of causality implicitly challenges the primacy of the original and the origin; thus it instances a challenge to authority and to the author. At the same time, in providing for the displacement of the origin and the original, Borges's minimal reference to Hume jeopardizes the privilege of presence and the present, which in Hume is figured as the primacy of the impression.

The problem of causality, which in "El arte narrativo y la magia [Narrative Art and Magic]" Borges identifies as the central problem of narrative (1.226–32) and which Hume identifies with temporal succession and custom or habit, thus with a certain distraction or irresolution, which Hume calls belief, is essential to Borges's considerations of *attribution*. Attribution is at the heart of any determination of authority or authorship, but it is also central to the privilege of the original over the translation. But the operation of attribution is also fundamental to identity or to the possibility of identification. It is necessary, then, to determine the ground of attribution. Hume's text provides one possible understanding of this ground in the indivisible and self-present impression. This is the empirical ground, which goes unchallenged in Hume, his critique of personal identity notwithstanding. In order to see how the Borgesian text responds to the empiricist solution to the problem of attribution it will be necessary to track closely Hume's understanding of time, the constitution of causality, and the formation of belief. The implications of Borges's conception of the consubstantiality of letters and translation will ultimately be legible—if not exactly *visible*—in the production of authority in the impossibility of attribution.

## *The inscription of impression*

On Hume's account, experience is founded on impressions, which he holds to be more *vital* than ideas, which are themselves but "the faint image[s] of [impressions] in thinking and reasoning" (Hume 1978, 1). Hume characterizes the difference between impressions and ideas according to the force and violence "with which they strike upon the mind": "Those perceptions, which enter the mind with most force and violence, we name *impressions*" (1). Impressions "comprehend all our sensations, passions and emotions, as they make their first appearance in the soul" (1). Ideas are "the faint images of these in thinking and reasoning" (1). Hume argues that of every impression "there is a copy taken by the mind, which remains after the impression ceases; and this we call an idea" (8). The idea *follows* (from) the impression. In short, "*all our simple ideas in their first appearance are deriv'd from simple impressions, which are correspondent to them, and which they exactly represent*" (4). It is this *derivation* that is important. Simple ideas derive from simple impressions; they represent impressions and are therefore fainter and weaker, less forceful and vivacious copies of them. The difference between impressions and ideas, then, is *vital.* Impressions are the *sign* of life, of the presence of life, of its force. Ideas *represent* impressions and are thus marked by their difference and distance from impressions and life. Ideas are dead.

It is worth noting two things. *First,* Hume recognizes that his description of the impression's imprint is potentially misleading. The problem lies in the suggestion that the mind or soul exists prior to the inscription or striking of the impression. It does not. The impression neither enters nor strikes the mind or soul. It does not leave an imprint there as if the mind or soul were a substance that existed prior to and that remains after the impression. Hume writes: "The mind is a kind of theatre, where several perceptions successively make their appearance; pass, re-pass, glide away, and mingle in an infinite variety of postures and situations" (253). From the incessant succession of perceptions and their mingling, which constitutes the infinite variety of postures and situations, hence positions and contexts, Hume draws two conclusions. The first is that "There is properly no simplicity in it [the mind] at one time, nor identity in different [times]" regardless of "whatever natural propension we may have to imagine that simplicity or identity" (253). On the one hand, insofar as it makes simplicity impossible, temporal succession ruins identity; on the other hand, and at the same time, it is temporal succession that makes identity possible in that succession allows for the synthesis effected by the imagination. Borges's articulation of the aporetic relation between time and identity finds one of its sources in this passage from Hume. The second conclusion Hume draws is that the theater metaphor is not especially apt: "The comparison of the theater must not mislead us. They are the successive perceptions only, that constitute the mind; nor have we the most distant notion of the place, where these scenes are represented, or of the materials, of which it is compos'd" (253). We have no impression of the mind; on the contrary, the impression of the mind is the inscription or the impress of the idea of the mind. The mind is nothing in itself. It is not that which coordinates impressions and ideas. It is not that which unifies and synthesizes the succession of perceptions. Thus the figure of interiority (the mind or the stage) is constituted in the exteriority of the inscription or marking of the idea. This inscription, however vital or vivacious it may be, is not an impression. Or, more exactly, the impression is always and only the inscription or imprint of what never was. The impression is writing, hence exteriority, or the movement of exteriorization. The interiority of the subject is constituted or composed from the outside, in the mark or impress that, *qua* writing, is never present.

*Second*, Hume himself jeopardizes the notion that the idea derives from, and is therefore the less vivacious copy of, the impression. After arguing that "[w]e cannot form for ourselves a just idea of the taste of a pine-apple, without having actually tasted it," he notes a "contradictory phenomenon, which may prove, that 'tis not absolutely impossible for ideas to go before their correspondent impressions" (5). Hume admits that were one shown the spectrum of all the shades of blue with one shade missing, one would nonetheless be able to form an idea of that shade without ever having a prior impression of it. In short, one will be "sensible," Hume writes, "that there is a greater distance in that place between the contiguous colours, than in any other" (6). One thus forms an idea based on the impression of nothing. One senses the insensible, in that one senses the absence of a color never before seen. Hume asks "whether 'tis possible for him, from his own imagination, to supply this deficiency, and raise up to himself the idea of that particular shade, tho' it had never been conveyed to him by his senses?"; and he responds: "I believe there are few but will be of opinion that he can; and this may serve as a proof, that the simple ideas are not always derived from the correspondent impressions" (6). Consequently, even simple ideas do not necessarily correspond to or follow from impressions. It is always possible, and perhaps it is at times necessary, that the imagination produces a simple idea that corresponds to no impression whatsoever in order to supply the lack of sensibility.[9] The continuum of presence is thus preserved or guaranteed by an imagination that does not depend upon presence. The imagination is unhinged from sense perception. At stake in the possibility of a simple idea that does not follow from or correspond to a prior impression is the chance but also the threat that the copy comes before the original, that the original represents the copy, that the dead is more vital than the living. But the possibility that the idea could come before the impression ought to make Hume's philosophy tremble, because it threatens Humean empiricism. If the copy (or the repetition) comes before the original, then the original becomes the trace or impression of an originary repetition. The origin—and this means presence and life—is virtual. Although he never references this passage in Hume's *Treatise*, the possibility of a copy coming before the original is legible throughout the Borgesian archive. It is this possibility that will become legible, for instance, in "Pierre Menard."

Hume, however, discounts this instance of a noncorresponding simple idea: "This instance is so particular and singular, that 'tis scarce worth our observing, and does not merit that for it alone we should alter our general maxim" (6). This is what philosophy does: it dismisses the "particular and singular" as irrelevant and meaningless in order to promulgate a "general maxim." Aristotle will already have claimed that there can be no science of the singular or the particular. Hume thus suggests that the founding principle of his skeptical empiricism—namely, "that all our simple ideas proceed either mediately or immediately, from their correspondent impressions" (7)—need not be altered to account for an instance to which such empiricism does not apply. The possibility of an idea that neither mediately nor immediately follows from its correspondent impression (which means the idea does not belong to the impression) has severe consequences. Once Hume admits the possibility of noncorrespondence, he must also grant that it will never be possible to discern the relation of any idea to any impression. If all ideas do not follow from impressions, then no one idea ever follows necessarily from an impression. Further, if simple ideas do not follow or correspond to impressions, then the life of the impression, which is always measured in relation to that of the idea (the vitality of the impression can be discerned only relative to the diminished vitality of the idea), becomes impossible to determine, in that it will always be possible that the impression copy the idea. Indeed, the impression is the imprint or inscription of an idea that is the trace of the trace of an originary copy of what will never have been.

## *The force of imagination*

If the impression is the copy of the copy, then from the first its imprint is an effect of the imagination. This means that any simple impression has the same status as, for instance, the idea or impression of the mind, that "theatre" through which perceptions "pass, re-pass, glide away, and mingle in an infinite variety of postures and situations" (253). The passing and re-passing, which is to say coming-into-being and passing-away, of perceptions (whether impressions or ideas), although necessary for Hume, nonetheless troubles him and results in his determination, on the one hand, that time is succession, and, on the other hand, that it is composed of *indivisible* elements.

It should be clear why time cannot be composed of indivisible elements. An indivisible element would be present to itself such that it would *be* in itself. As such, this element would neither come into being nor pass away. It would be impossible for it to succeed itself since, *qua* being or presence-in-itself, it could not be destroyed by another instant, since in that case two temporal instants would exist simultaneously, which is impossible. There is temporal succession, and thus the possibility that perceptions "pass, re-pass, glide away and mingle in an infinite variety of postures and situations," only insofar as no perception, hence no temporal instance, is indivisible. Hume acknowledges as much when he claims, "there is no impression constant and invariable" (252). This corresponds to what Hume asserted of the idea of the mind: that there is "properly no simplicity in it at one time, nor identity in different" regardless of the "natural propension we may have to imagine that simplicity and identity" (253). Because the mind is the imprint or the impression of an idea, it is like any other idea: it results from the irreducible train of perceptions, no one of which is "constant and invariable." If this is the law or principle of perception, then it is clear that perception is impossible, that is, no perception ever presents itself as such, simple and self-identical. The natural tendency to imagine simplicity and identity results not from the *nature* of perception, that is, not from the incessant train, but from the *imagination*, which associates or synthesizes perceptions, composing them *as such—as if* there were impressions and ideas *as such*. All perceptions are composed. The imagination makes possible the synthesis necessary to the inscription of impressions and ideas such that they can be recognized as "passing, re-passing, gliding away and mingling in an infinite variety of postures and situations."

But the imagination is nothing in itself. It has no more substance or unity than what Hume calls the "idea of *self*," which must derive, he says, from "some one impression" (251). "But self or person is not any one impression, but that to which our several impressions and ideas are suppos'd to have a reference" (251). For Hume this is the problem, for if self or person were grounded in a single, simple impression then "that impression must continue invariably the same, thro' the whole course of our lives; since self is suppos'd to exist after that manner" (251). But this goes against the general rule of impressions, which states that "there is no impression constant and invariable." Consequently, Hume explains, "For my part, whenever I enter most intimately into what I call *myself*, I always stumble on some particular perception or other, of heat or cold, light or shade, love or hatred, pain or pleasure. I never can catch myself at any time without a perception, and never can observe any thing but the perception" (252). Rather than being the stable and invariant point of reference, the self or person is composed of the succession of particular or singular perceptions that do not add up or refer to a self-identical, unified or simple self. For Hume, further testimony of the absence of a substantial self that unifies the multiple perceptions lies in the fact that "[w]hen my perceptions are remov'd for any time, as by sound sleep; so long as I am insensible of *myself*, and may truly be said not to exist" (252). The point is that one is never sensible of *one self*: the self is nothing but the train of particular and singular impressions that ruin the possibility of the self as unified presence. As Hume puts it, "Ourself, independent of the perception of every other object, is in reality nothing" (340). According to Hume, then, all of "mankind" is "nothing but a bundle or collection of different perceptions, which succeed each other with inconceivable rapidity, and are in a perpetual flux and movement" (252). And this collection has no simple point of reference: there is no "single power of the soul, which remains unalterably the same, perhaps for one moment" (253). Borges writes that according to Hume, one cannot "speak of the mind's perceptions, inasmuch as the mind is nothing but a series of perceptions. The Cartesian 'I think, therefore I am' is thus invalid: to say I think is to postulate the I, a *petitio principii.*" Then he refers to Lichtenberg who argued that "instead of 'I think,' we should say impersonally 'It thinks,' as we say 'It thunders' or 'There is lightning' " (1996, 2.139/SNF 321). And he concludes, much as he had done in "The Nothingness of Personality [La nadería de la personalidad]" some twenty-five years earlier, that "there is not, behind the face, a secret self governing our acts or receiving our impressions; we are only the series of those imaginary acts and those errant impressions" (2.139/SNF 321). Borges refers to this as Hume's "nearly perfect disintegration" of the subject (2.139/SNF 321).[10] The implications of this "disintegration" both for causality and the institution of authority will become clear.

To say that we are imaginary acts is to say that "we" are an effect of the imagination, of its capacity or force. As a power of the soul, the imagination is nothing in itself. It too is a bundle of perceptions rapidly succeeding each other without simplicity in any instant nor identity in any two. The imagination is composed in the "passing, re-passing, gliding away and mingling in an infinite variety of postures and situations" of perceptions inconstant and variable. Indeed, the imagination is that power that makes possible such intermingling through the inscription and thus the *exposure* of perception. The imagination marks time; it marks the passing, re-passing, and gliding away of perceptions such that perception *happens* in the first place. There is no perception without the marking of perception. This marking, moreover, makes possible the relation of perceptions in their passing, re-passing, and gliding away. Without such marking there will be neither perception nor the intermingling of perceptions. But because there is such inscription (which is nothing in itself, which is never present as such as an impression), the intermingling of perceptions is infinite: it cannot be controlled or limited naturally. The association or relation of one perception to another cannot be read off from the objects of perception, which are themselves constituted through the infinite intermingling or play of perceptions, that is, through the "power" of the imagination. Moreover, although the imagination exposes perceptions, thereby relating or associating them, this activity or capacity is not the operation of a substantial subject or of the mind. Hume's philosophy is not a psychologism. On the contrary, as Francisco Pereira points out, "The relations or principles of association are natural given that they operate in the imagination mechanically, that is, *automatically*, *unconsciously* and *irreflexively* [*Las relaciones o principios de asociación son naturales debido a que operan en la imaginación mecánicamente, esto es, de forma* automática, inconsciente *e* irreflexiva]" (2009, 151; emphasis added).

On the one hand, given that there is no impression "constant and invariable," relation is necessary in order to constitute or compose the impression in the first place. In other words, relation or association is necessary for the self-identity of any given impression or idea. On the other hand, such relation, because it is not necessary *as such*, that is, because it is an effect of the imagination and not the result either of the objects of perception or of perceptions themselves, opens onto the problem of the *fiction* of identity. Put simply, identity or identification is both inevitable and impossible. Because there is no necessary identity, identity is possible. And it is possible as a *mistake*, an *accident*. Identity is an inevitable accident. In his discussion of personal identity, Hume explains how diversity—the succession of different objects—becomes mistaken for identity: "Tho' these two ideas of identity, and a succession of related objects be in themselves perfectly distinct, and even contrary, yet 'tis certain, that in our common way of thinking they are generally confounded with each other" (1978, 253). Hume understands identity as an "object, that remains invariable and uninterrupted thro' a suppos'd variation of time" (253). Diversity is "several distinct objects existing in succession, and connected together by a close relation . . . as if there was no manner of relation among objects" (253). Given that there is no impression constant and invariable and, as Hume points out, "Our eyes cannot turn in their sockets without varying our perceptions" and that "Our thought is still more variable than our sight" (252–253), it follows both that what is posited as self-identical is diverse and that the structure of diversity is the structure of identity. That is, identity is conceivable only on the basis of the succession of diverse objects of perceptions that are themselves constituted as self-identical or present impressions or perceptions only through the power of the imagination to relate that which has no necessary correspondence. Hume recognizes this when he writes: "That action of the imagination, by which we consider the uninterrupted and invariable object, and that by which we reflect on the succession of related objects, are almost the same to the feeling" (253–254). The imagination makes possible the discernment of both identity and difference in that it produces the relation that "facilitates the transition of the mind from one object to another, and renders its passage as smooth as if it contemplated one continu'd object" (254), which, of course, is what it does when it posits the identity of any one object or perception in order, then, to determine the difference between any two. Relation—understood as resemblance—"is the cause of the confusion and mistake, and makes us substitute one notion of identity, instead of that of related objects" (254). Identity is a mistake: "However at one instant we may consider the related succession as variable or interrupted, we are sure the next to ascribe to it a perfect identity, and regard it as invariable and uninterrupted" (254). The resemblance upon which identity is grounded is the ancillary effect of relation and relation is the effect of temporal succession and the associative faculty of the imagination. The imagination relates one perception to another and this act of relation gives rise to the "perception"—the attribution—of identity. Hume writes: "Our propensity to this mistake is so great from the resemblance above-mention'd, that we fall into it before we are aware; and tho' we incessantly correct ourselves by reflexion, and return to a more accurate method of thinking, yet we cannot long sustain our philosophy, or take off this bias from the imagination" (254). To remove the bias of the imagination would require the removal of the imagination in that the imagination is nothing other than the associative faculty. Insofar as there is perception, there must be imagination and insofar as there must be imagination, there must be mistakes or accidents of the imagination, namely, the possibility of taking for identity what is, finally, only the passing, re-passing, and passing away of the infinite variety of perceptions. On Hume's account, "our last resource is to yield" to the imagination "and boldly assert that these different related objects are in effect the same, however interrupted and variable" (254). We cannot *not* yield to this propensity. The possibility of resisting it affirms it, in that it requires that we assume the identity of our impressions and ideas even as we deny the identity of the object of our perception. Hume argues that "[i]n order to justify to ourselves this absurdity, we often feign the continu'd existence of the perceptions of our senses, to remove the interruption; and run into the notion of a *soul*, and *self*, and *substance*, to disguise the variation" (254). Soul, self, substance—even mind—are fictions of identity. They name the fiction of self-presence, of sameness over time, of invariability and constancy.

They also provide a certain security: "We may further observe, that where we do not give rise to such a fiction, our propension to confound identity with relation is so great, that we are apt to imagine something unknown and mysterious, connecting the parts, beside their relation" (254). Not to fall into the illusion and generate the fictions of the soul, self, substance or mind is, in fact, to fall into the illusion and imagine "something unknown and mysterious" that organizes the object as constant and invariable, that is, as that which establishes the object's identity, rather than such identity being the mere effect of relation or associative succession. Both the production of the fiction and the production of "something unknown and mysterious" are capacities of the imagination: "There is no foundation for any conclusion *a priori*, either concerning the operation or duration of any object, of which 'tis possible for the human mind to form a conception. Any object may be imagin'd to become entirely inactive, or to be annihilated in a moment; and 'tis an evident principle, *that whatever we can imagine, is possible*" (250).

## *Auto-imagination, or belief*

The imagination is always already at work in its automatic labor of association. That the imagination works automatically means that it is both necessary and accidental. It is necessary insofar as it operates to relate perceptions—both to themselves, thus synthesizing perceptions as such, and to other perceptions—mechanically, without any reflection or consciousness, without any decision or intervention of the soul. The imagination is not an operation of the soul, the self, or the person; it is not an operation of the mind. It does not wait on these "substances." The accidentality of the imagination demonstrates itself precisely in the production of such fictions, which are by no means necessary, according to Hume. But insofar as the imagination works, it necessarily runs the risk of producing such fictions. The propensity for them cannot long be avoided, but the inevitability of this propensity nevertheless does not make either the fiction of identity or the determination of "something unknown or mysterious" necessary, for according to Hume causation is itself a mere fiction, an accident that results from a certain forgetfulness. What is forgotten, however, is that identity or what is taken for necessary connection or relation is "mere repetition" (Pereira G. 163).

Pereira writes, "constant conjunction consists in the regular repetition of the conjunction of relations of contiguity and temporal priority between two events . . . on various occasions [*la conjunción constante consiste en la repetición regular de la conjunción de las relaciones de contigüidad y prioridad temporal entre dos eventos . . . en varias ocasiones*]" (162). Constant conjunction—which, at the level of the constitution of the present impression, Borges translates as "imaginary unity [*imaginario conjunto*]"[11]—is Hume's name for the mere repetition of successive impressions *as if* this repetition were necessary and thus *as if* there were a relation of causality from one instance to the next. Constant conjunction does not produce the idea of causality or of necessity. This is so because, Hume explains, "The repetition of perfectly similar instances can never alone give rise to an original idea, different from what is to be found in any particular instance, as has been observ'd, and as evidently follows from our fundamental principle, *that all ideas are copy'd from impressions*" (1978, 163). In short, neither contiguity in space and time, nor the temporality of one impression in relation to another, nor the constant conjunction of events provides for the new idea of causation or necessity.

It is important to understand that the idea of causality is not the copy of an original impression of causation. There is no such impression. Consequently, what is required is what Hume calls "NECESSARY CONNECTION" (77). The attribution of necessity to any connection or relation between successive impressions, however, does not depend on anything *in* the objects that are related to each other. Hume contends that "'tis evident . . . that the repetition of like objects in like relations of succession and contiguity *discovers* nothing new in any one of them" (163). What, then, is necessary connection? Pereira writes that "the idea of necessary connection is introduced as the fundamental element of causality understood as natural relation, that is, as the natural principle of association of the imagination [*la idea de la conexión necesaria se introduce como el elemento fundamental de la causalidad entendida como relación natural, es decir, como principio natural de asociación de la imaginación*]" (Pereira G. 165–166). Put simply, necessary connection enables the *anticipation* of what comes. That the relation is natural means it is nonreflexive, mechanical, automatic; as such, it is necessary. Although such relation is predictable, it is also unrelated to the objects—*qua* successive and contiguous—themselves. Necessity inheres not in the object but in the imagination. It is the imagination that allows for the possibility of trespassing "the barrier of perceptions present to the mind or of ideas of memory [*la barrera de las percepciones presentes a la mente o de las ideas de la memoria*]" (168). Pereira further remarks that it is "only insofar as it is a natural relation that causality permits us to project ourselves beyond the present testimony of the senses and the perceptions of memory [*es solamente en cuanto relación natural que la causalidad nos permite proyectarnos más allá del testimonio presente a los sentidos y de las percepciones de la memoria*]" (157). What Hume calls natural relation or necessary connection is an effect of the imagination. Only the imagination is free from the tyranny—the limit—of the present. Without such freedom, causality would be inconceivable in that it would be impossible to anticipate what comes. Thus everything would come as a surprise.

Causality is natural only insofar as it is automatic, mechanical. It is not a natural law that can be read from objects themselves. It is an effect of the mechanicity and automation of the imagination. If we "naturally" anticipate what follows from one perception, we do so on the basis of belief, which is the effect of the assumption of the repetition of what has appeared before as constantly conjoined. The repeated but nonetheless particular and singular association of successive impressions results in the belief that such particular and singular impressions are essentially related one to the other such that the one always and necessarily comes after the other. In this way, according to this belief, one sees what's coming.

Belief is an effect of the imagination. It is impossible not to believe; that is, it is impossible that one perception not be associated with another perception and it is impossible not to forget that the relation between them is neither of identity nor of causality but of mere contiguity and succession. The universality or naturalness of the imagination's associative operation means that belief is also universal and as such it is neither subjective nor reflexive. It is automatic, mechanical. Without the imagination and its freedom from the present of impressions and therefore its associative capacity, there would be no belief; there would be no chance to anticipate what comes. The promise of the imagination is the structural—hence nonsubjective—opening to the future. Without this opening to the future, to the other, *here and now*, it would be impossible to anticipate what comes and thus to posit an idea of causality or necessity. The opening to the future is the structural freedom of the imagination, what Hume calls the imagination's nonrestriction to the present of sense impressions. In Hume's account, the imagination—unlike memory, for instance—is not grounded in sense impressions; it is not restricted by what will have been present, and thus by *being* or *presence*. On the contrary, whatever can be conjured by the imagination is possible. The promise of the imagination, then, is both the chance and the threat of what comes. The structural opening to the other, to the future, *here and now*, makes possible the coming of the other, succession. This is the chance of what comes and it is the chance of belief, the chance, then, of seeing or anticipating what comes. But it is also the unmitigable and unrelievable threat of what comes, the threat that anything may or may *not* come, and that it may or may *not* come without anticipation, that it may take us by surprise, from behind, as it were. It is in this sense that belief is deception. Believing in what comes, believing that what comes can be anticipated or known, nonetheless exposes us to what comes. And what comes always arrives, if it ever does, unannounced.

### *Belief, in secret*

It is not a question of a subjective belief. Belief is the inevitable result of the no less inevitable imagination, which means that in Hume an automatic, mechanical and universal belief results from the no less automatic, mechanical and universal imagination. It is impossible *not* to believe; or, put another way, all skepticism depends on this more fundamental, because universal, belief. Precisely because belief is universal, and because it plays an important role in Borges's conception of the relation between original and translation, it is essential to follow Hume a little further.

According to Hume, belief "attends the present impression" and "arises immediately, without any new operation of reason or imagination" (102). Indeed, he remarks: "The custom [i.e., belief] operates *before* we have time for reflexion. The objects seem so inseparable, that we interpose not a moment's delay in passing from the one to the other. But as the transition proceeds from experience, and not from any primary connexion betwixt the ideas, we must necessarily acknowledge, that experience may produce a belief and a judgment of cause and effect by a *secret operation*, and without once being thought of" (104). Belief is *not* an impression. Rather, it *supplements* the present impression in order to allow for the possibility of its experience. Hume notes, "on its first appearance, I can draw no conclusion" from an impression, but "when I have had experience of its usual consequences" it "may afterwards become the foundation of belief" (102). Although Hume suggests that belief is an effect of the repetition of irreducible, indivisible impressions, in fact, belief—a certain mechanical and automatic belief—makes the impression possible. It is precisely this automatic belief that makes possible the constitution of the impression as what Borges calls a *conjunto imaginario* (imaginary unity). In other words, belief must be operative *before* its foundation is established. This is the upshot of originary repetition. Such repetition—the originary passing and re-passing—is the inscription of temporalization or spacing. The impression is the effect of originary copying—tracing, iteration, repetition—that passes, re-passes, glides away and intermingles in an infinity of postures and situations. The impression, then, is never present as such; it is not. And this means that belief cannot come *after* the experience of the usual consequences of the impression. Rather, belief names the *secret operation* of synthesis that composes the impression (and brings it to appearance) in the first place. Belief "attends" the impression in order that the impression (re) present "itself" *as such*, as if it were the foundation of belief. Belief is not a new operation of the imagination or reason. It is the synthetic function of the imagination. If the imagination exposes what passes to what comes, then belief is the name of the synthesis *qua* the anticipation of what comes as what will have come before. It is a secret operation because it is *not* an impression and thus never leaves the impression of itself as present or presence. On the contrary, belief leaves no trace of *itself* between or within the impression it synthesizes. It is as if the impression took no time. It is as if what passes, re-passes and glides away did not pass. It is as if impressions were simple—as if they were not imaginary unities—and therefore the foundation of all experience.

If belief is a *secret* operation, it is—like all secrets—structurally *open*. In other words, what is most proper to the possibility of experience—namely, the synthesis of passing and re-passing—cannot *belong* to either the subject or the object of experience. Belief is foreign to the self or the person; it is foreign to experience as the possibility of experience. It is essential to any possible experience in that it attends to the impression such that the impression can be said to pass (to happen, to arrive, *pasar, suceder*) in the first place. Belief is the secret operation that is foreign to and makes possible the perception of the self or the person. Hume admits as much when he writes, "I never am conscious of any such operation, and *find nothing in the subject, on which it can be founded*" (102, emphasis added). It is impossible to found the operation of belief *in* the subject because on Hume's account the subject (or soul, or self, or person, or mind) has no proper interiority. The interior of the subject, the subject *proper*, is exterior to the subject. The inside comes from the outside.

Yet insofar as belief is not discernible within the object of perception, it does not simply come from the outside. Rather, Hume calls belief "that certain *je-ne-scais-quoi*, of which 'tis impossible to give any definition or description, but which everyone sufficiently understands" (106). It is impossible either to define or to describe belief because it is neither subjective nor objective, neither inside nor outside the subject. Hume is clear that belief is not an impression, for otherwise causality would also be an impression, which must be impossible in that causality or necessity names the ineluctable transition from one present impression to another without itself being anything present. Nevertheless, he claims that belief is "somewhat more than a simple idea" (97). Belief is "a lively idea produc'd by a relation to a present impression" (97). The characterization of belief as a lively idea complicates Hume's distinction between impressions and ideas in terms of vitality or vivaciousness. A lively idea is either still an idea, which means belief is a copy of an impression; or it is an idea that has the vitality of an impression, in which case the difference between impressions and ideas is compromised. Hume effectively argues that an idea attends the present impression such that the impression—and therefore the present—composes itself. Belief, which is nothing in itself, names the *force* or the *vitality* constitutive of impressions (hence, of sense). "To believe," Hume writes, "is . . . to feel an immediate impression of the senses, *or repetition of that impression in the memory*. 'Tis merely the force and liveliness of the perception, which constitutes the first act of judgment and lays the foundation of that reasoning, which we build upon it, when we trace the relation of cause and effect" (86, emphasis added).

But we have already seen that the present or living impression is the copy of the copy; it is the impression or imprint, the tracing, of the idea, however lively, of belief. Now, if the present or living impression results from the attention of belief, from the supplement of a secret operation that cannot be said to be present, but that nonetheless traces, as Hume claims, the relation of the present impression to itself as to what comes, that is, it traces the relation of the *no longer* to the *not yet*, then belief has the structure of writing. And this means that the living impression is a "posthumous act,"[12] which is another name for the act of the imagination. The *authority* of the impression *qua* ground for experience lies in its presence. Indeed, when sense impressions are not present, Hume argues, *we do not exist*. This authority depends on the inscription of belief, on the posthumous act of writing, on the dead imagination, which is constitutively segregated from the present. The living present depends on the dead letter. The impression, then, is always already *in memoriam*.

Life is the inscription of death. Although this is the upshot of a reading of the *Treatise*, it is not Hume's thesis. The *Treatise* merely provides the resources for reading the determination of the living present of sense perception as the accident of the necessary (but no less arbitrary) synthesis of belief. In fact, Hume attempts to secure the living impression from death by distinguishing belief and memory from the imagination. This gesture against the imagination is legible in the understanding that to believe is either "to feel an immediate impression of the senses" (this is the present-tense of immediate life) or "the perception of that impression in the memory." Strictly speaking, there is no impression in memory. There are no *past* impressions. Past impressions are ideas and all ideas, insofar as they derive (according to Hume's own argument) from impressions, are memorial. This means that all experience is the experience of mourning: originary mourning is the experience of life. To live is to believe and to believe is to remember and to remember is to mourn.

To mourn is to imagine. But Hume never says this. On the contrary he wants to distinguish memory and imagination in order to maintain the immediate sense and presence of life. Everything comes down to the measure of life. Although he points out that it is "a peculiar property of the memory to preserve the original order and position of its ideas" and that this distinguishes memory from imagination in that "the imagination transposes and changes them, as it pleases" (85), nevertheless, Hume cautions that it is "impossible to recall past impressions, in order to compare them with our present ideas" (85). In short, the only way to determine the authority or the originality of the order of ideas is to compare the sequence of ideas to the sequence of impressions; yet, because it is impossible to recall past impressions (except as ideas), there is no certain way to verify the validity of the order of the ideas preserved and presented in memory. It is always possible that memory will misrepresent the order of ideas. Nothing is more common. Consequently, Hume asserts that the difference between memory and imagination "lies in [memory's] superior force and vivacity" (85). Following this declaration Hume offers a series of examples the upshot of which is to demonstrate that memory is endowed with a force and vivacity that "mere fictions of the imagination," which are "fainter and more obscure" (85), cannot match.

According to Hume: "An idea assented to feels different from a fictitious idea, that the fancy alone presents to us: and this different feeling I endeavor to explain by calling it a superior *force,* or *vivacity,* or *solidity,* or *firmness,* or *steadiness*" (629). For Hume, the difference between memory and imagination hinges on this *feeling* in the mind that is belief. Memory, by virtue of this feeling, "renders realities more present to us than fictions, causes them to weigh more in the thought, gives them a superior influence on the passions and imagination" (629). Although, "The imagination has command over all its ideas, and can join, and mix, and vary them in all the circumstances of place and time"—this is precisely the "passing, re-passing, gliding away and intermingling" of impressions "in an infinite variety of postures and situations"—it may even, Hume writes, "set them . . . before our eyes in their true colours, just as they might have existed," which means the imagination may do the work of memory; nevertheless, "it is impossible that that faculty can ever, of itself, reach belief" (629). The imagination, then, can *present* ("set . . . before our eyes") things "in their true colours, just as they might have existed" and yet be incapable of the feeling in the mind ascribed to belief and, thus, to ideas of memory.

## *Imagination, fiction, deception*

It is clear that Hume seeks to marginalize the imagination, both its automation and its freedom from the impression. The problem is that without the imagination's freedom from the present and presence of the impression, there would be no possible relation to either the past or to the future, thus there would be neither memory nor belief. Yet, it is also clear that the imagination jeopardizes both memory and belief insofar as it undermines the link to impressions as the ground for experience and truth. If truth is grounded in experience and experience is necessarily grounded in and on the present impression, then it can be argued that error is an aberration rather than a constitutive part of truth. On Hume's account, the difference between truth and fiction, between memory and imagination, will literally be *felt*. Although Hume confesses "that 'tis impossible to explain perfectly this feeling or manner of conception," nevertheless, he affirms "everyone sufficiently understands [it] in common life" and that "in philosophy we can go no farther, than assert that it is something *felt* by the mind, which distinguishes the ideas of the judgment from the fictions of the imagination" (629).

Hume goes on to explain, for instance, that the difference between poetic enthusiasm, which derives from the mere fiction of the imagination, and what he calls "serious conviction," which derives from belief and memory, from custom and constant conjunction, "proceeds in some measure from reflexion and general rules" (631). This is so because without such reflection and general rules it will be impossible to tell them apart. "We observe," Hume writes, "that the vigor of conception, which fictions received from poetry and eloquence, is a *circumstance merely accidental, of which every idea is equally susceptible*" (631, emphasis added). The mechanicity of the imagination's associative faculty—without which there would be no constant conjunction, no belief, no memory, no impressions—subjects every perception to accidentality. Because the imagination—just like the belief that depends on it—is automatic, *all* relations between perceptions are accidental.

Consequently, accidentality also affects the vivacity and force of perceptions: "And as an idea of the memory, by losing its force and vivacity, may degenerate to such a degree, *as to be taken for* an idea of the imagination; so on the other hand an idea of the imagination may acquire such a force and vivacity, *as to pass for* an idea of the memory, and counterfeit its effects on the belief and judgment" (86, emphasis added). Because there is no perception constant and invariable, such "degeneration" must always be possible.[13] It is always possible that ideas—

perceptions in general—will counterfeit *themselves*. Indeed, perceptions are constitutively counterfeits, copies, representations. Belief is another name for constitutive deception. That is, insofar as belief is generative of ideas, then it necessarily and unexceptionally—mechanically—generates the possibility of deception. The counterfeit that belief generates is the counterfeit of belief. There is no belief without this counterfeit, without this necessary deception. But this also means there is no belief without the imagination. "This is so noted in the case of liars; who by the frequent repetition of their lies, come at last to believe and remember them, as realities; custom and habit having in this case, *as in many others*, the same influence on the mind as nature, and infixing the idea [here, the idea of imagination] with equal force and vigor" (86, emphasis added).

The upshot of this reading of Hume is that while belief is necessary for any determination of causality, it is no less the case that belief can never be secured *in itself* from the imagination upon which it depends. Thus, that which makes possible "necessity"—repetition, technicity or automaticity—also forecloses the possibility of protecting belief from corruption or deception, from the accidents of fiction. Because belief is only possible if there is referral, hence an opening to exteriority in general, it is always possible to be deceived and to deceive oneself, to take lies, fictions, for truth. It is not only possible to do so, it is a structural necessity that we do so as the condition of possibility of truth and of the truth of experience, thus of any possible authority, including the truth, experience, and authority of skepticism.

The attempt to ground truth, experience, and authority on the indivisible and present impression inevitably results in a circular argument. According to Hume, belief *both* makes possible the repetition constitutive of the impression as the definitive ground of all experience *and* results from such repetition. What Hume cannot account for, and what troubles the conceptions of truth, experience, and authority articulated in the *Treatise*—whether authority is conceived as the origin or the original, the sovereign or the author—founded upon self-presence, and therefore on autonomy, is the *secret operation* of the imagination that synthesizes, thereby composing, the present out of the passing, re-passing, and gliding away of perceptions that are not. This is the limit of Hume's skeptical empiricism. Ultimately, in order not to give up on the value of presence, which Hume (and not just Hume) considers the time of life, he grounds skepticism on the inviolable certainty of sense impression. He invests in the truth of punctual sense certainty in order to declare all *a priori* ideas—including that of causality—unfounded. The problem is that his certainty of the impression—that there *is* sense impression and that it *is* indivisible and present—both undermines his skepticism and ruins the self-presence of life as *lived*. Indeed, this is the upshot of Borges's "A New Refutation of Time," when he cites near the conclusion the fifth-century Buddhist treatise, the *Visuddhimagga* (*The Path to Purity*): " 'The man of a past moment . . . has lived, but he does not live nor will he live; the man of a future moment will live, but he has not lived nor does he now live; the man of the present moment lives, but he has not lived nor will he live' " (2.148/SNF 331). If the time of life is the indivisible present, if man lives in the present, then nothing will have happened nor will ever happen to him. And if nothing has ever happened nor ever will happen, then he will not have lived nor ever will live. He will be unaffected, thus dead. If, as Borges asserts in "A New Refutation of Time," "[e]very instant is autonomous" (2.140/SNF 322), then the life of the so-called "living" present is always already dead.

### *Fidelity to the text*

Borges is correct to criticize Hume for the failure to push his skepticism beyond the impossibility of a temporal succession given in and guaranteed by indivisible sense impressions. But this criticism does not amount to a refutation of time; rather, it is a refutation of Hume's (and Berkeley's and Schopenhauer's) understanding of time as grounded in indivisible instants and, therefore, it is a refutation of time *qua* existent or being. It is the being or substance (*ousia*), the presence, of time that is at stake in Borges's claim that time is neither indivisible nor divisible: "It is not indivisible, for in that case it would have no beginning to connect it to the past nor end to connect it to the future, nor even middle, because whatever has no beginning or end has no middle. Neither is it divisible, for in that case it would consist of a part that was and another that is not. Ergo, the present does not exist, and since the past and the future do not exist either, time does not exist" (2.147–148/SNF 330–331). Borges's analysis of time is correct: time does not *exist*; it is not of the order of *being*. Time is not a *substance*. The mistake is to think that the refutation of time *qua substance* refutes time. It does not. Indeed, the nonsubstantial conception of time, that is, the understanding of time as divided between the *no longer* and the *not yet*, no part of which *is*, makes possible *both* the critique of substance (the *in itself* or the *as such*) *and* the belief in substance *qua* sameness or identity over time.

Borges admits that he *does not believe* ("I myself do not believe [*yo mismo descreo*]") in this refutation of time. He claims that it results from "a life dedicated to belles-lettres and, occasionally, to the perplexities of metaphysics" (2.137/SNF 318). Borges further acknowledges that the principal targets of his critique, Berkeley and Hume, "abound in paragraphs that contradict or exclude [his] thesis"; nevertheless, he *believes* (*creo*: I believe) that he has "deduced the inevitable consequence of their doctrine" (2.135/SNF 317). What does it mean to be given over to the "perplexities of metaphysics," to be, then, "an Argentine adrift on a sea of metaphysics" (2.135/SNF 317)? It means to be caught within the horizon of belief. Borges discerns that metaphysics involves, necessarily, inevitably, a suspension of disbelief. Even the skeptic *must* believe. Borges does not believe in the refutation of time he promulgates, but he does believe that such a refutation follows logically from Berkeley and Hume. As the *inevitable* consequence of their philosophical arguments, the refutation of time *in which Borges does not believe* would not, in fact, admit of such disbelief. Borges believes this.

In "A New Refutation of Time," however, Borges does not criticize the role of belief in Hume. According to "the inevitable consequence" of Hume's *Treatise*, belief cannot be grounded upon sense impressions or an indivisible element of any sort; it cannot therefore be conceived or experienced as present. Yet, it is that which sustains or supports—insofar as it synthesizes—sense impressions and, therefore, the sense certainty of life *qua* present to itself. The point, however, is that because it is an effect of belief—the secret operation that belongs neither to the subject nor to the object, that is neither an impression nor an idea—the certainty of the impression, hence the impression *itself*, can never be given empirically. The ground of Hume's empirical skepticism, that which guarantees or supports such skepticism, cannot be experienced. Belief names the impossible ground of any possible experience.

Borges's refutation of time, in which he does not believe, but which he believes is an inevitable consequence of Berkeley's and Hume's respective philosophical projects, which means it is the unavoidable result of both idealism and empiricism, comes to him when he is tired. He writes that the refutation of time that he has "glimpsed or foreseen [*divisado o presentido*]" "tends to visit me at night and in the weary twilight [*en el fatigado crepúsculo*] with the illusory force of an axiom [*con ilusoria fuerza de axioma*]" (2.137/SNF 318). Elsewhere, in "The Homeric Versions," Borges suggests that a certain exhaustion makes possible the belief in what he calls the definitive text: "The concept of the *definitive text* does not correspond except to religion or exhaustion [*cansancio*]" (1.239/SNF 69). Hume, of course, was a dedicated critic of religion, but Borges's positioning of Hume's notion of causality—the belief that results from forgetting or distraction, *una distraída experiencia*—in relation to the possibility of the definitive text, suggests that for Hume the "modest mystery" of letters (alphabetic characters, literature, handwriting) is that they are composed through faith, as a matter of belief. As Borges notes, the question always asked of translation concerns its faithfulness: "Which of these many translations is faithful?, my reader will want to know. I repeat: none or all of them . . . except for the literal versions, whose virtue lies entirely in their contrast to contemporary practices" (1.243/SNF 74). The problem or limit of the *literal* translation haunts Borges: the literal translation is both the *most* faithful and the *least* faithful; it is the least faithful because it is the most faithful. Ultimately, it is the literal translation that exposes the role of belief in translation and in the original.[14]

Fidelity to a definitive text—a fidelity that is by definition exhausted—appears to delimit translation.[15] Commenting on *Don Quijote*'s first sentence, Borges remarks that he does not know if that sentence "would be considered good by an impartial divinity; I only know that any modification would be sacrilegious and that I cannot conceive of any other beginning for the *Quixote*" (1.239/SNF 70). Whereas it is possible that Cervantes "ignored this slight superstition and perhaps never noted [*no hubiera identificado*] that particular paragraph," Borges claims to be incapable of anything but repudiating any divergence (1.239/SNF 70). He confesses: "The *Quixote*, due to my *congenital practice* [*congénito ejercicio*] of Spanish, is a uniform monument, with no other variations except those provided by the publisher, the bookbinder, and the typesetter" (1.239–240/SNF 70; emphasis added). The congenital practice of Spanish is accidental. It is an accident of birth and circumstance.

This accident "grounds" what Borges considers the necessity of the *Quijote*. In "Sobre los clásicos [On the Classics]" Borges writes: "A classic is that book which a nation or a group of nations or history [*el largo tiempo*] have decided to read as if [*como si*] in its pages everything was deliberate, fatal, profound as the cosmos and capable of interminable interpretations [*capaz de interpretaciones sin término*]" (2.151). In sum, according to Borges, a classic "is a book that generations of men, urged on by diverse reasons, read with . . . a mysterious loyalty" (2.151), which Borges also calls "a reading that demands an act of faith [*una lectura que reclama un acto de fe*]" (2.151). Some two decades earlier, in "The Homeric Versions," he explained, "With famous books, the first time is actually the second, for we approach them [*los abordamos*] already knowing them. The prudent common phrase 'rereading the classics' is the result of an innocent truth [*de inocente veracidad*]" (1.239/SNF 69–70). The first time is always (at least) the second time. There is no reading that is not from the beginning a re-reading. In the context of "The Homeric Versions," Borges means that it is impossible within any given culture to approach that culture's foundational texts without presuppositions, without pre-understanding. Inasmuch as these remarks occur in the context of a discussion of the privilege of the original over the translation, however, it is impossible not to consider their import for any discussion of authority grounded on the privilege of priority. The *first* time is always already the *third* time, for were the impression absolutely singular, hence unrepeatable, it would be unanticipatable and unrecognizable as such.

According to the logic of "La supersticiosa ética del lector [The Superstitious Ethics of the Reader]," this "mysterious loyalty" to the text, this "act of faith," entails "an inattentive [*distraída*: distracted, absentminded, irresolute] reading that favors partial affectations [*de atenciones parciales*]" (1.202/SNF 52). The constitution of the classic and by extension of the text *itself* or *as such*—hence as inalterable, as necessary—requires a certain distractedness, an absentmindedness, an irresoluteness; in short, it requires accidentality, contingency, chance.[16] In order to *believe* in the classic, attention can only be partial, distracted.[17] But, importantly, Borges is not only concerned with the determination of classic texts. The *hrönir* of Tlön—those secondary objects—"were the coincidental offspring of distraction and forgetfulness" (1.439/CF 77).

### *Accidents of the origin, or congenital translation*

The assertion that for one whose use of Spanish is congenital the *Quijote* is untranslatable, immune to any variation except that introduced by chance or error and thus without any authority, must nonetheless be read next to the first sentence of "Las versiones homéricas." For Borges, translation is consubstantial to letters. Despite the *Quijote*'s monumentality and definitiveness, the introduction of editor's and typesetter's errors—which are in the main variations of the letter, of the graphic element of the text—indicates that every text is constitutively open—in its very production—to chance, to change, to alteration, hence to a necessarily accidental corruption that cannot be ascribed to any authority or authorial intention. In his autobiographical essay, Borges embraces such errors as essential to the *Quijote*: "Later I made a friend obtain for me the Garnier edition [of the *Quijote*], with the same engravings, the same footnotes and also the same erratas [*también con las mismas erratas*]. For me all these things form part of the book. I consider that edition to be the true *Quijote*" (1999, 26). "Erratas" are printer's errors, often of the typographical variety. The possibility of such corruption without authority, such translation, is what Borges calls the "modest mystery" of letters. It is this mystery that leads the narrator of "Tlön, Uqbar, Orbis Tertius" to report that he was always amazed to open a book in the morning to find the letters in the same places as they were the night before. The possibility of such unauthorized additions and deletions, of typographical and editorial errors, makes clear that, in fact, letters do not always remain where they were. On the contrary, letters wander, stray.

Although Borges admits that, due to congenital limitations, he cannot bear the *Quijote* in translation, he confesses that he first read the Spanish classic in English and when he later read the novel in Spanish it seemed to him "a bad translation" (1999, 26). Borges is not the only one to have thought the English version was the original. The de-authorization—or what Lisa Block de Behar calls "un *auto/des/autor/ización* [an auto/dis/author/ization]" (1987, 109)—of the *Quijote* began much earlier when Cervantes himself made Cide Hamete Benengeli responsible for the "redaction of the manuscripts that tell the adventures . . . of Don Quijote" (109). *Auto-des-autorización* is a kind of *auto-de-fe* of authorship and authority that nonetheless reasserts authority in the name of another. This first instance inevitably gave rise to others. For example, the close proximity of the publication dates of the first Spanish edition and the first English translation resulted in the attribution of the authorship of the *Quijote* to Francis Bacon, while the Spanish version "was nothing but the translation of a minor official named Cervantes" (109).

Cervantes thematized this problem when, late in the novel, don Quijote enters a print shop and becomes involved in a conversation about translation. Ultimately he concludes: "It seems to me . . . that translating from one language to another, except from those queens of all languages, Greek and Latin, is rather like looking at Flemish tapestries on the wrong side, because even though you can make out the figures, they're partially hidden behind this thread and that thread, and you can't ever see them as clearly and with all the detail you can find on the right side." (1985, 2.998/1999, 694).[18] Cervantes exempts Greek and Latin from the law of translation, because they can sustain translation *without losing themselves*. Such languages, according to Walter Benjamin, are "unconditionally translatable," because there is no gap between the letter ("the literal quality") and the meaning or the "true language," the "Truth" (1996, 262). Benjamin writes that in Holy Writ "language and revelation are joined *without tension*" (262–263, emphasis added). In Cervantes's *Quijote*, Greek and Latin take the place of Holy Writ. Don Quijote concludes his discussion of translation by suggesting that there are actually less profitable ways to spend one's time than in translation and by remarking that two translations in particular "are so well done that it's hard to tell which is the translation and which the original" (1985 2.999/1999, 694). The translations Cervantes praises—but perhaps also fears—are not only secular texts, but vulgar texts, neither Greek nor Latin. The perfect translation of such vulgarity jeopardizes and undermines the origin and the original. Cervantes anticipates the problem of authority that the *Quijote* will encounter from its first appearance in English, in Spanish. Yet, in exempting Greek and Latin, he secures the possibility of authority and of authorship. The indivisibility of translation and original in the perfection of translation effectively absolutizes sovereignty in and as the origin, the original. Greek and Latin—queen, thus sovereign languages—are absolutely self-identical in Cervantes's account.

Borges, however, thinks translation and original differently. Rather than suggesting the possibility of perfect translation such that translation and original become indistinguishable, he describes the aporia of translation. On the one hand, translation is necessary to the original in that it instances the consubstantial problem of the letter. On the other hand, the congenital—which is also to say the accidental—relation to a mother tongue means translation is constitutively foreign to the original. Translation, then, is necessarily internal and external, necessary and accidental to the original. It comes both before and after the original. It comes before the original insofar as the original can only be constituted in a consubstantial relation with translation; thus there is no original before the problem of translation. It comes after the original insofar as one has a congenital use of an original or mother tongue, which makes all other tongues foreign. We can only ever write in one language. Yet, on account of the consubstantiality of letters and translation, the language in which we write is always foreign to us. We write in translation as the condition of possibility of writing in the mother tongue.[19] This is the aporia: the original and the translation are constitutively heterogeneous *and* indissociable.[20] Necessary *con*substantiation explains why we never get beyond the letter, why we never arrive at any transcendence that secures or guarantees meaning and therefore the authority or sovereignty of either original or translation.

"The Homeric Versions" anticipated by seven years Borges's first *ficción*, which he claims to have written in order not to have failed a different writing assignment. After suffering from septicemia and struggling between life and death for a month, Borges feared he had lost his mind. After he had begun to recover and after he knew that he had not lost the capacity to understand, he nevertheless was terrorized by "the idea that [he] would never write again" (1999, 110). Having already written a good number of poems and brief articles or reviews, he explains, "I thought that if in that moment I attempted to write a review and failed, I would be finished intellectually. But if I tried something that I had never done before and failed, that would not be so bad and perhaps it would even prepare me for the final revelation [*la revelación final*]" (110). This "new and different" something is "Pierre Menard," which itself proposes an impossible project.

Like "The Homeric Versions," albeit in a very different and more oblique way, "Pierre Menard" addresses the problem of translation. The list of Menard's *visible* work includes translations of two Spanish texts, one by Quevedo, *Aguja de navegar cultos*, and one on chess, *Libro de la invención liberal y arte del juego del axedrez*. The list of *visible* works also comprises Menard's *trasposición* into Alexandrines of a poem by Paul Valéry. It is possible to argue against transposition as translation, but in fact transposition might be as close as one ever comes to *literal* translation in the sense that it effects a literal movement or displacement within the same language. Transposition literally instances the movement of the letter. It is thus a kind of *errata*. It is this movement that haunts the narrator of "Tlön, Uqbar, Orbis Tertius." Despite the documented interest in translation, Borges does not suggest that Menard translates or transcribes the *Quijote*. Block de Behar observes that one of the limitations of George Steiner's and Maurice Blanchot's respective readings of "Pierre Menard" is that both "see Pierre Menard as a translator, the ideal translator" (1987, 115).[21] Indeed, Steiner writes, "Arguably, 'Pierre Menard, Author of the *Quixote*' . . . is the most acute, most concentrated commentary anyone has offered on the business of translation. What studies of translation there are . . . could . . . be termed a commentary on his commentary" (Steiner 70). For his part, Blanchot notes, "When Borges suggests that we imagine a contemporary French writer writing, starting with thoughts that are his own, some pages that would textually reproduce two chapters of *Don Quixote*, this memorable absurdity is nothing other than that which is accomplished in all translation" (1959, 142/2003, 95).

*Contra* Steiner and Blanchot, Block de Behar asserts that Menard "is not a translator of the *Quijote* . . . ; nor can his labor be confused with plagiarism" (1987, 117). Of course, we already know that Borges considered all of his *ficciones* to have been plagiarized. Nevertheless, the narrator of "Pierre Menard" agrees with Block de Behar: "Nor, surely, need one add that he never aimed at a mechanical transcription of the original; he did not propose to copy it" (Borges 1996, 1.446/CF 91, translation modified). Pierre Menard's *Quijote* is "Neither transcription, nor translation; neither plagiarism, nor adaptation," Block de Behar insists, "If a necrological note is dedicated to Menard as the author of the *Quijote*, it is because Borges was increasingly incapable of not confusing [*cada vez más . . . no puede dejar de confundir*], in the same entity, in the same function, author and reader" (1987, 117). The importance of Block de Behar's investment in the identity of author and reader becomes transparent once she indicates the etymological connection of *leer* (to read; *legere*) and *ley* (law; *lex, legis*).[22] Her concern is to put authority in its proper place. With the postulation of the unity (a *conjunto imaginario*, Borges might have said) and necessary indivisibility of author and reader, of authority and law, Block de Behar ascribes an absolute sovereignty to the Borgesian text.

The indivisibility of author and reader, which Block de Behar sites as the theoretical and perhaps practical principle of the Borgesian text, is problematic for two related reasons. First, it leads Block de Behar to posit an untenable interpretation of Derrida. Second, it results in an authority of the text that manifests itself as the tyranny of the origin. According to Block de Behar's account, Derrida has taught us that "In the beginning was the text. Always a pretext: the anterior text, the first reason of writing proper, foreign writing (reading)" (1987, 118).[23] It is easy to see that writing and reading, author and reader, authority and law, must all be the same, indivisible, once the text takes the place of the word in the beginning. Block de Behar concludes: "the text does not change [*no se altera*], but it is the principle of alterity [*es prinicipio de alteridad*]" (122). With this remark Block de Behar misinterprets Derrida's understanding of the text. When, at the outset of "Plato's Pharmacy," Derrida writes, "A text is not a text unless it hides from the first comer, from the first glance, the law of its composition and the rules of its game"; and when he continues, "A text remains, and moreover, forever imperceptible. Its law and its rules are not, however, harbored in the inaccessibility of a secret; it is simply that they can never be booked, in the *present*, into anything that could rigorously be called a perception" (1981, 63), his definition of text is such that it is marked by movement, alterity and alteration, by displacement. Hence, the text is temporal or temporalized through and through. Block de Behar's rendering of Derrida's understanding of text, however, makes the text stand still, as if it were *in itself* the origin and thus the inalterable beginning or principle of alteration. Like Cervantes and Benjamin before her, she posits the sovereign authority of the origin, whether understood as queen languages, Holy Writ, the original, or, in Block de Behar's case, the text that is and always will be. Her conception of the text, in short, books it in and as the *present*. For Block de Behar, that which does not move provides the rule for the condition of possibility of movement. On her account, "text" is another name for the unmoved mover or God. "Text" thus becomes an onto-theological concept.

No doubt this makes sense if one desires an indivisible and absolute sovereignty of the text such that there can be no difference between author and reader, authority and law. But it is important to distinguish Block de Behar's notion of the text from Derrida's, whose "concept of the text," Rodolphe Gasché writes, "in no way implies" what Derrida has called a "theology of the text" (1986, 278; Derrida 1981, 258). In Derrida there can be no theology of the text, because the text—if there is one—is marked by the movement of *différance*, of the trace. Far from being that which institutes and rules over the text or the trace of the text, God is but an effect of the trace.[24] Block de Behar's understanding that the inalterable text is the *principio*—beginning and principle or rule, thus also the prince (*príncipe*)—of all alterity, does not concur with Derrida's assessment of *différance*, of which he writes: "[*D*]*ifférance* is not. It is not a present being, however excellent, unique, principal, or transcendent. It governs nothing, reigns over nothing, and nowhere exercises any authority. It is not announced by any capital letter. Not only is there no kingdom of *différance*, but *différance* instigates the subversion of every kingdom. Which makes it obviously threatening and infallibly dreaded by everything within us that desires a kingdom, past or future presence of a kingdom" (1982, 21–22). It is necessary to read Derrida's claim that "*différance* instigates the subversion of every kingdom" in the strongest possible sense, and thus as including the most basic sovereignty, that of the *autos*, of ipseity and the proper. *Différance* not only marks the sovereign decision; it also marks—remarks and *solicits*—sovereignty itself. *Différance* decides indivisible sovereignty within itself. There is no sovereignty without such decision. Nothing is immune from the double operation of *différance*, including the trace. Derrida writes, "Always differing and deferring [*Toujours différante*], the trace is never as it is in the presentation of itself. It erases itself in presenting itself, muffles itself in resonating, like the *a* writing itself, inscribing its pyramid in *différance*" (23). "Therefore," Derrida concludes, "the concept of the trace is incompatible with the concept of retention, of the becoming past of what has been present. One cannot think the trace—and therefore *différance*—on the basis of the present, of the presence of the present" (21). The trace opens an economy of death,[25] of finitude and absence that cannot be construed as modifications of presence.

The trace responds to the problem that most preoccupied Borges and that also vexed Hume, namely, that of the synthesis of succession or of the time that passes and the identity that endures. In Derrida, the trace provides for a synthesis of temporality that does not recur to the impossible thought of an indivisible now.[26] The thought of an unmoved, incorruptible original—whether Greek, Latin, Holy Writ, the text, or Hume's indivisibly present impression—depends on a conception of temporality grounded on an indivisible now as the origin or the original. Only such an indivisible now could, as Benjamin writes, provide "a stop" to translation and its effects or, as Block de Behar notes, be inalterable. The problem, however, is that an inalterable and indivisible origin could never afford the possibility of any movement whatsoever. There could never be an account, therefore, of the translatability, in Benjamin's terms, of the original, if the original, Holy Writ, were in itself capable of determining the rule or the "stop" of translation. In Hume's terms, the simple, indivisible present impression can have no necessary or causal relation to any other impression. This must be the case, for in order for an indivisible now to be related to another now, two nows must exist at the same time. Since this is impossible, the now cannot be indivisible but must rather be divided in itself. Hume never provides an account of this latter possibility, although his description of belief as that which secretly or mysteriously relates impressions and ideas (Borges's "imaginary unity")—with a rapidity that cannot be registered phenomenally—suggests that such a synthesis *composes* impressions *as such*. Belief is, as Hume writes, that "*je-ne-scais-quoi*," which is neither sensible (it is not simply an impression) nor intelligible (it is not simply an idea). Although never present, belief nonetheless makes possible the repetition, hence ideality, necessary to any perception, whether sensible or intelligible. Belief thus makes possible the recognition of the impression in the first place *as* the first impression.

## *Attributing authority to context*

If we take seriously Borges's considerations of Hume, translation, and time in "The Homeric Versions" and "A New Refutation of Time," then it follows that Borges is acutely aware of the problem or limit of sensibility and perception. Indeed, "Pierre Menard, Author of the *Quijote*" turns on the impossible distinction between Menard's *visible* and *invisible* work. If "Pierre Menard" concerns the limit of perception, and therefore the distinction between the sensible and the intelligible, between the visible and the invisible work, it nevertheless does not provide a key for making this decision. Rather, in "Pierre Menard" Borges attempts to mark or inscribe the synthesis that makes any perception—whether of the visible or the invisible—possible.

Pierre Menard's *visible* work, therefore, must already be marked by a synthetic operation that is no less mysterious, secret, than the operation of Hume's belief. This has at least one important implication. Any discussion of the difference between Cervantes's *Quijote* and Menard's *Quijote* that depends on context misses the point. This is so because context is always thought on the basis of presence. Context is always thought as *visible*. What is at stake in such readings is the question of value: one text determined in this or that context or historical or cultural moment is better, richer, more sophisticated, subtle, less arcane, etc., in comparison to another. This is how Menard's literary necrologist evaluates the two *Quijotes*. It would be easy enough to outline the way too many critics have simply repeated this gesture. One example will suffice.

Susan Petrilli observes, "Borges insistently returns to the question of translation, which he considers of great importance on the level of experience. Direct writing does not enable us to perceive that mystery of the text which, on the contrary, is indistinctly revealed by translation" (153). Yet, despite Petrilli's understanding that "A kind of praise of translation runs through the whole corpus of Borges's writings" (165), in her account translation works to save the original insofar as it *reveals* the mystery that remains inherent to the original. In her argument, as in Block de Behar's, the "text" is something beyond the operation of translation, untouchable. Nowhere is the distinction between original and translation clearer, however, than in Petrilli's observation that "A translation is *obviously not identical* to the original . . . not even Menard's *Quijote* with respect to Cervantes's *Quijote*" (162, emphasis added). If one considers Menard's *Quijote* a translation of Cervantes' *Quijote*, and there are good reasons for not doing so, at the very least one would have to concede their literal or material identity. In other words, Petrilli's statement is absurd. Without the assumption of the determinative effects of context, it would be impossible to distinguish Cervantes's *Quijote* from Menard's. Petrilli grants the *visible* importance of contextual and historical difference, otherwise she would have to notice the obvious:

the two *Quijotes* are strictly identical. If she acknowledges the influence of contextual difference, it follows that she should also acknowledge the historicity of the text itself, namely, that the text is susceptible to change and, therefore, to the effects of time.

Yet, despite noting that "time plays its part as well," Petrilli does not consider the temporalization necessary to the problem of the identical non-selfsame. In her determination of the relation between Menard's *Quijote* and Cervantes's she insists that the translation "is obviously not identical to the original" (156), but rather that Menard's translation "is only *verbally* identical to Cervantes's *Quijote*" (158). The obviousness of the non-identity of Menard's translation and Cervantes's original, which is in any case undermined by Petrilli's concession of a *verbal* identity, hinges on the reader's accession to the narrator's authoritative (authorized and authorizing) understanding of how to interpret the difference between the two texts.[27] The narrator's interpretation suggests the possibility of contextual determinations of verbal or textual events, as if context were not also open to the same translation effects.[28]

The determination of contextual difference hinges on the assumption—the belief or the superstition (which here, as in Hume, passes for fact)—that we know what it means for a text to be written in Spain in the early seventeenth century and how this differs from the production of a *verbally* identical text in France—by a symbolist poet, no less—in the twentieth century.

## *Monsters of attribution, or acts of faith*

The conclusion of "Pierre Menard" makes such determinative attribution suspect: "Menard has (perhaps unwittingly) enriched the slow and rudimentary art of reading by means of a new technique—the technique of deliberate anachronism and fallacious attribution. That technique, requiring infinite patience and concentration, encourages us to read the *Odyssey* as though [*como si*] it came after the *Aeneid*, to read Mme. Henri Bachelier's *Le jardin du Centaure* as though [*como si*] it were written by Mme. Henri Bachelier" (1996, 1.450/CF 95). The technique of deliberate anachronistic attribution is possible only if the text is constitutively out of context. It is only because the text is *never present* to itself or *in itself*, that it is possible to attribute Mme. Henri Bachelier's *Le jardin du*

*Centaure* to Madame Henri Bachelier as if she had authored it; that is, as if we *believed* it were so. And, moreover, it is clear that attribution is constitutively fallacious: we can only ever have faith in the attribution of this or that work to this or that author. Authority, then, is false, fallacious, deceptive; it is known only insofar as it is believed. Authority is a matter of faith.

The implications are even more severe, however. If Borges's technique of fallacious attribution—and there is only fallacious attribution—models Hume's understanding of belief, then belief—which is neither subjective nor objective—is strictly speaking a *technical* operation. At the heart of the human—as the condition of possibility of self-recognition, of auto-affection or self-positing, and thus as the condition of possibility of experience—is a machine, a prosthetic device. The heart of the human is mechanical; it beats automatically.

Perhaps it is more appropriate to speak of the mechanical substitution not of the heart, but of the voice. In "Sobre el doblaje [On Dubbing]," after listing examples of combinatory monsters, one of which is the Trinity, Borges writes, "Hollywood has just enriched this frivolous [*vano*: vain, empty] museum of teratology: by means of a perverse artifice they call dubbing, they devise monsters that combine the famous face of Greta Garbo with the voice of Aldonza Lorenzo" (1.283/SNF 262). According to Petrilli, it would be a mistake to identify the monstruous effects of dubbing with translation. She argues, "The relation of iconic similarity distinguishes translation from dubbing. Dubbing produces . . . the arbitrary grafting onto a person's body, onto his or her features, gestures and movements, of another voice, in another language" (Petrilli 165). Moreover, Petrilli notes that Borges "takes a stand against dubbing." In Petrilli's analysis, "Dubbing is substitution. Translation would also seem to be a substitution, but only as a result of idolatry of the 'original' " (165). And it is certainly the case that Borges calls dubbing a "phonetic-visual anomaly" and argues that its "central defect" is "the arbitrary implant of another voice and another language" (1996, 1.283/SNF 262). At the conclusion to "Pierre Menard," however, Borges celebrates just such arbitrary attribution.

In "On Dubbing," Borges insists that "The voice of Hepburn or Garbo is not accidental [*no es contingente*] but, for the world, it is one of the attributes that define them [*es, para el mundo, uno de los atributos que las definen*]. Similarly, it is worth remembering that gestures are different in English and Spanish" (1.283–284/SNF 262). To the end of this sentence Borges appends a footnote: "More than one spectator will ask himself: Since they are usurping voices, why not also faces? When will the system be perfect? When will we see Juana González playing the role of Greta Garbo playing the role of Queen Christina of Sweden?" (1.284n/SNF 262n1). The suggestion of the perfection of dubbing opens onto the question of reference and of the relation of copy to original, of the counterfeit to the authentic. Borges does not suggest that Queen Christina plays the role of Queen Christina, that between Queen Christina and Queen Christina a certain dubbing and doubling necessarily takes place. Nor, for that matter, does the note explicitly suggest that the voice and figure of Queen Christina—and by extension the voices and figures of everyone, of Garbo and Hepburn included—are contingent, arbitrary, accidental. The reference to Queen Christina, however, signals an oblique reference to Schopenhauer, who, in *The World as Will and Representation*, cites Queen Christina in a discussion of the right to deceive the other: "In all cases in which I have a right of compulsion, a perfect right to use *violence* against others, I can, according to the circumstances, just as well oppose another's violence with *cunning* without doing wrong, and consequently I have an actual *right to lie*" (1.340). Schopenhauer concludes: "If anyone should deny this, he would have still more to deny the legality of any ruse adopted in war, of stratagem; this is just the lie founded on fact, and is proof of the saying of Queen Christina of Sweden that 'The words of men are to be esteemed as nothing; hardly are their deeds to be trusted' " (1.340). Schopenhauer's point is that right and wrong are mere moral determinations. Borges pushes the problem of such deception to its logical extreme: the possibility of deceiving the other necessarily entails the possibility of self-deception. When a footnote in "Sobre el doblaje" concerning Queen Christina is read in conjunction with the remark that it is not necessary to watch the original, but only to *believe* that one watches the original, it becomes clear that the attribution of voice to figure (and of both to an unchanging identity) is itself an effect of dubbing, of doubling and duplicity, of self-deception. That a voice belongs—is proper—to anyone at all is an effect of faith, of belief, of that secret *je-ne-scais-quoi*. It is an *act of faith* to attribute one's *own* voice to one self. Consequently, it is necessary to take the naturalness—the givenness—of the relation between voice and figure on credit.

Such credit is an effect of auto-deception, of *auto-doblaje*. What distinguishes Juana González and Greta Garbo from Queen Christina is nothing more and nothing less than that González and Garbo know that to be González and Garbo is finally no different from playing Queen Christina. In order to be Garbo, Garbo necessarily plays "herself": there is an entire repertoire of gestures, features, necessarily reproducible, imitable, that sign "Garbo," even in the absence of "Garbo." Garbo's voice is properly her own only insofar as from the beginning, from the very first word she speaks, it is already dubbed, doubled, repeated. There is, then, no identity without the possibility of dubbing and doubling and deception, without the possibility of the counterfeit. There is no voice properly Garbo's own without or outside the substitution—mechanical, technical, monstrous, both accidental and necessary—of that voice.

In "Sobre el doblaje," however, Borges distinguishes translation from dubbing on the grounds that dubbing practices arbitrary thus accidental implantations. Apparently, like Garbo's voice, according to the narrator, translation is *not* accidental; it is not an implant, a prosthesis in and of the original. This understanding of translation retreats from the furthest implications of "Las versiones homéricas," which established the problem or limit of translation as consubstantial to literature, to letters and to the *hand*. There is always already prosthesis. This limit, which must be trespassed in the instant of its delimitation, provides the *technical* support for literature *as such* in that it makes literature repeatable, translatable, and thus *visible*, in the first place. As the limit of literature, translation is necessarily *foreign* to literature. Yet, it marks literature's possibility as original and thus as belonging *congenitally*—thus by the accident of its singular inscription—to a national imaginary. In this, too, deception will have been necessary.

More effectively perhaps than any other text in the Borges archive, "Pierre Menard" spells out the necessary operation of translation. It does so marginally, not unlike "Sobre el doblaje," in a footnote attached to the end of the list of Menard's *visible* work. The note marks the border or limit between Menard's visible and invisible work: "Madame Henri Bachelier also lists a literal translation of Quevedo's literal translation of St. Francis de Sales's *Introduction à la vie dévote*. In Pierre Menard's library there is no trace of such a work. This must be an instance of one of our friend's droll jokes, misheard or misunderstood" (1.446/CF 90). The only traces of Menard's *Quijote* are ashes: Menard will have consigned his notebooks to the pyre. The narrator unwittingly registers his inability to think the effects of the *invisible* work to its furthest conclusion, for what makes possible the narrator's discovery and recognition of Menard's *visible* work as his own operates as well in the irreducible interval between and within the literal translation of the literal translation of San Francisco de Sales's *Introduction à la vie dévote*. Heidegger's claim that "As soon as one makes a literal translation everything is changed" must be doubled: if everything is changed in the appearance of the literal translation, then the literal translation (into French) of the literal translation (into Spanish) *returns in* and *as* the *original*. The literal translation of the literal translation haunts the original like a ghost. It neither is nor is not. At stake in this non-phenomenological—neither sensible nor intelligible—*literal* translation from French to Spanish to French is the impossibility of the original and the origin, of their impossibility as the condition of their possible institutionalization. In "Pierre Menard," the original is an effect of translation. This has at least two implications. *First*, such an operation takes time, which means it makes a difference in that it differs and defers the relation to itself that constitutes or composes the "itself"—the proper, the original—as such. The literal translation of the literal translation instances what Rodolphe Gasché has called "the operator of différance" (1985, 114), where translation is thought as arbitrary, accidental, *and* necessary. For the very desire for the origin and the original depends on translation. "Pierre Menard" literally spells out that there can be no original and thus no origin, neither *principium* nor *arkhe*, without the operation of translation. No sovereignty, then, without that which will already have compromised it *in the first place*, as its condition of possibility. *Second*, the literal translation of the literal translation does not inaugurate the origin by way of a transcendental rule or law. This would serve to establish translation or "the operator of différance" *as* the origin and original and thus *beyond* the effects of translation. "Pierre Menard" indicates that the operation of translation leaves traces behind, but, importantly, these traces are *not* permanent. On the contrary, because translation is subject to the same temporalization as the original it puts in place, the traces of this operation are necessarily perishable. The traces of the translation of the translation remain as ashes: Pierre Menard incinerates the drafts of his work. The *work* of translation goes up in smoke.

Contrary to George Steiner's inclination "to believe that 'a literal translation of Quevedo's literal translation' of Saint François de Sales was, indeed, to be found among Menard's papers" (Steiner 70), the narrator finds no traces of the literal translation of the literal translation. The inability to see this text is perhaps to have been expected, for the traces—the *rastros* or *huellas* of such translation—are always already erased in the appearance and institutionalization of the original as the trace of the trace of translation; as the *erasure*, the smudge mark of the original. The note *re*marks and *marks out* the necessary but unheard-of and unseen operation of translation that makes possible the monstration of the original *as* a monstrosity, *as* technically determined.

And the narrator, who looks right at the literal translation of the literal translation on a shelf in Pierre Menard's study, does not believe that he sees it as the condition of possibility of the ungrounded belief in the original.

# 3

# Kant's Dog

In a certain way it is always too late to ask the question of time.

Jacques Derrida, *Margins of Philosophy*

Kant was notorious in Königsberg for his strict adherence to routine. He was so regular, Ernst Cassirer reports, that the citizens of Königsberg set their clocks by his movements (9–10).[1] The most public articulation of this regularity was his daily walk through the city. Although it is doubtful Kant took a dog along on his constitutional, nevertheless, at the moment in the *Critique of Pure Reason* that he determines the possibility of the conceptualization of sense perception, which Heidegger considered the heart of Kant's Critical project and which ultimately turns on the regulation of the synthesis of time,[2] Kant trots out man's best friend. Although he needs a dog to demonstrate the trick of temporal synthesis that makes any sensible conceptuality possible, it is also clear that he needs to keep this dog on a tight leash. He cannot afford to let it run off or go astray. On one reading, then, the *Critique of Pure Reason* institutes a sort of philosophical leash law. Kant holds the dog so tightly that it is always already a dead dog, philosophical road kill.

In literature there is perhaps no more memorable instance of the problem of conceptuality than Borges's "Funes el memorioso [Funes the Memorious]."[3] And within that text, the key moment is the unforgettable example of Ireneo Funes's particular observation of the manifold that others reduce to—or synthesize as—a dog: "Not only was it difficult for him to see that the generic symbol 'dog' took in all the dissimilar individuals of all shapes and sizes, it irritated him that the 'dog' of three-fourteen in the afternoon, seen in profile, should be indicated by the same noun as the dog at three-fifteen, seen frontally" (1.489/CF 136). The frustration for Funes derives from his "experience" of the manifold of perceptions that nonetheless must be synthesized under a general concept in order to be remembered. The dog seen in profile at 3:14 is not the same dog when seen in full frontal view at 3:15. Inasmuch as the dog does not repeat itself, Funes could never say that he has seen a dog at all. This experience of the manifold contaminates the possibility of self-recognition. Funes always takes himself by surprise: "His own face in the mirror, his own hands, surprised him every time he saw them" (1.489/CF 136). At stake is the possibility of propriety. For Funes, identity conceived as self-identity and, accordingly, as self-possession over time, is suspended.

"Funes the Memorious" is dedicated to what, in "El jardín de senderos que se birfurcan [The Garden of Forking Paths]," Borges calls the riddle of time. If in "Pierre Menard," Borges addressed the act of faith necessary for any possible attribution and which is the effect of a nonempirical and non-sensible operation of translation, in "Funes," Borges stresses time's effect on the possibility of thought in general. If the last chapter sought to demonstrate that the empirically determined imagination must nonetheless be marked by a certain transcendentality, namely, a certain automaticity or mechanicity that cannot be ascribed to the subject, this chapter reads the necessary inscription of the empirical as the impossible condition of possibility for the transcendental determination of thought and experience. In other words, this chapter reads Borges's implicit challenge to Kant by taking up, once again, the force of the imagination. Insofar as the imagination names neither the simply passive nor the simply active exposure to the other—thereby designating the vanishing limit between sensibility and the understanding, between interiority and exteriority—it also names the privileged place for thinking the complicated relations between empiricism and transcendental philosophy, between literature and philosophy, between the accidental and the necessary, between the singular and the universal. In short, the operation of the imagination inscribes or marks, singularizes, the transcendental, thus ruining it in its institution. The operation that makes it possible to see and name, to know or to recognize, a dog *as* a dog, makes it impossible that the dog will ever be one.

### *Chronometrics, memory, and the fall*

That "Funes" concerns the temporality of memory is clear from the story's opening paragraph, in which the verb *recordar* (to remember) is used six times in the first five sentences and parenthetically referred to as the "sacred verb" (1.485/CF 131). From the beginning, Borges situates the narrator's memory—fallible, always already a matter of faith, governed by belief (*creer*)—in opposition to the infallibility of sacred memory, which only one man has a right to claim. "Funes el memorioso," therefore, presents the fallible memory of the one whose memory is infallible. The narrator's first memory of Funes, however, has nothing to do with his memory. Instead, it highlights his peculiar ability to tell time: "I recall the short baggy trousers . . . , the straw-soled cotton slippers, the cigarette in the hard visage, all stark against the now limitless storm cloud. Unexpectedly, Bernardo shouted out to him—*What's the time, Ireneo?* Without consulting the sky, without a second's pause, the boy replied, *Four minutes till eight*, young Bernardo Juan Francisco. The voice was shrill and mocking" (1.485–6/CF 132). "Chronometric Funes" (1.486/CF 132), as everyone calls him, always knows the time, like a clock, hence mechanically, but without the need to consult a watch or any other external device for marking or counting time. Funes has the most radical sort of *internal* time consciousness, which nonetheless determines his experience of time according to the calculation of time that could only be figured on the basis of a technological prosthesis. Such time consciousness, however, according to Husserl, is not internal at all; rather, it characterizes what he calls objective time, the "datable, measurable, historical, and cosmic time" of daily life (Zahavi 81). Consequently, "chronometric Funes" is characterized by the capacity to intuit objectively determined time.

In *Signs of Borges*, Sylvia Molloy figures the shift from "chronometric Funes" to "Funes the memorious" in terms of affectivity. Before the accident, in which he falls from a horse, when he is still "chronometric Funes" and capable of what appears to be the immediate intuition of calculable time, Funes is described in a way that locates him in his circumstances: the clothes, the sandals, the cigarette, the look, the sky.

He appears entirely determined by or through his context. After the accident, however, when he is no longer capable of forgetting, he is described as being "as monumental as bronze" (1.490/CF 137), entirely cut off from the circumstances of life, thus, dead (Molloy 74–75). This seems the opposite of what might be expected. On the one hand, the ability to calculate time immediately but without recourse to external technology ought to remove Funes from circumstances, for to be seamlessly immersed in one's context seems contrary to the possibility of the objective calculation of time. We become absorbed in the minutiae of life and lose track of time. Yet, before the accident, Funes never fails to calculate time. On the other hand, Funes's later ostensible inability to forget signals his absolute immersion in circumstances; he literally has lost "himself" in time, but being lost in time implies not only the impossibility of time's objective calculation, but also—and contrary to Molloy's account—the impossibility of *not* being affected by time. On one reading, then, "Funes el memorioso" is a story about a fall into time. It is clear, however, from Borges's insistence on Funes's preoccupation with time both before and after the fall, that the fall *into* time is no less a fall *out* of time; or, to credit Borges's reading of Saint Augustine, perhaps it is a fall *with* time.[4] But it will be necessary to recall how Borges describes Funes's voice both before and after the fall: in both cases it is mocking. Before the fall: "The voice was shrill and mocking [*aguda y burlona*]" (1.486/CF 132). After the fall: "Then suddenly I heard Ireneo's high, mocking voice" (1.487/CF 134). The lack of any difference in his voice, which here figures his personality (mocking), indicates that before and after the accident, Funes remains the same. In this case, the accident makes no difference. There is no opposition, then, between these two determinations of Funes and thus no opposition between these two modalities of time. "Cronométrico" Funes is Funes "el memorioso" because no perception and no memory—however "absolute" and infallible—are ever possible without the possibility of affection, of both self-affection and being-affected. Time is the form of affection. According to Kant, time is the pure, *a priori* form of the intuition of sensibility. In Kant, there can be no cognition of being affected without the *a priori* intuition of time, without time necessarily informing—literally giving form—to such affection. This will have been the case for Funes both before and after the fall.

Only after the accident, when he is "hopelessly crippled" (1.486/CF 132), does Funes realize that ". . . he had been what every man [*todos los cristianos*] was—blind, deaf, befuddled, and virtually devoid of memory" (1.488/CF 134).[5] For nineteen years he had lived as in a dream: "he looked without seeing, heard without listening, forgot everything, or almost everything [*de casi todo*]" (1.488/CF 134–5). The phrase "almost everything" (*casi todo*) speaks volumes about "chronometric" Funes and his apparent conversion into Funes "the memorious": only in forgetting *almost everything* was he capable of telling time, which means the objective calculation of time becomes possible only if one forgets time, if one forgets that time affects one incessantly, thus disturbing every instant, every calculable and calculated now. Furthermore, forgetting "*casi todo*" makes possible the telling of the story in the first place. Borges remarks: "I will not attempt to reproduce the words of it, which are now forever irrecoverable. I prefer to summarize truthfully the many things Ireneo told me" (1.487/CF 134). The possibility of telling the story is an effect of forgetting the story. In principle, therefore, Funes "the memorious" could never tell his own story, not because he forgets himself but, on the contrary, because in remembering everything he cannot forget *in order to remember* himself. Indeed, upon recovering sense, in coming back to consciousness after the accident, Funes literally appears to have recovered his senses and at the same time lost himself: "[T]he present was so rich, so clear, that it was almost unbearable, as were his oldest and even his most trivial memories. . . . Now his perception and his memory were infallible [*Ahora su percepción y su memoria eran infalibles*]" (1.488/CF 135).

Borges ultimately concludes that despite his vast and infallible memory, Funes was incapable of thought: "He had effortlessly learned English, French, Portuguese, Latin. I suspect, nevertheless, that he was not very good at thinking. To think is to forget differences, to generalize, to abstract. In the teeming world of Ireneo Funes there was nothing but almost immediate details" (1.490/CF 137). Eleven years earlier, in "La postulación de la realidad [The Postulation of Reality]," Borges had already arrived at this conclusion: "The conceptual simplification of complex states is often an instantaneous operation. The very fact of perceiving, of paying attention, is selective; all attention, all focusing of our consciousness, involves a deliberate omission of what is not interesting. . . . For us, living is a series of adaptations, which is to say, an education in oblivion" (1.218/SNF 61).[6] It will be necessary to take up the understanding that would posit Funes's "almost immediate" (*casi inmediato*) experience, on the one hand, and the often (*muchas veces*) instantaneous operation of discrimination (forgetting) constitutive of reality, on the other hand. Borges subtly undermines these ostensible positions through the qualification of immediacy (it is only "almost" and therefore not immediate at all) and instantaneousness (which is only "muchas veces" instantaneous, hence, not universally instantaneous and therefore not structurally necessary). In both cases, he inscribes time as the condition of possibility both of Funes's infallible memory and of the operation of forgetting necessary to thought.

## *The forgotten language*

Before turning to the problem of time, however, it is worthwhile considering the list of languages Funes learned "without effort," if only in order to recall what appears to have been forgotten. In 1918, during his family's residence in Lugano, Switzerland, Borges taught himself German with the help of an English-German dictionary. He was inspired to do so by reading Thomas Carlyle's *Sartor Resartus*, the protagonist of which is a professor of German Idealism. Borges remarks: "In the beginning I tried to read Kant's *Critique of Pure Reason*, but it defeated me, as it does the majority, including the majority of Germans" (1999, 44). In fact, Borges suggests that it would be better to read the first *Critique* in any language other than German.[7] According to Emir Rodríguez Monegal, German was the first language Borges chose to learn, but was his fifth language after English, French, Latin, and Spanish.[8] Borges claims German came to him fairly easily and within two or three months he was able to read Heine's poetry without a dictionary. Despite his apprenticeship to German through poetry, and despite the claim in his autobiographical essay that "German is a beautiful language, perhaps more beautiful than the literature it has produced" (Borges 1999, 46), for Borges "German was . . . the language of the philosophers" (Rodríguez Monegal 136). He appears to share this predilection with at least two (German) philosophers, Hegel and Heidegger.

In the *Science of Logic* Hegel claims, "German has many advantages over other modern languages; some of its words even possess the further peculiarity of having not only different but opposite meanings so that one cannot fail to recognize a speculative spirit of the language in them" (32). Heidegger was perhaps a bit blunter when, in the posthumously published *Der Spiegel* interview, he remarked that the German language had an "inner relationship . . . with the language of the Greeks and with their thought." This was confirmed for him, he noted, by the French, who "When they begin to think, they speak German, being sure that they could not make it with their own language" (1993, 113). Borges apparently agreed with Heidegger on this point, remarking that French "is . . . rather ugly. Everything becomes trivial when one says it in French" (1999, 46). Given his relation to German, it seems unlikely that in 1942 he would have forgotten the language. We should recall that from 1937 to 1945 Borges dedicated a series of texts in *Sur* to German culture and Nazism, as well as to Argentina's (in)famous Germanophilia.[9] This series culminates in "*Deutsches Requiem*," which appeared in the collection *El aleph* (1949) and which concerns the Nuremburg trials of 1945–46. In the "Afterword" to *El aleph*, dated 3 May 1949, Borges explains: "During the last war, no one could have longed more earnestly than I for Germany's defeat; no one could have felt more strongly than I the tragedy of Germany's destiny; '*Deutsches Requiem*' is an attempt to understand that destiny, which our own 'Germanophiles' (who know nothing of Germany) neither wept over nor even suspected" (1.629/CF 287). Many years later, however, in a story included in *El informe de Brodie* (1970), Borges continued to fret, however obliquely, the relation of German (and German philosophy) to the anti-Semitism he clearly despised. He did so by referring to Martin Heidegger.[10] The reference is not flattering.

"Guayaquil" displaces the confrontation between Simón Bolívar and José San Martín concerning the final strategy for expelling the Spaniards from Perú. The upshot of the meeting was that San Martín abandoned his army, leaving the liberation of Perú to Bolívar. In Borges's "Guayaquil" the meeting takes place between two historians—the narrator and Eduardo Zimmermann—from different universities in Argentina who are to decide who would retrieve from Sulaco certain recently discovered letters of Bolívar. The story plays out much like the meeting between Bolívar and San Martín in that the narrator abandons the field, by staying home, and Zimmermann goes to retrieve the letters. No reasons are given for Zimmermann's victory and the narrator's capitulation. The reference to Heidegger takes place early in the story at the moment the narrator describes the circumstances of Zimmermann's exile from Prague. "Dr. Eduardo Zimmermann . . . is a foreign-born historian driven from his homeland by the Third Reich and now an Argentine citizen. Of his professional work . . . I know at first hand only an article in vindication of the Semitic republic of Carthage (which posterity has judged through the writings of Roman historians, its enemies) and an essay of sorts that contends that government should function neither visibly nor by appeal to emotion. This hypothesis was thought worthy of refutation by Martin Heidegger, who proved decisively (using photocopies of newspaper headlines) that the modern head of state, far from being anonymous, is in fact the *protagonistes*, the *khoragos*, the David whose dancing (assisted by the pageantry of the stage, and with unapologetic recourse to the hyperboles of the art of rhetoric) enacts the drama of his people" (2.439/CF 391). Up to this point it seems Borges mocks Heidegger's troubling language about the destiny of a people.[11] But the paragraph concludes: "Heidegger likewise proved that Zimmermann was of Hebrew, not to say Jewish descent. That article by the venerable existentialist was the immediate cause of our guest's exodus and subsequent nomadism" (2.439/CF 391). According to Bioy Casares, Borges described the plot of a story based on the "mystery of Guayaquil" as early as October 1953 (90). This means that by the early 1950s, Borges was already concerned with the cultural implications of Heidegger's philosophy. In "Note on (toward) Bernard Shaw," which is dated "Buenos Aires, 1951" and which appeared in *Otras inquisiciones* in 1952, he refers to these implications as "immoral" (2.127/OI 166).[12] Borges's reference to Heidegger thus does cultural work in that it provides for the foreign intervention in Argentine history: the Argentine historian capitulates before the moral superiority (Bioy Casares 90) of the European historian, but does so only because the European's—Zimmermann's—Jewishness left him vulnerable to a certain Germanic—if not more broadly European—"immorality," that is, anti-Semitism. "Guayaquil" thus indicates the danger of identifying too closely with *any* culture, whether in terms, say, of Argentina's Germanophilia, or of any culture-philia more generally. Love of Latin American history and culture, for instance, according to Daniel Balderston, results in the narrator's "irrational hatred of his Jewish rival" (1993, 117).

There can be little doubt that the commitment to exposing the risks of cultural identification means Borges did not simply forget

German during the composition of "Funes el memorioso." Indeed, that Funes never learns German and thus German is conspicuously absent from Funes's capacious memory, haunts "Funes el memorioso," for no Borgesian text more thoroughly and more overtly takes up the problem of language and conceptualization. No text more obviously considers the problem of philosophy, the problem and possibility of what we know, as a problem of language. That German, the language of the philosophers in Borges's account, will not have been learned is no simple oversight, but another of Borges's riddles.

### *Imagining numbers*

Borges's confessed inability to read Kant becomes ironic in "Funes el memorioso" and the example of the dog. After all, it is Kant's dog. In the *Critique of Pure Reason*, in the section devoted to "The Transcendental Doctrine of the Power of Judgment," Kant points out that it is not images of objects "that ground our pure sensible concepts" (1998, 273; A141/B180),[13] but rather schemata. The schema, according to Kant, is "the transcendental time-determination which . . . mediates the subsumption of" appearances under the categories (272; A139/B178). In effect, the schema answers the question how pure concepts of the understanding, necessarily *a priori* and thus void of any empirical content, can be applied to intuitions of sense and therefore to objects of sense (appearances) with which they must be homogeneous.[14] The possibility of the homogenization of the fundamentally heterogeneous faculties of sensibility and understanding depends on the production of the schema, which, as the "mediating representation" between sensibility and understanding, "must be pure (without anything empirical) and yet **intellectual** on the one hand and **sensible** on the other" (272; A139/B178). The possibility of sensible concepts thus depends on schematism's temporalization of the categories. In other words, only by way of a transcendental time-determination can categories, which are universal but empty, be made homogeneous with intuitions of sense, which are temporal but without rule. Kant explains: "The concept of the understanding contains pure synthetic unity of the manifold in general. Time, as the formal condition of the manifold of inner sense, thus the connection of all representations, contains an *a priori* manifold in pure intuition. Now a transcendental time-determination is homogeneous with the **category** (which constitutes its unity) insofar as it is **universal** and rests on a rule *a priori*. But it is on the other hand homogeneous with the **appearance** insofar as **time** is contained in every empirical representation of the manifold" (272; A138–9/B177–8).

As "in itself always only a product of the imagination" (273; A140/B179), but nevertheless not an image, schematism names the "general procedure of the imagination for providing a concept with its image" (273; A140/B179–80). This image, however, should not be misunderstood as the ground of either transcendental or empirical concepts, for, as Kant writes, "it is not images of objects but schemata that ground our pure sensible concepts. No image of a triangle would ever be adequate to the concept of it. For it would not attain the generality of the concept, which makes this valid for all triangles . . . but would always be limited to one part of this sphere. The schema of the triangle can never exist anywhere except in thought, and signifies a rule of the synthesis of the imagination with regard to pure shapes in space" (273; A140–1/B180).[15] Moreover, it would be a mistake to think that images could more adequately supply empirical concepts: "Even less does an object of experience or an image of it ever reach the empirical concept, rather the latter [the concept] is always related immediately to the schema of the imagination, as a rule for the determination of our intuition in accordance with a certain general concept" (273; A141/B180).

Put simply, although the faculty of sensibility, through the mediation of the imagination, provides representations (images or appearances) to the faculty of the understanding, the understanding is concerned only with the unity of this synthesis and not with any individual or particular intuition. Therefore, the understanding is not concerned with an image of sense, but only with the formal and pure condition of possibility of the image. The pure concept—as "referring" only to the schema of sensibility and not to any particular intuition—is thus necessarily *a priori*, hence free from and uncontaminated by any sensible intuition. Kant's examples are several, beginning with the image or representation of number in five dots (. . . . .) as opposed to the schema of the number five in general. At stake for Kant is the ostensible purity of the non-imagistic number 5 so long as it is not represented empirically in any sensible figure.

To be sure, in "Funes el memorioso" Borges takes up the example and the problem of number in Funes's development of a numbering system that fails any conceivable criterion for a system that could perpetuate itself, synthetically, *ad infinitum*, which is what a numbering system must accomplish. Rather than Kant, however, here Borges's philosophical referent is Locke's understanding of number in the *Essay Concerning Human Understanding* in which number, in conjunction with the name, provides the possibility of the synthetic unity of consciousness or of the mind "itself." Locke writes: "Amongst all the *Ideas* we have, as there is none suggested to the Mind by more ways, so there is none more simple, than that *of Unity*, or One" (2.16, §1/205). Not only is number the simplest idea, it is also the most universal: "[E]very Object our senses are employed about; every *Idea* in our Understandings; every Thought of our Minds brings this *Idea* along with it. And therefore it is the most intimate to our Thoughts, as well as it is, in its Agreement to all other things, the most universal *Idea* we have" (2.16, §1/205). For Locke, number's intimacy and universality, combined with its simplicity, necessarily results in the postulate that every number is absolutely different from every other number: "*The simple modes of Number are of all other the most distinct*; every the least Variation, which is an unite, making each combination, as clearly different from that, which approacheth nearest to it, as the most remote; two being as distinct from one, as Two hundred; and the *Idea* of Two as distinct from the *Idea* of Three, as the magnitude of the whole Earth, is from that of a Mite" (2.16, §3/205).

What is it, then, that ties this idea—and any idea, whether complex or simple—together, thus unifying and distinguishing it? It is the name. In his discussion of the formation of complex ideas, Locke asserts, "Though therefore it be the Mind that makes the Collection, 'tis the Name which is, as it were the Knot, that ties them fast together" (3.5, §10/434).[16] The possibility of complex ideas depends upon the synthesis of what Locke calls the "train of *Ideas*, which constantly succeed one another" (2.14, §3/182). The determination of complex ideas is structurally the same as that of simple ones, which are also determined in the synthesis—by means of "attention" or perception, which Locke calls "the first faculty of the Mind" and which is "for the most part, only passive" (2.9, §1/143)—of the constant succession of sensations.

Insofar as each succeeding number in the series of numbers, once it is named, becomes a unity and a distinct idea, it follows that counting or calculation requires a faculty of retention or memory: "By the repeating . . . of the *Idea* of an Unite, and joining it to another Unite, we make thereof one collective *Idea*, marked by the Name *Two*. And whosoever can do this, and proceed on, still adding one more to the last collective *Idea*, which he had of any Number, and give a Name to it, may count, or have *Ideas* for several Collections of Unites, distinguished one from another, as far as he hath a Series of Names for following Numbers, and a Memory to retain that Series, with their several Names" (2.16, §5/206).

The outlines of "Funes the Memorious" should already be apparent in that Locke's conception of number and counting or calculation depends not on a mental faculty that synthesizes a system of numbers, but rather on a memory capacious enough to retain a series of names without any necessary relation of one to another. Borges's interest in this problem, however, becomes even more transparent at the moment Locke suggests that to be able to count is to be able to tell: "So that he, that can add one to one, and so to two, *and so go on with his Tale* [emphasis added—DEJ], taking still with him the distinct Names belonging to every Progression; and so again by subtracting an Unite from each Collection retreat and lessen them, is capable of all the *Ideas* of Numbers, within the compass of his Language, or for which he hath names, though not, perhaps, of more" (2.16, §5/206). Locke opens the door for Borges's critique, for, according to Locke's criteria, Funes's number system, which is no system at all, *counts*: each idea of number is distinct from every other and a unity in itself. And because Funes's memory is absolutely capacious he has no difficulty recalling or retaining the names. Indeed, it would be impossible for him not to do so. Borges has already made clear, however, that an absolute memory is incapable of thought and, therefore, incapable of calculation or the accounting necessary to narrative. In his understanding of the unity and uniqueness of each number, Locke stresses that in order for numeration to be useful beyond relatively small numbers, the names for numbers must be systematized. But a system becomes possible only if all the terms are organized according to the same principle. Without a principle of organization, without a system, one plus one might well equal two, but not always and not necessarily. One plus one might also equal, as Borges points out, "*a poncho full of meat* [*manta de carne*]" (1.489/CF 136).

With the problem of number Locke comes to the limit of his empirical determination of thought. At the moment he ties the possibility of number to the name and memory, he implicitly acknowledges the inevitable confusion—the heap of names—that will arise if everyone does not have an infinite memory: "And I doubt not but we our selves might distinctly number in Words, a great deal farther than we usually do, would we find out but some fit denominations to signifie them by; whereas in the way we take now to name them by Millions of Millions of Millions, *etc.* it is hard to go beyond eighteen, or at most four and twenty decimal Progressions, without confusion" (2.16, §6/207).

The problem of number warrants two additional comments before turning back to the problem of schematism in Kant.

*First*, Kant agrees with Locke that every number is a distinct unity, which is why Kant asserts that all arithmetical or mathematical judgments are synthetic rather than analytic. That is, in Kant's account, in the phrase "two plus three equals five," there is nothing in either of the concepts two or three that gives us the concept five. The judgment is not analytical. Synthetic judgments are those judgments that in their combination of concepts produce a new concept that cannot be derived from either of its constitutive concepts. All mathematical judgments, Kant claims, are synthetic. By itself this does not distinguish Kant from Locke, for whom numbers are also distinct from one another and for whom, therefore, in order for there to be the possibility of mathematical knowledge there must be synthetic judgments. The difference between them lies in Kant's assertion of the *a priori* apodicticity of such synthetic judgments. This determination, in principle, allows Kant to set aside Locke's claim that empirical memory was necessary to avoid mathematical confusion, because for Kant mathematics is not empirically determined. On the contrary, mathematics is organized by a transcendental principle. For example, although it is always possible that in adding two and two, this or that subject will arrive at the sum of three or five, for Kant this empirical determination will never jeopardize the *a priori* certainty that two plus two equals four, which according to Kant must be the case no matter how many times one arrives at a different sum. Locke cannot make this claim. His consideration of number makes clear that numeration, and thus all mathematics, depends upon an empirical certainty which is only possible through naming and memory: "For without such Names or Marks, we can hardly well make use of Numbers in reckoning, especially where the Combination is made up of any great multitude of Unites, which put together without a Name or Mark, to distinguish that precise

Collection, will hardly be kept from being a *heap in Confusion*" (2.16, §5/207, emphasis added). On Locke's account, therefore, there is no transcendental, *a priori* guarantee of mathematical certainty: all calculation is secured empirically and thus requires for the synthetic operation the name or the mark, which are necessarily empirical determinations.

*Second*, number, which is the idea of unity and thus in itself simple, serves one purpose: namely, to unify every idea as *one* idea. In short, number (unity) makes possible the determination of any *one* idea in the incessant "train of *Ideas*." Without the idea of number, which is in itself nothing but unity, but which accompanies all other ideas as the condition of possibility of the unity of the idea, there would only be the train of ideas, which, Locke writes, "constantly succeed one another" (2.14, §3/182). More exactly, in order to think the train of ideas at all, number must already be on the train. In order for there to be a train of ideas, there must be an idea of the train. Such an idea is always already named, numbered, unified. Nevertheless, the *train* of ideas is both an attempt to represent temporality, its incessant succession, and an effect of temporality. Locke writes, "There is another sort of Distance, or Length, the *Idea* whereof we get not from the permanent parts of space, but from the fleeting and perpetually perishing parts of succession. This is Duration" (2.14, §1/181). At stake in this conceptualization of time is the possibility of presence or of what is present, for if what passes through the mind—the train of ideas, say—is "fleeting and perpetually perishing" even in its parts, then Locke necessarily subscribes to infinite divisibility and the impossibility of ever presenting or making present any idea *as such* or *in itself*. Consequently, without a synthesis of time—and a synthesis of time already thought as spacing, as another kind of distance or length, and thus another thought of space, one that necessarily and simultaneously becomes time—the train cannot be thought in the first place. The difficulty for Locke stems from the need to think the synthesis of time empirically, as always experientially determined, when, of course, the condition of possibility of any experience in fact depends upon the synthesis of temporality. Consequently, Locke's theorization of number as the first moment of intellectual synthesis, the first operation in which the incessant succession of ideas becomes unified as *one* idea, is inadequate.[17]

## *Walking the dog*

Although Borges spends a good deal of time describing Funes's number system in order to dismiss it as lacking a transcendental principle, the most arresting figure in "Funes el memorioso" is the dog Borges borrows from Kant's last example of the operation of transcendental schematism. It is this dog that Borges takes for a philosophical walk in the park. Kant writes, "The concept of a dog signifies a rule in accordance with which my imagination can specify the shape of a four-footed animal in general, without being restricted to any simple particular shape that experience offers me or any possible image that I can exhibit *in concreto*" (1998, 273; A141/B180).[18] This is the dog Borges trots out.

All objects of experience, according to Kant, can be such only insofar as they are temporally determined, for time, in Kant's understanding, is the pure form of intuition and there can be no objects of cognition that are not grounded in possible intuitions of sense.[19] Concepts, however, are not themselves temporal. How, then, does Kant arrive at the conceptual unity of the object that is only a manifold of appearances and therefore as yet unconstituted "as such"? In order to answer this question Kant sketches out the threefold synthesis necessary to any possible conceptuality: the syntheses of the apprehension of appearances in the intuition, of the reproduction of representations in the imagination, and of recognition under concepts of the understanding. The synthesis of reproduction in the imagination—whether empirical or transcendental—is the most important of the three, in part because without this synthesis sensibility could never be accommodated to the understanding and thus no knowledge would be possible.

Were the synthesis of reproduction impossible, there could be no cognition, but not because there would be no concepts of the understanding. On the contrary, Kant contends that without the synthesis of reproduction, "Not even the purest and most fundamental representations of space and time, could ever arise" (230; A102), which means there would be no intuitions of sense to provide content to concepts. Thus concepts would remain empty. This means that *before* the possibility of the *a priori* intuition of space and time, there is *already* repetition, reproduction. Hence, *before* the forms of space and time there is *already* temporalization in that there is already repetition, a doubling that cannot *not* take time even as it makes possible the consolidation of time "itself" as an intuition of sense. On Kant's account, therefore, there must be temporalization *before* either the intuition or the concept of time. The place or site—the citation—of this temporalization is the imagination, which Kant says operates spontaneously, automatically.

The synthesis of reproduction makes possible retention, which is necessary to thought, because without retention we could not sustain a thought from its beginning to its end. But Kant does not figure retention as uninterrupted perdurance or absolute self-sameness or constancy. Instead, he understands retention as the *transcendental* necessity of repetition. "Now it is obvious," Kant asserts, "that if I draw a line in thought, *or think of the time from one noon to the next*, or even want to represent a certain number to myself, I must necessarily first grasp one of these manifold representations *after another* in my thoughts. But if I were always to lose the preceding representations (the first parts of the line, the preceding points of time, or the successively represented units) from my thoughts and *not reproduce them when I proceed to the following ones*, then no whole representation and none of the previously mentioned thoughts, *not even the purest and most fundamental representations of space and time, could ever arise*" (230; A102, emphasis added). Although time is the formal condition of all sensibility and thus the ground of all cognitions of experience, what it gives to consciousness in the form of appearances or representations is unknowable outside of or before their homogenization with a concept of the understanding in schematism. There is no cognition, hence no experience of time prior to the schematization of representations of sense with categories of the understanding. What is cognizable must therefore be determined temporally. It follows, then, that insofar as in sensibility time is the form of succession, in order for there to be the *cognition* (and thus the *experience*) of time, time must be determined in the transcendental operation of the imagination. The possibility of the cognition of time thus depends on the retention—hence the repetition—of the representation of sensibility in the synthesis of reproduction. The temporalization of the concept of time determines it precisely in order to (re)produce—i.e., synthesize—time as an object of cognition. Were time not (re)produced and thus (re)presented as an object of cognition, we could not know either that there is time or that it is experienced as succession.

In sum, Kant's determination of time as the *a priori* form of inner sense is only possible in the transcendental possibility of repetition in the spontaneous operation of the imagination. And this means time can only be posited as being in itself, or as Kant puts it, as "Time itself" and as that which "does not elapse" (275; A144), only if "time" is always already temporalized in the transcendental imagination.[20] Kant can conceptualize an unchanging time and can argue that "change does not affect time itself" only if schematism provides *a priori* for the possibility of sensibility—and of time as pure form—as a sensible concept of the understanding.

## *The signature of the imagination*

Despite its necessity, Kant remains troubled by the possible side effects of the imagination, so much so that he attempts throughout the *Critique of Pure Reason* to delimit its field of play and in the *Critique of Practical Reason* he excludes it altogether, although in *Kant and the Problem of Metaphysics* Heidegger suggests that practical reason may well be grounded in the transcendental imagination: "Insofar as freedom belongs to the possibility of theoretical reason, however, it is in itself as theoretically practical. But if finite reason as spontaneity is receptive and thereby springs forth from the transcendental power of imagination, then of necessity practical reason is also grounded therein" (1997, 109). Moreover, even in the pages of the *Critique of Judgment* in which Kant discusses aesthetic judgments of reflection, which are not determinant judgments of the understanding and thus not judgments of cognition, he nonetheless restricts the imagination in relation to what he calls "the power of judgment" with regard to the production of beautiful art.[21] The task of bringing genius—and thus the imagination—"in line" falls to taste: "Taste . . . is the discipline (or corrective) of genius, clipping its wings and making it well behaved or polished" (197/5:319). Consequently, although it remains necessary for the production of beautiful art, Kant is always prepared to sacrifice the imagination.[22]

In the context of the *Critique of Pure Reason*, which concerns the conditions of possibility of cognition and thus of determinative judgments, Kant recognizes, on the one hand, that we could never take the dog for a walk without the operation of the transcendental imagination; but, on the other hand, because schematism is spontaneous, and thus unruly, it is always possible that the dog will run away.[23] In short, Kant needs a leash. The question becomes, once attached to the leash, what will keep the dog from coming to its end?

It should be obvious that Kant is in a bind. On the one hand, the imagination is necessary to cognition. On the other hand, it threatens the very security of transcendental philosophy. In Kant's account, because schematism is always an operation of the productive or transcendental imagination, it is the synthesis that makes possible sensible conceptualization. It is therefore the possibility of the *cognition* of temporalization, hence of time as movement, change. But as productive, it is also spontaneous. Because the imagination is necessary to cognition, it is not subjectively determined. On the contrary, the operation of the imagination is objectively valid for everyone; thus it is universal. Transcendental schematism, then, is automatic, hence necessary. There is no experience without it. But because the imagination is automatic, it operates indiscriminately; it happens by accident, without determinate cause. In short, it is free. Consequently, the spontaneity of the imagination names a freedom without autonomy. It is an automatic freedom. Although it is free, inasmuch as it is automatic, mechanical, the imagination cannot give itself its own rule or law. Indeed, according to Kant's most extensive analysis of it in *Anthropology from a Pragmatic Point of View*, the imagination cannot be said to have an "itself."

Because anthropology is an empirical science, Kant's *Anthropology* rightly concerns only the empirical imagination, which Kant calls the "productive faculty of sensibility" (2006, §31/67).[24] For precisely this reason, Heidegger dismisses "[t]he attempt to experience by means of Anthropology what is more original about the power of imagination" as "unsuccessful" (1997, 93). Despite the *Anthropology*'s limitation, Rodolphe Gasché argues that the operation of the empirical imagination "reveals certain traits and presuppositions that must have their corresponding structures in transcendental imagination" (1994a, 38). The most important operation of the imagination in the *Anthropology* is the synthesis of temporality in the faculty of designation or that of "using signs": "The faculty of cognizing the present as the means for connecting the representation of the foreseen with that of the past is the faculty of *using signs*.—The mental activity of bringing about this connection is *signifying* (*signatio*), which is also called *signaling*, of which the highest degree is call *mark-*

*ing* [*Auszeichnung*]" (Kant 2006, §38/84). According to this account, the present is the site of signaling, of making or marking a distinction, hence of making something stand out. In sum, for Kant, the present is the horizon of signaling or marking such that the past is determined in a way that relates it to the future. Accordingly, the faculty of marking or signaling is the faculty of attribution. Insofar as the present is the site of such attribution, structurally the present can never point to itself; rather, it distinguishes itself *in itself*: it can only point away from "itself" in pointing toward, *signaling*, the relation of past and future. Past and future are associated with one another in a present that can never be present "in itself," which means the imagination incessantly dislocates "itself." The present names the irreducibly vanishing limit of designation. As Heidegger put it, referring to the transcendental imagination, "The transcendental power of imagination is homeless" (1997, 95). The imagination, therefore, is the infinitely divisible site of temporalization. Ceaselessly pointing away from any possible "itself" in relating past and future, the imagination temporalizes.

One of the effects of such temporalization is the possibility of the failure of the understanding, for in pointing away from "itself" and toward another, it is always possible that the imagination misses its mark. "All language," Kant writes, "is a signification of thought and . . . the best way of signifying thought is through language, the greatest instrument for understanding ourselves and others. Thinking is *speaking* with oneself . . . ; consequently, it is also *listening* to oneself inwardly (by means of the reproductive power of imagination)" (2006, §39/86). Thus, we talk to ourselves in the same way we talk to others. We understand ourselves, our thought, through language. Nevertheless, although language is "the greatest instrument for understanding ourselves and others," it is never secure: "But even those who can speak and hear do not always understand themselves or others" (§39/86). Because it is always possible that one understands neither oneself nor others, the possibility of misunderstanding must be considered a *necessary* part of the structure of signaling or marking.[25] The temporalization necessary to communication, and therefore to the economy of sense and the calculation of meaning, also ineluctably inscribes within the economy of communication the possibility of *not* making sense. In Kant there is no meaning without a synthesis of temporality and there is no synthesis of temporality without the faculty of designation, hence a marking, an inscription, which requires, as the condition of possibility of making sense, the constitutive look away from the site traditionally designated as the guarantor of meaning and of sense, namely, the present. The faculty of designation necessarily inscribes the effects of time within the ostensibly closed circuit of sense, thus opening it toward the possibility of having been always already shorted out.

The unruliness of the imagination gives Kant pause, for the imagination is that which makes possible knowledge: "The principle of the necessary unity of the pure (productive) synthesis of the imagination prior to apperception is thus the ground of the possibility of all cognition, especially that of experience" (1998, 238; A118). What Kant elides in this passage is the constitutive dis-unity and dis-location of the imagination. The synthesis of the imagination makes possible all cognition, but because the imagination cannot be unified, because it has no "itself," because it is never present to itself, the imagination also makes cognition impossible. Cognition is an accident of the imagination.

According to Kant, the highest degree of the faculty of designation "is called *marking*" (2006, §38/84). If, as Gasché argues, the operation of the empirical or reproductive imagination reveals presuppositions and traits of the transcendental or productive imagination, then it is necessary to ask in what way the highest degree of transcendental imagination can be understood as marking or signalizing and thus as the possibility of attribution. The answer has already been suggested: Kant argues that between sensibility and understanding "it is clear there must be a third thing, which must stand in homogeneity with the category on the one hand and the appearance on the other, and makes possible the application of the former to the latter. . . . Such a representation is the **transcendental schematism**" (1998, 272; A138/B177). Here it is not necessary to rehearse yet again the operation of schematism. Of interest is only its mediating function, on the one hand, and its elision, on the other. In making possible the subsumption of appearances to categories, schematism works like the faculty of designation insofar as it attributes images to concepts and applies concepts to images. Yet, the schema is not of the order of either images or concepts.[26] Schematism is the rule of their possible homogenization. As that which mediates images and concepts, the schema is necessarily temporal: "an application of the category to appearances becomes possible by means of the transcendental time determination, which, as the schema of the concept of the understanding, mediates the subsumption of the latter under the former" (272; A139/B178). In mediating sensibility and the understanding, schematism necessarily points away from "itself." It never shows up "as such." As Kant explains: "This schematism of our understanding with regard to appearances and their mere form is a hidden art in the depths of the human soul, whose true operations we can divine from nature and lay unveiled before our eyes only with difficulty" (273; A141/B180–1).[27] Kant here comes close to Hume's concept of belief as the *je-ne-scais-quoi* whose secret operation cannot be observed but which everyone sufficiently understands. Schematism cannot be unveiled before our eyes, because it is not an appearance, but only the transcendental time-determination that makes possible the homogenization, the coming-together or synthesis, of the category and appearances, of the universal and the particular. Following Kant's logic, it must be *impossible*—not simply difficult—to perceive schematism, to have sensible intuition of it, although the condition of possibility of seeing anything at all depends on schematism.

The necessary impossibility of perceiving transcendental schematism, of bearing witness or testifying to its operation is problematized in Kant's suggestion that the operation of the transcendental imagination leaves a mark: "We can say only this much: the *image* is a product of the empirical faculty of productive imagination, the *schema* of sensible concepts (such as figures in space) is a product and as it were a *monogram* [emphasis added—DEJ] of pure *a priori* imagination" (1998, 273–74; A141/B181). A monogram is a single line, a *graphe*, an inscription, but also a signature. The imagination signs; it leaves a mark. The transcendental imagination only signs in the case of its relation to sensible concepts, that is, in the instance where images "first become possible" (274; A142/B181). According to Kant, "The schema of a pure concept of the understanding, on the contrary, is something that can never be brought to an image at all, but is rather only the pure synthesis, in accord with a rule of unity according to concepts in general" (274; A142/B181). The problem concerns the possibility of a *pure* synthesis, one that leaves no mark or trace; one that leaves no monogram. A synthesis is necessary because of the infinite succession or divisibility of time, specifically, that time is divided between the *no longer* and the *not yet*, and that no part of time *is*. A synthesis of time, therefore, necessarily requires a trace or mark of the *no longer* that remains for the *not yet*. The monogram names the *borrón*, the smudge that remains as the trace of the erased inscription. It is the mark of erasure and the erasure of the mark. In Kant, a pure synthesis "is a transcendental product of the imagination, which concerns the determination of the inner sense in general, in accordance with conditions of its form (time) in regard to all representations, insofar as these are to be connected together *a priori* in one concept in accord with the unity of apperception" (274; A142/B181). At stake here is an *operation* of the imagination that takes no time: it is a synthesis of time that takes no time and, consequently, that leaves no trace of time. Nevertheless, on the surface, it would seem that the monogram, the single line, is the hyphen or the *trait d'union*, that connects representations *a priori* in one concept. The monogram, its linearity, its signature or inscription, its initialization, is the name (the metaphor) for the schema of the imagination; it literally *marks* time in that it makes possible the synthesis of the categories, that is, their unity.[28]

According to the logic of empirical imagination and the faculty of designation, insofar as schematism names the transcendental operation of attribution, *mis*attribution or *mis*marking must be possible, which possibility must therefore be constitutive of the relation of sensibility and understanding. In other words, because temporalization is necessary to the operation of attribution—whether empirically as the referral of past and future in an infinitely divisible present that cannot present "itself" *or* transcendentally as the attribution of images to concepts in a schematism that disappears in its mediating operation—it is always possible, hence necessary, that *mis*attribution happen. It is always possible that appearances be *mis*marked, that they be *mis*attributed to concepts, just as it is always possible that in talking to ourselves we *mis*understand ourselves. Kant had already recognized this possibility in the first *Critique*: "I note only that when we compare the thoughts that an author expresses about a subject, in ordinary speech as well as in writings, it is not at all unusual to find that we understand him even better than he understood himself, since he may not have determined his concept sufficiently and hence sometimes spoke, or even thought, contrary to his own intention" (1998, 396; A314/B370).[29]

### *A philosophical leash law*

It is one thing to admit, as Kant does, the possibility of such misapprehension in the *Anthropology*, because, inasmuch as anthropology is an empirical science, misapprehension there has the same status as the empirical determination of two plus two equals five: it does not jeopardize the apodicticity of the transcendental principle of reason. To admit in the *Critique of Pure Reason* that it is possible that images and concepts can be mismarked or misattributed, however, undermines Kant's claim to have determined and explained the universal structure of cognition. Transcendental misattribution is not an empirical accident, but is the necessary effect of the imagination's spontaneity, which means it is the inevitable conclusion of Kant's understanding of schematism as temporalization. Accordingly, in order to save Critical philosophy, Kant must find a way to restrain the imagination and its temporalization, to put it on a leash in order to choke off its infinite referral, its free play. He does so by positing an unchanging point of reference.

Although the transcendental schematism of the imagination is necessary for all knowledge, it is also the case, Kant insists, that "without consciousness that that which we think is the very same as what we thought a moment before, all reproduction in the series of representations would be in vain" (1998, 230; A103). As the possibility of attribution, schematism makes possible the reproduction of representations and thus the homogenization of sensibility and understanding, but because schematism is constitutive temporalization, it cannot guarantee the identity necessary to thought. As Gasché points out, the imagination is always already distracted from "itself." Because schematism is not an immediate operation, but rather constitutive mediation, the referral it effects can never be certain. The identification it exercises between appearances and concepts can only ever be provisional. Kant solves this problem by positing the "I" as the unity of consciousness. The "I" that secures the synthesis of time is not, however, that which in the *Anthropology* Kant calls the "I" by virtue of which the subject "is a *person*, and by virtue of the unity of consciousness through all changes that happen to him, one and the same person" (2006, §1/15). This "I" cannot solve the problem of temporal synthesis precisely because it is a "representation"

(§1/15). It is therefore of the order of empirical apperception, which, as Kant explains in the *Critique of Pure Reason*, is "forever variable," hence, "it can provide no standing or abiding self in the stream of inner appearances" (1998, 232; A107). Insofar as it is a "consciousness of oneself" determined by "internal perception" (232; A107), empirical apperception cannot provide the formal unity of consciousness necessary for the possibility of cognition. This is so because empirical apperception is conditioned by intuitions of time and space. Yet, "no cognitions can occur in us," Kant writes, "no connection and unity among them, without that unity of consciousness that *precedes* all data of the intuitions, and in relation to which all representation of objects alone is possible" (232; A107, emphasis added).

It is worth recalling what is at stake here. Experience is only possible in the automatic operation of the imagination to schematize intuitions of sensibility and concepts of the understanding. Schematism is thus the tracing that effects a transcendental time-determination: the becoming-sensible of understanding and the becoming-conceptual of sensibility. In other words, schematism—the operation of the transcendental imagination—relates appearances of what never was to concepts of the understanding in order that sense perceptions be cognized in the first place, that is, in order that there be the experience of time as succession.[30] But because the imagination is temporal, that is, because the imagination cannot be located in itself, it is always liable to *mis*marking, to *mis*attribution, and it is this chance that makes Kant nervous. For this reason he ties the imagination to a ground that remains unaffected by time, to a "pure, original, unchanging consciousness" (232; A107), "the standing and lasting I" that "constitutes the correlate of all our representations" (240; A123), which he calls, "transcendental apperception" (232; A107).

Transcendental apperception is not a concept of the understanding, nor is it an object of sense. It is neither intuitable nor cognizable as such. Thus, transcendental apperception is not representable. Were it representable, it would necessarily be subject to the vagaries of time. As Hägglund points out, were transcendental apperception itself temporal, "the very ground for the synthetic unity of consciousness would itself be subjected to succession and thus in need of being synthesized by an instance other than itself, and so on" (2008, 23). Consequently, transcendental apperception provides the formal unity of consciousness, the "I think" that accompanies all my representations without itself ever being an object of representation. Without this "spontaneous source of synthesis" (23) as that which secures the formal unity of consciousness, Kant remarks, "There would . . . be no determinate connection" of these representations, "but merely unruly heaps [*Haufen*] of them" (1998, 239; A121). Kant's language is close to Locke's.[31] In his discussion of number as the necessary unity of ideas, Locke observes that without number, nothing would keep our thoughts from "being a heap in Confusion" (2.16, §5/207). Without number, Locke repeats, nothing would restrain our distinct ideas from "running into a confused heap, wherein the Mind loses itself" (2.17, §9/215). In Locke, therefore, the idea of number accompanies all the ideas in the mind in order to unify not only the idea as one idea, but also to sustain the unity of the mind as one mind and thus to keep it from losing itself in a heap of confusion. In Kant, transcendental apperception or the unchanging "I" accompanies all representations and provides for the unity of consciousness such that all my thoughts refer to one consciousness.

To put this in somewhat more Borgesian terms and to return to the example of the dog that Funes cannot perceive, transcendental apperception functions as the dog's leash: "It is this apperception that *must be added* to the pure imagination in order to make its function intellectual" (1998, 240; A124, emphasis added). According to Kant, on account of the unchanging "I" that is transcendental apperception, "We therefore have a pure imagination, as a fundamental faculty of the human soul, that grounds all cognition *a priori*" (241; A124). Transcendental apperception anchors or secures the operation of the transcendental imagination because—its necessity for the possibility of cognition notwithstanding—the imagination always threatens to go astray, to run off, wander, err. Transcendental imagination temporalizes and thus makes possible both the pure forms of sensibility (space and time) and cognition insofar as it determines the time of the concept. It is not the schema of time that determines time *qua* concept, however, but the promise of schematism, its noon, the impossible cite of its possibility. As a consequence, the imagination cannot be contained, leashed, precisely because it is not. The imagination always leaps away, toward another. In tying imagination to transcendental apperception, Kant holds the leash so tightly that it becomes a noose. The dog cannot run around. It has no time for life.

In *Radical Atheism*, Martin Hägglund argues that the trace structure of time, or spacing, makes possible the synthesis of time without recurring to an atemporal instant that would ground time. Thus it offers a way to think identity without positing an "unchanging I" or unity of consciousness. He locates in Kant's example of drawing a line in thought the resources for thinking the operation of the trace. Hägglund explains:

> Since the temporal can never be in itself, it must be synthesized by something other than itself in order to appear as such. No alteration—and hence no passage of time—can be marked without something that persists as a measure of the change. Kant usually anchors the synthesis in the persistence of a transcendental apperception, but he here opens the way for a different solution. The synthesis is not effectuated by a spontaneous "I think" beyond the intuition of time, but by the act of spatial inscription that is the drawing of the line. The persistence of such spatial inscription is quite different from the persistence of a self-identical consciousness. The spatial inscription can archive time and thus make it possible to grasp alteration, but it is itself exposed to alteration at every juncture. Both the act of inscription and the reading of inscription necessarily take time. Thus, the drawing of the line marks not only the becoming-space of time but also the becoming-time of space as the condition for synthesis. (2008, 27)

The drawing of the line is the monogram, the *borrón*, of the imagination, which is *not* the atemporal "I think" of transcendental apperception. It is the *act* of inscription; it is therefore an act of faith. It is a promise.

## *The time of the heap*

It would be a mistake to try to make "Funes el memorioso" heel too strictly to Kant, but it is nonetheless clear that insofar as Funes perceives anything at all, he is capable of a synthesis of temporality. He is incapable, however, of reining in that synthesis, of limiting its spontaneity, its play. In Funes, the synthesis of the imagination in schematism has always already run off, been distracted, leaped away. Indeed, Funes tells Borges, "*my memory, sir, is like a garbage heap* [vaciadero de basuras]" (1.488/CF 135). Although *vaciadero de basuras* is perhaps better translated by "garbage dump," the translation of it by "garbage heap" is felicitous in that it makes clear Borges's philosophical investment. It would be a stretch to claim that in Locke and Kant "heap" (*Haufen*) becomes a philosophical concept, but that to which "heap" refers has, at least since Aristotle, troubled philosophy. On at least two occasions in the *Metaphysics*, both of which concern number and unity, Aristotle opposes the unity of number to a heap (σωρὸς). For instance, when he asks about the cause of the unity of number, he answers, "In the case of all things which have several parts and in which the totality is not, as it were, a mere heap [σωρὸς], but the whole is something besides the parts; there is a cause" (1984, 1045a10/2.1650).[32] A heap results from the absence of causal determination; it is a multitude or plurality without order or rule. A heap, then, according to Aristotle, is accidental, without rule or principle, without necessity or causality. An accident never adds up to more than its parts; it does not take place within the whole. It is not circumscribable. An accident has neither *arkhe* nor *telos*.

A long philosophical tradition leads to Kant's suggestion that a "heap" would be the exact condition of a consciousness at the mercy of a spontaneous imagination that synthesized intuitions of sense and concepts of the understanding without referring these sensible concepts to an always already unified consciousness. An unrestrained imagination would be without principle, without rule. It would be accidental. Understood within this Kantian frame, Borges's Funes lacks neither the empirical faculty of designation nor the transcendental possibility of schematism. Rather, he lacks the leash, transcendental apperception, that would turn the indiscriminate heap into a determined whole.

Borges does not therefore challenge the necessity of temporal synthesis for the possibility of thought. Such a challenge would be absurd. In the figure of Funes he both articulates the necessity of the synthesis of time and jeopardizes the Kantian solution to the imagination's constitutive distraction, namely, transcendental apperception, the unchanging "I." Yet, because the noon of time always comes back in such a way as to destroy the possibility of time's presence to itself, which makes impossible the possibility of any absolute calculation of time, there can never be an unchanging "I," just as there can be no absolute, infallible memory.

According to Borges, then, time is not, as Kant argues, simply the form of inner sense, as if there were no time outside the consciousness of the human being, which effectively determines the world external to consciousness as being in itself, noumenal, and thus beyond any temporalization and any possible understanding. But nor is time simply external to us, which would necessarily determine consciousness as the constant measure of time. Insofar as time can be located neither inside nor outside, and thus insofar as there can be no place beyond time from which to determine time, there is no opposition between the inside and the outside, no fundamental distinction, say, between the form of inner sense (time) and the form of outer sense (space). Time is the impossible limit of interiority and exteriority, a limit that cannot *not* be violated as the condition of possibility of its institution. Because the interior, in closing itself off from the exterior, necessarily exposes itself to the outside and thus disrupts and displaces itself, there is no possibility for the unification of time's constitutive ecstasy.

This does not mean that time cannot be determined. It means only that there is no irreducible present or now-point that makes possible the security of any unity whatsoever, including the unity of consciousness. In his lecture on time, Borges writes: "There is no moment in which we can say to time: Stop. You are so beautiful . . . !, as Goethe wished. The present does not stop. We could not imagine a pure present; it would be null" (1996, 4.205). Earlier in the same lecture he asserted, "The present in itself is like the finite point of geometry. The present in itself does not exist. It is not an immediate fact of our consciousness" (4.202). In order for us to be conscious of the present, it must *not* be present. On the contrary, the present is divided between, thus constituted of, the *no longer* and the *not yet.* It is marked by passage, transit, translation.

If we acknowledge that, in order to remember, Funes must necessarily synthesize time, then we must also concede that he is capable of forgetting, for there is no operation of synthesis that does not open onto the possibility of forgetting. Funes must be capable of forgetting, otherwise nothing would happen to him because nothing would ever pass and pass away. The verb *pasar* means as much "to happen" as "to pass." Hence, to live in the absolute present absolved of the past, absolved of loss, is to be dead. As Molloy noted, Borges describes Funes as monumental, bronze. He is a statue, lifeless. He is apparently so absolutely alive, so full of himself, that he is dead. Further, Borges establishes the cause of Funes's death: pulmonary congestion refers to the literal filling up of the lungs with fluid. He dies from congestion, from the apparent fullness of his present. But in order to die, one must be subject to time, to alteration. Such alteration can happen only insofar as something happens, something passes. Dying is passing away, but if living happened in the present, dying would be impossible. Nor, of course, could one live, for to live is to be exposed to whatever or whoever comes, to the accidents of the future, *here and now*.

## *Schopenhauer's cat*

Funes, however, is not Borges's only example of the necessary failure of any attempt to think experience on the basis of the present or the now. "El sur [The South]," for instance, concerns the inheritance of a past, a legacy, which is never simply given or imposed, but which is elected, chosen, and which, ultimately, is too present for the protagonist Juan Dahlmann, who lives and dies in a past which is nevertheless determined in and as the present. At a given moment in the narrative, in a café that he has remembered, Dahlmann finds himself contemplating the difference between the human being and the animal while petting a cat: he "thought, while he stroked the cat's black fur, that this contact was illusory, that he and the cat were separated as though by a pane of glass, because man lives in time, in successiveness, while the magical animal lives in the present, in the eternity of the instant" (1.525–526/CF 176). The cat is characterized as having a "disdainful divinity [*divinidad desdeñosa*]" (1.525/CF 176). If the philosophical figure for Funes's experience is Kant's dog, then the figure to which Borges refers in "The South" is Schopenhauer's cat. Schopenhauer does not mention a cat, but he does distinguish between the human being and the animal and he does so precisely in terms of the animal's inability to project itself into the future or to recall itself from the past. It is not, however, that the time of the animal's existence is different from the human's. According to Schopenhauer, both exist only in the present: "Above all, we must clearly recognize that the form of the phenomenon of the will, and hence the form of life or of reality, is really only the *present*, not the future or the past" (278). Therefore, he concludes, "No man has lived in the past, and none will ever live in the future; the *present* alone is the form of life" (278). Nevertheless, unlike "the animal that does not think," which "lives fearlessly and heedlessly in the presence of annihilation, supported by the consciousness that it is nature herself and is as imperishable as she . . . man alone carries about with him in abstract concepts the certainty of his own death" (281). The abstract concepts that, by providing the human being the certainty of its death and thus distract it from the present, are themselves "only an empty dream of the imagination" (278). In other words, Schopenhauer believes that we live in the present. In "Funes el memorioso" Borges makes clear that there is no life, no living, in the present as such. Life can never be in itself and the attempt to tie the living dog, which is temporally determined, to the present, kills the dog. Schopenhauer's cat, however, appears to be something different: it is always already dead because nothing happens to it. It lives, as Schopenhauer suggests, in "an everlasting midday" (280). Pet the cat all you like, you will never touch it.[33]

## *Funes and language*

If, despite their apparently different relationships to time, Schopenhauer's cat is Kant's dog, then it follows that Funes' radical empiricism is Kant's transcendentalism; that is, empiricism and transcendentalism harbor fundamentally the same relation to the imagination. This is already evident from the discussions of the imagination in Hume and Kant, but the identity of empiricism and transcendental philosophy is also demonstrable in their respective relations to and reflections on language. On the one hand, grounded as it is in experience, and therefore upon perceptions, empiricism ought to (and did) demand that language be fundamentally particular, that is, grounded in the singularity of perception such that the singularity of impressions might be expressed. On the other hand, transcendental philosophy ought to be capable of articulating a universal language. Yet, in each case, the one necessarily corrupts the other.

For example, the infallibility of his memory leads Funes to reject a language analogous to the one Locke suggested and also rejected: "In the seventeenth century, Locke postulated (and condemned) an impossible language in which each individual thing—every stone, every bird, every branch—would have its own name; Funes once contemplated a similar language, but discarded the idea as too general, too ambiguous" (1.489/

CF 136).[34] In Locke's case, such a language is impossible because of the necessary ideality of language: "All Things, that exist, being Particulars, it may perhaps be thought reasonable, that Words, which ought to be conformed to Things, should be so too, I mean in their Signification: but yet we find the quite contrary. The far *greatest part of Words*, that make all Languages, *are general Terms*: which has not been the Effect of Neglect, or Chance, but of Reason, and Necessity" (3.3, §1/409). For Locke there are two reasons why the relation of words to things is necessarily ideal, hence, universal. *First*, because "it is beyond the Power of humane Capacity to frame and retain distinct *Ideas* of all the particular Things we meet with" (3.3, §2/409). Locke argues that inasmuch as it is considered "an instance of a prodigious Memory" for a general to recall all the names of his soldiers, "We may easily find a Reason, why Men have never attempted to give Names to each Sheep in their Flock, or Crow that flies over their Heads; much less to call every Leaf of Plants, or Grain of Sand that came their way, by a peculiar Name" (3.3, §2/409). *Second*, and more importantly, to give every particular thing its own proper name would go against the principal interest of language. Locke writes: "If it were possible [to have no general terms], *it would yet be useless*; because it would not serve to the chief end of language. Men would in vain heap up Names of particular Things, that would not serve them to communicate their Thoughts. Men learn Names, and use them in Talk with others, only that they may be understood: which is then only done, when by Use or Consent, the Sound I make by the Organs of Speech, excites in another Man's Mind, who hears it, the *Idea* I apply it to in mine, when I speak it. This cannot be done by Names, applied to particular Things, whereof I alone having the *Ideas* in my mind, the Names of them could not be significant, or intelligible to another, who was not acquainted with all those very particular Things, which had fallen under my Notice" (3.3, §3/409–10). Thus, for words to be as useful "as they ought to be" any given word must necessarily be capable of comprehending "*several particular Things*" (3.1, §3/402). In order for communication *with others* to be possible, which according to Locke is the chief end of language, language must be conventional, which means it must be universalizable.

Funes, too, rejects the idea of a rigorously empirical language, but not on the grounds that language must be universalizable in order to be communicable, hence, in order to be language at all. He does not argue, for example, that even the most radical empiricism must ultimately depend upon the possibility of ideality, which is, in fact, the consequence of Locke's understanding of language's dependence on general terms. Rather, a particular name for every particular thing, according to Funes, is already "too general, too ambiguous" (1.489/CF 136). An individual name for every individual thing is too general because it ignores the effect of temporality on perception: "Funes remembered not only every leaf of every tree in every patch of forest, but every time he had perceived or imagined that leaf" (1.488/CF 136). According to Funes, not only should every leaf of every tree in the forest have its own particular name, but, because of what Borges calls the "heavy-laden flight of time," every leaf of every tree *every time it is perceived or imagined* must be named particularly (*Inquisiciones* 104; SNF 9).

Funes's memory apparently makes possible the project of a radical empiricism, that is, of a perception rigorously grounded in experience. The example of the dog is instructive, for Borges no doubt could have done without the spatial reorientation—the shift from profile to frontal view—because for Funes the dog at 3:14 cannot be the same as the dog at 3:15, whether he changes position or not. Pushed to the extreme, it is obvious that in Funes's eyes the dog can never be identical to itself. The dog is always no longer and not yet the "same" dog; it is no longer and not yet "itself." Not an instant, no matter how short, goes by in which the dog appears as "itself." For Funes, there can be no identity if identity is understood as being-in-itself or as being-self-identical; there is no identity in that identity requires sameness over time, something Funes's memory obviates. This means that the concept "dog" is strictly speaking impossible, for in order to regulate—subsume or comprehend—the manifold of sense data, the concept must be self-identical. The impossibility of such conceptual self-identity mitigates the possibility of any language whatsoever. A radically empirical language is not a language at all.

Funes's too capacious memory, his inability not only to forget and thus to abstract or synthesize, but also to pull himself together as a unity of consciousness, results in his inability to think, for sure, but should also make it impossible for him to speak. A radically empirical or particular language would be jibberish, babel. More to the point, however, an absolutely particular language would be an absolutely universal language.

In 1942, the year that he wrote "Funes," Borges published "El idioma analítico de John Wilkins [The Analytical Language of John

Wilkins]," in which he dismissed the idea of a universal language.[35] In the note on Wilkins, Borges locates the origin of the project of a strictly universal language in a letter in which Descartes suggests, "by using the decimal system of numeration, we could learn in a single day to name all quantities to infinity, and to write them in a new language, the language of numbers; he also proposed the creation of a similar, general language that would organize and contain all human thought" (2.84–5/SNF 230). The reference is to Descartes's letter to Mersenne on 10 November 1629 in which Descartes responds to the six propositions for a universal language that Mersenne had sent to him. Descartes points out that what is being "sold" as a universal language is in fact little more than the master set of a universal translator. At stake is less a new language, than the possibility of easily allowing everyone, using the same "primitive" symbols, to translate from one language to another. Everyone would thus continue to understand everyone else in his or her own language. But Descartes notes important limitations. For one thing, he remarks that understanding a language is not simply a question of syntax and semantics. There is also the problem, in spoken language, of sound: the "discordant combination of letters . . . would often make the sounds unpleasant and intolerable to the ear. It is to remedy this defect that all the differences in inflexion of words have been introduced by usage; and it is impossible for your author to have avoided the difficulty while making his grammar universal among different nations; for what is easy and pleasant in our language is coarse and intolerable in German, and so on. The most that he can have done is to have avoided discordant combinations of syllables in one or two languages; and so his universal language would do only for a single country" (Descartes 1991, 11–12). In other words, accent is idiomatic and untranslatable.

The articulation or pronunciation of the specific combination of letters of the universal language ineluctably singularizes it. Usage necessarily corrupts language. *Langue* is corrupted by *parole*: "If you make a language with only one pattern of conjugation, declension and construction, *and with no defective or irregular verbs introduced by corrupt usage . . .*" (emphasis added). The corruption of such a universal language is ineluctable, but it is not simply a negative development. On the contrary, such usage (and thus such corruption) is necessary in order for language to be communicable in the first place, in order for it to be understandable and to facilitate understanding. The instant the universal language is articulated—pronounced, written—it is ruined and becomes both susceptible to and in need of translation. But the necessity of translation obviates not only the need for a universal language, but also its possibility. Descartes spells this out when he observes that the need for a dictionary makes the proposed universal language no different from any other language: "I am sure that if you gave M[onsieur Claude] Hardy [a friend of Descartes's] a good dictionary of Chinese or any other language, and a book in the same language, he would guarantee to work out its meaning" (10–11).

Because a universal language would require that the meaning of every word be unequivocal, such a language would in principle admit no translation, whether intra- or inter-lingual. This is the point of Borges's ironic remark about the Royal Academy of Spanish's claims for the expressiveness of the Spanish language at the same time that the "same Royal Academy produces a dictionary every few years in order to define those words [*que define las voces*]" (2.84/SNF 229–30). Spanish expresses nothing but more words, every word expressing "itself" only *in other words*, which are also other voices (*voces*). A universal language, however, could not sustain such reference, for at the moment one word refers to another, the universal language would require translation. And there is no language in which words do not refer to other words. Particularity will always already have crept into the universal system, interrupting it, forcing its repetition, definition.

According to Borges, Wilkins understood this: "In the universal language conceived by [*que ideó*] Wilkins in the middle of the seventeenth century, each word defines itself [*cada palabra se define a sí misma*]" (1996, 2.84/SNF 230). We know where this ends up: the wonderful arbitrariness of the Chinese encyclopedia, which nevertheless is neither more nor less arbitrary than any language.[36] "Notoriously, there is no classification of the universe that is not arbitrary and speculative," Borges writes, and the reason is simple, "there is no universe in the organic, unifying sense of that ambitious word" (2.86/SNF 231). Such arbitrariness marks the inscription of automaticity (necessity) and chance (accidentality). At stake here is the singularity of language, which singularity is both preserved and lost, inscribed and erased, in the name, the signature, the accent.

In Borges's account, there is no difference between so-called particular and universal languages. An absolutely universal language in which every thing is called by its own name, in which every word defines only itself, is finally nothing other than Funes's dream of an absolutely particular language. Both posit a language without referral, and thus a language that would not be temporal.[37] Yet, language depends on the possibility of saying things (words) *in other words*, on the possibility of referentiality, which possibility necessarily exposes language to the future, thus to arbitrariness and accidentality. A language in which every word defines itself, in which "cat" means "cat" without the possibility of further definition *in other words*, is both absolutely transparent and absolutely meaningless. It would be language as tautology. An absolutely particular language, which is also an absolutely universal language, would not be a language at all. In its absolute auto-identity or auto-affection, it would not be able to communicate anything, not even itself as communicative.

## *The monstrosity of copulation*

"There is something monstruous," Borges remarks, "about mirrors [*los espejos tienen algo monstruoso*]" (1.431/CF 68). This discovery, which late at night Borges says is "inevitable," spurs Bioy Casares's memory. "That was when Bioy remembered a saying by one of the heresiarchs of Uqbar: *Mirrors and copulation are abominable, for they multiply the number of mankind*" (1.431/CF 68). Bioy Casares's memory fails him, of course: what he remembers is not identical to what is cited in the *Anglo-American Cyclopaedia*, which "is a literal (though also laggardly) reprint of the 1902 *Encyclopaedia Britannica*" (1.431/CF 68). The *literal* reprint changes everything, introducing within literal duplication, a certain monstrosity, a certain difference. If mirrors and copulation are monstrous, it is because the copula is the operator of a doubling that ineluctably—but accidentally, arbitrarily—introduces an alterity that cannot be foreseen within the constitutive possibility of ideality. It is precisely this monstrosity, which is also the possibility of monstration, thus of visibility, that the dreams of absolutely particular and absolutely universal languages seek to exclude. Both seek to exclude the time of monstrosity and monstration, the time of identity, which is the time it takes to say, to write, A = A or "I am I." This is the time of copulation. This time inscribes the becoming-particular of the universal and the becoming-universal of the particular. To put it in Kantian terms, it marks the becoming sensible of the concept and the becoming conceptual of the intuition of sense, without, however, this operation ever being referred to a stable point of reference. The copula therefore notes the possibility of becoming, of temporalization without recourse to any unity, without the determination of a self-present unity of consciousness. As the minimal articulation of identity, "I am I" indicates the structure neither of the absolute nor of absolution, but of attribution and thus of finitude. This means that the doubling or mirroring instantiated in and by the copula necessarily inscribes difference, duplicity, within the structure of identity. It is always possible—precisely as the condition of possibility of identification in general—that in saying "I am," I am *not* and I am *not I.* This is because, insofar as attribution is necessary, no identity, no identification can ever be immediately given: I can never be present to myself. I can only ever be attributed to I. This is the law of identification. If this were not the case, if in fact there were the guarantee of identity and, thus, the guarantee of immediate auto-affection, not only would referentiality be unnecessary, it would be impossible. But so too would I, for I am only the possibility of referral. This is only to say that I am not one, that I am always at least two, always already doubled, always already dubbed. I am (the monster) that I am. This is God's madness no less than Swift's.[38]

Finally, this doubling that I am and that is constitutive of the possibility of perception in the first place—thus, as well, the very mark of perception's *im*possibility—already operates in Borges's description of Funes's self-perception. Recall that when seen in a mirror, and this is the only way one can ever see one's "own" face, Funes's visage appears new to him, surprising. It is not his own. Funes's perception of his face is always already mediated, temporalized, repeated, and repeatable. Funes's perception, if he has any, is marked by doubling and duplicity from before the beginning.[39] Time is the condition of possibility of any perception, however "almost immediate" (*casi inmediato*) it may be. It is indeed the impossible condition of possibility of such immediacy. Which means temporalization must also be constitutive of transcendental apperception, which is, in Kant, an ostensibly immediate or fixed point of reference that nonetheless can only be thought, that is, conceived, in and through its *perception*, thus, its being-posited. There is no immediate perception, contrary to Kant's occasional claim in the first *Critique*, and there is no atemporal unity of consciousness, because the condition of possibility of conceiving such apperception, of cognizing it, of *locating* it in the first place, necessarily displaces it into time.[40] As a consequence, Kant's unchanging I has no voice of its own, no voice that is not always already the voice of another, in which to call—to present or to make present—his dog. Borges has let him loose for good.

# 4

# Decisions of Hospitality

> Humanitarianism is always inhuman.
>
> —Jorge Luis Borges, *Evaristo Carriego*

> If metaphor, the chance and risk of *mimesis*, can always miss the true. . . .
>
> —Jacques Derrida, *Margins of Philosophy*

> They remembered that all nouns . . . have only metaphoric value.
>
> —Jorge Luis Borges, *Ficciones*

The preceding two chapters make clear that the contradiction of time that passes and the identity that endures can be solved through neither an empirical nor a transcendental determination of the relation of sense and understanding. The synthesis of succession, as Martin Hägglund characterizes the problem that most concerns Borges, can be anchored neither in the indivisible present impression *à la* Hume nor in the unchanging "I" of transcendental apperception *à la* Kant. Importantly, however, both Hume and Kant locate the synthesis of time and, thus, the act of translation that makes cognition possible in the imagination, which, according to both, operates spontaneously—automatically, mechanically—and secretly. Part of what has been at stake in the preceding chapters has been an attempt to come to terms with such spontaneous—which is neither subjective nor objective, neither simply free nor simply conditioned—translation. In neither Hume nor Kant is the imagination ever simply present; it is not of the order of being *qua* presence, hence it is not *natural*, not least in its necessary production of monsters. In both Hume and Kant, the imagination is of the order of artifice, of *techne* rather than *phusis*, of nonbeing, of time. In this sense, the automatic operation of translation has been conceived as an accident. If translation describes the movement across a border, a movement of transference to another site, of a *trans-duction* (*traductio* or *traducción*), then the accident of translation is metaphor.

## *The accident of metaphor*

In 1921, at the very beginning of his professional literary career, Borges published an essay dedicated to metaphor in the journal *Cosmópolis*. Some thirty years later, in 1952, he published a second essay under the same title, which he inserted into the *Obras completas* edition of *Historia de la eternidad*, which was first published in 1936. Although the two versions of "La metáfora" differ from one another, both concern metaphor's problematic relation to a reality that can only be said *in other words*. The interest of these two versions of "La metáfora" lies at their opposite ends. The 1921 version begins, "There does not exist an essential dissimilarity between metaphor and what professional scientists call the explication of a phenomenon. Both are associations woven between two distinct things, one of which is transferred into the other. Both are equally true or false" (1921, 395).[1] The 1952 version concludes with Borges's famous remark, "Some day the history of metaphor will be written and we will learn the truth and the error that these conjectures contain" (1996, 1.384). Taken together these propositions make clear that every indication or description, every nomination, of a thing is fundamentally metaphorical. Metaphor enters language *at* and *as* the possibility of language. But insofar as metaphor is constitutive or originary, truth and error will never be sorted out.

The 1921 version continues: "To explain pain, for example, in terms of histology, of a shock to the nervous system, of cavities . . . , amounts to making what is explained disappear. Of course, this nomenclature can offer a practical utility, similar to the intellectual relief that, in an algebraic operation, the fact of assigning a value [*el hecho de rotular*] to the quantities *x*, *y* or *z* apportions. But it is absurd to believe that these symbols can change or clarify in any way the things that they label" (1921, 395). Put simply, words abstract from a reality that cannot be explained otherwise. As Borges argues, "Light—the photic sensation, for instance—is something definitively demarcated from the vibrations into which the optics translate it" (395). A *rótulo*, however, is not just the determination that manifests itself as a word or a phrase, a sign or a symbol, a value. A *rótulo* is an inscription, a mark. Metaphor is another name for—thus a metaphor for—the singularity of inscription, of writing, and thus of *material* determination. At the same time, however, the singularity of inscription, *qua* inscription or mark, is necessarily open to repetition and appropriation. In short, the possibility of metaphor depends on temporal finitude, for determination is impossible outside the horizon of movement or alteration. And, as Aristotle points out in the *Physics*, temporal change is negation, destruction: "A thing, then, will be affected by time, just as we are accustomed to say that time wastes things away, and that all things grow old through time. . . . For time is by its nature the cause rather of decay" (1984, 221a30–221b1/1.374). Metaphor is another name for corruption.

Borges's understanding that there is no essential difference between metaphor and the scientific description of phenomena challenges the important Aristotelian distinction between science (*episteme*) and philosophy, on the one side, and the more practical concerns of rhetoric and poetry (as well as history), what might be called the arts of persuasion and delight (hence the arts of *movement*), on the other side. This is the distinction between necessity and chance or fortune, that is, between what happens always or for the most part and what may always be otherwise (which includes the possibility of not being at all). Aristotle explains: "Since, among things which are, some are always in the same state and are of necessity (not necessity in the sense of compulsion but that which means the impossibility of being otherwise), and some are not of necessity nor always, but for the most part, this is the principle and this is the cause of the accidental" (1026b27–32/2.1621). The accidental names the horizon of what is neither always nor for the most part. As such, it is not the concern of philosophy (or science, determinate knowledge) but of rhetoric, which, unlike philosophy, is exercised in public arenas such as the tribunals or the *agora*, and thus within the sphere of human affairs where necessity in fact plays no part and where a decision must be made. Aristotle outlines rhetoric's parameters thusly: "There are few facts of the necessary type that can form the basis of rhetorical deductions. Most of the things about which we make decisions, and into which therefore we inquire, present us with alternative possibilities. For it is about our actions that we deliberate and inquire, *and all our actions have a contingent character*; hardly any of them are determined by necessity . . ." (1357a23–33/2.2157, emphasis added).[2]

Rhetorical argument proceeds through enthymemes and examples, both of which "deal with what is for the most part capable of being otherwise" (1357a14–15/2.2157). An enthymeme is a rhetorical deduction based not on necessity but on probability, which means that enthymemes are discursive strategies for deciding cases that are fundamentally undecideable, unpredictable. Rhetoric, then, is not concerned with truth because truth in Aristotle is eternal, and as such, it is necessary. Rather, rhetoric concerns practical knowledge, hence action; and action—the decision to act—takes place in relation to an irreducibly undecidable outcome or end; in other words, chance (contingency, accidentality) plays its part in every act. Because it concerns the accidental, thus that which is not essential, what Aristotle calls *onoma ti monon*—the merely nominal—, rhetoric is "concerned with appearances" (1404a/2.2238). Nevertheless, Aristotle admits that "we cannot do without" rhetoric: "The right thing in speaking really is that we should be satisfied not to annoy our hearers, without trying to delight them: we ought in fairness to fight our case with no help beyond the bare facts: nothing, therefore, should matter except the proof of those facts. Still . . . other things affect the result considerably, owing to the defects in our hearers. The arts of language cannot help having a small but real importance, *whatever it is we expound to others*: the way in which a thing is said does affect its intelligibility" (1404a1–10/2.2238, emphasis added).

Rhetoric (the "arts of language") ought to be ruled out of discussions, but cannot be. It is unessential (the apodicticity of facts alone ought to be persuasive), but nonetheless necessary: "we cannot do without it" for "whatever it is we expound to others." In short, there is no possibility of deciding *what to do* or *how to act* without rhetoric.

This is so regardless of Aristotle's claim that "nobody uses fine language when teaching geometry" (1404a11–12/2.2238). To the extent language is necessary to teach geometry, so too is rhetoric. This means that in order for truth to be known and communicated—however apodictically—it *must* pass through rhetoric. Truth must, finally, *appear*, but in order to do so it must appear in and through language. In doing so, it is exposed to accidentality, to nonessentiality and nonbeing. No truth without language and no language that does not say itself, articulate itself, in and through, *as* the arts of language. Philosophy thus needs rhetoric even as it dismisses it. Philosophy needs rhetoric in order to be philosophy, in order to concern itself with truth, with being rather than appearances. But because rhetoric is concerned only with appearances—with what may be otherwise—it is not bound to truth or fact: it can always mislead, deceive.

But it is not simply that rhetoric *can* mislead. On the contrary, as an art of language without any essential relation to truth, rhetoric can *only* mislead, deceive. Hence, the condition of possibility for determining or saying the truth is its impossibility. Truth (essence) can only be said through appearance, thus *as* what it is not. Consequently, truth appears *in name only*, in the mere name. And this means truth can only ever be said metaphorically, *in* and *as* metaphor. This is what Borges suggested in his assertion that there is no *essential* difference between metaphor and the scientific description of phenomena. Elsewhere, in an essay published in *Sur*, Borges claimed, "to speak is to metaphorize; to falsify" (1999b, 33). This claim undermines the Aristotelian distinction between philosophy and rhetoric, truth and appearance, necessity and accident.

This chapter pursues the furthest implications of Aristotle's understanding of metaphor and its relation to time and being in order to open a reading of the possibility of decision in Borges. Is a decision possible? If a decision is possible and necessary only in those circumstances that are not governed by what always or for the most part happens, then the decision is, by definition, governed by what may always be otherwise. Accordingly, the decision is always rhetorically determined, which suggests that there is no decision that is not, *essentially*, touched by metaphor, that is, by constitutive metaphoricity. The question that this chapter attempts to answer concerns the relation of metaphor or metaphoricity to possibility and to time. Specifically, is metaphor (and thus possibility) related to being and therefore to the present or is it related to the future? And if metaphor (and therefore possibility) is structurally open to the future, then is a decision ever possible? For Borges, as will become clear, the question of decision—of its impossible possibility—has implications for politics and the political.

### *Metaphor, analogy, homonymy*

In the 1952 version of "La metáfora," Borges invoked Aristotle's definition of metaphor: "In the third book of the *Rhetoric*, Aristotle observed that all metaphor arises from the intuition of an analogy between dissimilar things" (1996, 1.382). The definition of metaphor offered in the *Rhetoric* is identical to the one offered in the *Poetics*: "Metaphor consists in giving the thing a name that belongs to something else; the transference being either from genus to species, or from species to genus, or from species to species, or *on grounds of analogy*" (1457b7–9/2.2332, emphasis added).[3] Although Aristotle does not say as much in the *Poetics*, analogy is the condition of possibility of all metaphor, of metaphoricity in general. Analogy is the combinatory mechanism that makes possible all relations and determinations. In the *Poetics*, Aristotle discusses metaphor under the heading of "diction" (*lexis*) and he concludes: "the greatest thing by far is to be a master of metaphor. It is the one thing that cannot be learnt from others; and it is also a sign of genius, since a good metaphor implies an intuitive perception of the similarity in dissimilars" (1459a5–8/2.2334–2335).

The problem of metaphor and its mastery announces the maximal problem of philosophy. According to W. K. C. Guthrie's interpretation of Aristotle and Ancient Philosophy more generally, in which "motion and change are the most characteristic marks of nature," the most pressing philosophical problem facing Greek philosophy is "how to bring within the compass of scientific knowledge a world of unstable phenomena, always changing, coming into being and passing away, never the same for two instants together" (102). Guthrie argues that in large measure Aristotle rejected Plato's theory of Forms because Plato conceived such Forms as "a set of substances existing apart from the sensible world" (103). Instead, he postulated that "the trained mind can, by a process of thought, analyse this continual flux [of the sensible world] and find underlying it certain basic principles (*archai*) which do not change"

(102–103). These *archai* or principles are not substances separate from the sensible world. They are observable in the sensible world through an act or operation of thought. They are, then, an effect of abstraction, but such abstraction requires analogy or metaphor in that what is apparent and therefore mutable must be seen as if it were constant. Metaphor or analogy is the articulation—the inscription or *rótulo*—of the instability of *what is*, of incessant coming-to-be and passing-away. Rodolphe Gasché's remark that "[w]hether or not certain philosophers explicitly reflect on the problem of analogy, all metaphysics, insofar as it is concerned with the unity in difference, must be understood itself primarily as a philosophy of analogy" (1986, 296) points in the direction of Borges's Tlön, where philosophy is a branch of fantastic literature, not because all science finally is psychology, but because of the as-structure of language. Indeed, because language is analogical the "as if" inscribes nonessential or accidental relation at the heart of being.

In the *Poetics* Aristotle considers analogy as simply one of four types of metaphor. Nevertheless, in implicit agreement with Borges, Derrida writes, "Analogy is metaphor par excellence" (1982, 242) and he claims Aristotle insists on this in book three of the *Rhetoric*, the book to which Borges refers in the 1952 version of "Metaphor." Aristotle professes, for instance, "Of the four kinds of metaphor the most taking is the proportional kind" (1984, 1411a1/2.2251).[4] Further, in Aristotle, analogy not only refers to mathematical proportionality. Following Franz Brentano's reading of the Scholastics, Gasché argues that analogy also refers to attribution and correspondence. That is, in addition to determining the proportional relation of two terms, analogy also constellates any number of terms as corresponding to a central or dominant term, figure, or name. But if "analogy is metaphor par excellence," then Aristotle cannot restrict metaphor to rhetoric and poetics. On the contrary, analogy—and therefore metaphor—belongs no less to metaphysics (and to the *Metaphysics*) as the condition of possibility of saying Being. Aristotle writes: "There are many senses in which a thing may be said to 'be,' but they are related to one central point, one definite kind of thing, and are not homonymous" (1003a32–33/2.158). Aristotle thus establishes important limits on the saying of Being, namely, the several ways to say Being all refer to a *central point*, to one definite kind of thing. Consequently, Being is said neither ambiguously, nor accidentally, nor equivocally. Being is not said through homonymy.[5]

According to Aristotle, Being is certain of itself. The problem, however, is that Being cannot call itself in or by its proper name. This is what is at stake in the categories, which, Derrida explains, "answer the question of knowing in what ways Being is said" (1982, 183). Indeed, Derrida notes, "at the moment when Aristotle sets categories, and the category of category, in place . . . he intends to answer the question which does not admit . . . the distinction between language and thought" (182–183). The importance of this cannot be overstated in that "the system of the categories is the system of being's turns of phrase. It brings the problematic of the analogy of Being, its equivocalness or unequivocalness, into communication with the problematic of the metaphor in general" (183–184). From the beginning, the problem of saying Being and of Being saying itself is haunted by metaphoricity. Thus, when Aristotle outlines the science that studies "being as being" (1984, 1003a22/2.1584), the *as* already introduces essential metaphoricity. In order for Being to name itself, to designate or point to itself, it cannot avoid the displacement constitutive of metaphor. Being can only ever call itself *as* Being, and the necessity of this *as* makes Being a homonym of itself.

Perhaps this explains why Aristotle opens his *Categories* with the problem of homonymy: "When things have only a name in common [*onoma monon koinon*] and the definition of being which corresponds to the name is different, they are called *homonymous* [*Homonuma legetai*]" (1984, 1a1–2/1.3).[6] As an example of homonymy, Aristotle indicates that both a man (*anthropos*) and a portrait (*gegrammenon*) can be called animals (*zoon*). The essence or being (*ousia*) of a man and that of a portrait are not the same, yet they can be called by the same name: *zoon*. A portrait, then, is an animal equivocally, ambiguously, *in name only* (*homonuma*), that is, homonymically. Aristotle follows the discussion of homonymy with a similar account of synonymy. "When things have the name in common and the definition of being which corresponds to the name is the same, they are called *synonymous* [*Sunonuma de legetai*]" (1a6–7/1.3).

All metaphors require the recognition of *homoiosis* (likeness, similarity) in dissimilarity. Insofar as metaphor depends on "the intuitive perception of similarity in dissimilars [*to gar eu metapherein to homoion theorin estin*]"[7] (1459a7–8/2.2335), metaphor becomes possible in the synthetic operation that determines differences as similarity or likeness through a structure of referral or analogy. As Derrida observes, "*Mimesis* is never without the *theoretical* perception of resemblance or similarity, that is, of that which always will be posited as the condition of metaphor. *Homoiosis* is . . . that without which the metaphorical operation is impossible" (1982, 237). But insofar as likeness (*homoiosis*) always results from difference, at bottom metaphor is not only analogical but *essentially* homonymical. Consequently, metaphor is essentially without essence. This has implications for language in that metaphor instances the possibility of language.[8] It is this understanding of language that informs Borges's claim that there is no essential difference between metaphor and scientific description, which means both metaphor and scientific denomination are *equally* true and false.

## *The homonymy of being*

In his 1931 lectures on Aristotle's *Metaphysics*, Heidegger observed that the unity of Being is neither equivocal (*homonumos*) nor univocal (*sunonumos*). Rather, the unity of Being is analogical, which means Being is said in many ways without, however, being reduced either to *mere* homonymy or to synonymy. The unity of Being *corresponds* to the unity of analogy, which depends on transference: "This corresponding, *analegein*, is intrinsically an *anapherein pros to proton* . . . : 'a carrying onto the first' of the meaning and securing it there" (1995, 33). Heidegger refers to *Metaphysics* IV where Aristotle notes: "[S]ince there are many senses in which a thing is said to be one, these terms also will have many senses, but yet it belongs to one science to consider them all; for a term belongs to different sciences not if it has different senses, but if its definitions neither are identical nor can be referred to one central meaning. And since all things are referred to that which is primary, as for instance all things which are one are referred to the primary one, we must say that this holds good also of the same and the other and of contraries in general" (1984, 1004a22–28/2.1586). Heidegger goes on to elaborate the regulatory principle of analogy: "The manner of the carrying back and forth of the meanings to the first is different in each case. The first, however, is the *sustaining and guiding basic meaning*; it is always that from out of which the meaning which carries itself to it and corresponds to it is capable of being spoken. In Greek, the 'from and of which' is the *arkhe*" (1995, 33–34). There must be a rule or principle that governs the *pollakos legomena*. Heidegger writes, "For *on* [being] is said neither *homonumos* nor *sunonumos* (as the *genos*)"; rather, "it is said *koinon*" (34). "How, then," he asks, "is the unity of this universality of being to be conceived as a sort of analogy?" (34) and he stresses Aristotle's qualification of homonymy: Being is not said by means of a *merely accidental* homonymy.

For Heidegger, this is important for two reasons. *First*, although Aristotle claims in the *Nicomachean Ethics* that the unity of the good is *not* the unity of homonymy, Heidegger remarks that in *Metaphysics* IV (1019b8), "being is used in the sense of a homonym" (36). But Heidegger insists on the distinction between the spurious unity of an accidental homonym and the unity of Being indicated by non-accidental or necessary homonymy. *Second*, Heidegger's reading of the opening sentence of Aristotle's *Categories* allows for no alternative to homonymy or synonymy: because Being is *not* said through synonymy, it *must* be said through homonymy, for "what is not συνωνυμως is a ομωνυμως" (36). Were it said through synonymy, Being would be a genus; this would, however, limit Being, restricting it from saying *all* that *is* in that there is no universally determinate genus.[9] Therefore, the unity of Being—the way Being says itself in whatever is—must be of the order of homonymy, but it cannot be accidental, otherwise it would not be the case that Being *must* be and is said in whatever is. "Being is not purely and simply an accidental ομωνυμον, but a sort of one, in the sense of analogy" (36).

Heidegger nonetheless cautions that the analogy of Being does not solve the "being question." To the contrary, it is "but the title of the most stringent *aporia*, the impasse in which ancient philosophy, and along with it all subsequent philosophy right up to today, is enmeshed" (38). There is no way out of the aporia that does not recur, finally, to analogy. In this sense analogy is irreducible.[10] Heidegger senses as much when, in his consideration of the meanings of *dúnamis*, he returns once again to the problem of analogy. Following Aristotle in his deferral of an accounting for what he calls the group of meanings related only nominally, Heidegger writes: "[W]hat is to be excluded are those meanings which belong to δυναμις ομωνυμως λεγομενη, to the meaning of force which is stated in the sense of nominal identity" (48). According to Heidegger, Aristotle recurs to "another form of analogy, although he does not differentiate between the two forms with a specific designation" (48). This is an important gesture in that it implicitly acknowledges that the distinction between *analogia attributionis* and *analogia proportionalitatis* is the legacy of Medieval Scholasticism. The distinction ultimately makes little sense in that whether via attribution to a given meaning (the *arckhe* or regulatory principle) or via correspondence according to proportional resemblance, both forms of analogy *refer* different or dissimilar things to each other according to a principle of likeness, *homoiosis*.

The issue is whether the identity, the *homoiosis*, of the analogy, its unity, is accidental or not. Taking up Aristotle's example of the analogy between bodily eyes and the eyes of the soul, Heidegger writes: "In the correspondence a *transfer* occurs from the proportionality between the eyes and vision in the physical onto the proportionality in the mental—a transfer: a μεταφορα; every 'metaphor' is an analogy (but not in the sense of an *analogia attributionis*). Eye and eye mean here something different, but this is by no means a mere accident and unfounded identity of the name, but rather a certain correspondence (ομοιοτης τις) in the matter" (48).

Every metaphor is an analogy, but not an analogy of attribution. On the contrary, analogy must be determined in and by "a certain correspondence" not of the name, but of the matter, *Sache*. On Heidegger's account, likeness (*homoiosis*) cannot simply be an effect of referral, attribution, chance. It must be proportional, hence *measured*. There must be "a certain correspondence in the matter." Only proportion appears to guarantee and secure reference and correspondence. Only proportional correspondence avoids the risk or chance of nominal identity and thus of equivocation.

It is worth recalling that Aristotle does not *nominally* distinguish these two types of analogy. The problem of maintaining the distinction becomes apparent to Heidegger as he begins to calculate the various senses of *dúnamis*. In the end, he asks, "But where does all this lead us?" (61). His answer is instructive: "Let us leave such indeterminate, undecided, fleeting, and polymorphic things to language! What would be the point of a sum of fixed definitions with words grafted onto them and thereby made unequivocal? That of course would be the decline and death of language" (61).[11] The interest of this passage lies in Heidegger's concession that without homonymy language would decline, die. Equivocation—

hence, nominal identity and accidental homonymy—therefore is *essential* to the *vitality* of language. This also means that synonymy is an effect of homonymy insofar as homonymy marks the possibility of language as such. A language dies precisely to the extent homonymy—accidentality, contingency, equivocality, chance, misattribution—is restricted, delimited. The reduction of referral (temporality, analogy)—of all that is indeterminate, undecided, fleeting, and polymorphic—would spell, univocally, the death of language. Yet, at the same time, these very characteristics, which constitute language's vitality, also and inevitably, irreducibly, jeopardize the possibility of language as meaningful and communicative. The upshot is that in order for language to communicate and to be meaningful, it must be temporally determined. Consequently, as the very condition of its possibility, language necessarily threatens meaning and communication. As the condition of its possibility, language threatens itself. Synonymy—meaningful, unequivocal correspondence—thus depends on homonymy. The success of language depends on its failure. This is the case, moreover, *both* for living *and* dead languages. There is no language, living or dead, free of homonymy. If language is to mean and to communicate, equivocation must be possible.

Heidegger knew this. Gasché explains: "[T]he primary disclosure achieved by the as-structure is at the same time a primary covering-up. Indeed, since the as-structure uncovers 'with regard to,' it veils and reveals in the same gesture. Thus, Heidegger has inscribed an originary falsehood into the very articulation of the logos, which will allow him, with one structure, to explain why propositions *can* be wrong" (1986, 301). Despite the apparent recognition of the constitutive possibility of equivocation or errancy as the condition of possibility of meaning and communication, Heidegger attempts to restrict this necessary accidentality to the horizon of language, thus preserving Being itself from its deleterious effects. "Let us leave such indeterminate, undecided, fleeting, and polymorphic things to language!" As a consequence, although Heidegger is clear that "Being is nothing outside the determined existent" (Derrida 1978, 143) and therefore the articulation of Being cannot "avoid the ontic metaphor" (138), Heidegger nonetheless desires to save Being *as such*, by placing it beyond the corruption of constitutive metaphorization. Derrida writes: "Being itself is *alone* in its absolute resistance to every metaphor" (138).[12] *On the one hand*, Being resists every metaphor and thus resists metaphoricity and analogization. Being withholds itself as such from analogy and therefore from any possibility of being named. Being *as such* or *in itself* cannot be determined by analogy, by or within the as-structure of thought insofar as Being resists absolutely every metaphor. *On the other hand,* insofar as "Being is nothing outside the determined existent," it goes without saying that Being "would not appear as such without the possibility of speech. Being *itself* can only be thought and stated" (143). But if Being can only ever be thought and stated, then being can only ever be analogous to itself, which means Being can never be *in itself* or *as such*. It can only *be* metaphorically or analogically. Consequently, Being can never call itself in its *own* name. No name is *proper* to Being, which means Being is *merely* a name. Being is always equivocal, in name only, homonymous.[13]

If Being, however, is only nominally, equivocally, identical to itself, then it stands to reason that no other word or entity is self-identical either. *Whatever is* is *in name only*. Being thus suffers the same indeterminateness, the same indecision, the same fleeting stability as anything and everything else. Whatever is must be thought, posited, conceived—*said*—within language. Heidegger's attempt to preserve Being from this fate by isolating it from metaphor parallels Borges's understanding of Aristotle's position in the 1952 version of "Metaphor": "Aristotle . . . grounds metaphor on things and not on language" (1996, 1.382). Borges attributes to the twelfth-century Icelandic historian, mythographer, and "double traitor [*doble traidor*]" (1.371), Snorri Sturluson the determination that metaphors have no anchor in the real world, which would mean that the so-called real world would be so *in name only*, homonymically. "The tropes conserved by Snorri are (or seem) the results of a mental process that does not perceive analogies but rather that combines words; some can impress . . . but they neither reveal nor communicate anything" (1.382). That metaphors neither reveal nor communicate any*thing* is owed to their indeterminateness and indecision, which no doubt depends on the constitutive temporality of referral or correspondence without anchor in Being. Metaphors are ships adrift in a sea without horizon or harbor: they never run aground on the shoals of a substance (*ousia*, being) that is not itself a substantive, a noun and thus a name. The ground of metaphor, and of language therefore, is the name and thus constitutive homonymy. Any decision *about* the world—any decision *in* the world—necessarily remains ungrounded, provisional. Every decision is, consequently, a decision *in name only*. In itself, necessarily, every decision is already mistaken, equivocal.

### *The inscription of hospitality*

In the 1921 version of "Metaphor" Borges acknowledges the constitutive instability of language and, by his choice of example, of the world: "I believe that in Arabic there still endure many words that translate at the same time two opposite things. Without going so far, I will recall the amphibological meaning of the Spanish word, *huésped*" (1921, 401). *Huésped* means both "a person sheltered, welcomed, in a foreign house" and "a person who hosts in his house another."[14] *Huésped* derives from the Latin *hospes*, *hospitis*, which, Emile Benveniste explains, "designates the one who receives as well as the one who offers hospitality" (261).[15] There is, then, a reciprocity or economy between *hospes* and *hostis*, or between two types of stranger: "to explain the relation between 'guest' and 'enemy,' in general we admit that the one and the other derive their meaning from 'stranger,' to which the Latin again attests, where 'favorable stranger > guest [*hôte*]' and 'hostile stranger > enemy' [*pour expliquer le rapport entre «hôte» et «ennemi», on admet en général que l'un et l'autre dérivent du sens de «étranger» qui est encore attesté en latin; d'où «étranger favorable > hôte» et «étranger hostile > ennemi»*]" (Benveniste 1969, 92).[16]

The *hostis*, however, is not simply a stranger. It is a stranger with the rights of the citizen, a stranger who lives within the borders of the state: "a *hostis* is not a foreigner in general. Different from travelers that live outside the limits of the territory, *hostis* is 'the foreigner insofar as we recognize in him rights equal to those of the Roman citizen' [*Un* hostis *n'est pas un étranger en général. A la différence de peregrines qui habite hors des limites du territoire,* hostis *est «l'étranger, en tant qu'on lui reconnaît des droits égaux à ceux des citoyens romains»*]" (93). The stranger, the foreigner, therefore, is not the barbarian; he is not the absolute other. This is so, Derrida argues, because "*xenos* indicates relations of the same type between men linked by a pact which implies precise obligations also extending to their descendents" (2000b, 21). The foreigner occupies the same space and has the same rights as the citizen without being a citizen. The foreigner is different: a stranger, but equal; he or she is different (from us) but equal (to us). Both aspects—the difference and the equality—must be accounted for; neither is naturally subordinate to the other.

Benveniste observes that "the history of *hostis* summarizes the changes that were produced in the Roman institutions [*l'histoire de* hostis *résume le changement que s'est produit dans les institutions romaines*]" (1969, 95) and that in Homer's Greece *xénos* ultimately came to mean "simply 'foreigner,' non-national [*simplement l'«étranger», le non-national*]" (96). Indeed, "In Attic law, there is a *graphe xenius*, an action against a foreigner who attempts to pass for a 'citizen' [*Dans le droit attique, il y a une* graphe xenius, *poursuite contre un «étranger» qui veut se faire passer pour un «citoyen»*]" (96). This law or edict of the foreigner, this *graphe xenius*, protects the border—by marking or drawing it—of the citizen. This law, this writing, makes possible the relation *to* the foreigner *as* foreign, *as* foreigner, but in doing so it necessarily conditions this relation through the institution of an economy, a pact, which is also a contract, a promise. The foreigner, the stranger, finds him- or herself among us, citizens, under the law, subject to the law. But the law also determines citizens in their self-relation. The citizen can be such only insofar as he or she is responsible for the foreigner *qua* foreign. In short, by not granting the foreigner citizenship, the citizen becomes responsible to and for the foreigner *as* foreign. The demand that citizen and stranger, host and guest, be separate and equal necessarily runs the risk that the one will be taken—mistaken, but also that one will take him- or herself *or* the other—for the other. A *graphe*—a writing and thus a line—must be drawn between them and thus between us. It is the line in the sand, the border (the law) that *marks out* (outlines) the difference between them and us and that, in the same stroke, marks *out* (erases) the possibility of their—that is, our—equality. For at the moment the line is drawn distinguishing host from guest, citizen from foreigner—from the moment the pact is signed and the promise sealed, the invitation extended, which are the conditions for the institution and recognition of equality—equality is necessarily crossed out. The line—*graphe*, law, edict, border—circumscribes the scene, imposing order, rules. The line determines the pact and establishes parameters. By dividing citizen from foreigner, the line conditions the relation of one to the other. The line puts each in (his, her, its) place.

The *graphe* is also a signature, an *autographe* and an *auto-bio-graphe*, a birth certificate, a passport. It delimits and describes, nominates, both sides of its border, citizen and foreigner. The *graphe* divides. It marks the inscription of decision. The *graphe xenius* therefore not only draws the line between but, in marking the limit, also draws the line, the circle, around it. It circumscribes the citizen and the foreigner, the host and the guest. This is what is at stake in Benveniste's elaboration of the etymological relation of *hospes* to **pot(i)*, which means "chief," and to **pet-*, meaning "himself." The Latin example is of especial importance for Benveniste, not least because what issues from the **pet-/*pot(i)* complex is the language of power, of potentiality, and of property and properness. As Benveniste explains, "There is a homophony between this **pet-/*pot(i)-* 'chief' and a particle of identity, **pet-/*pot(i)-*, which means 'same, self' " (1971, 259). In short, that which is most one's own and the possibility of sovereignty and, in particular, what might be considered the minimal condition of sovereignty, mastery over one's own house (259–264), are signaled in *hospes*, the Latin root of hospitality, which indicates the pact between citizen and foreigner, host and guest.

Hospitality is tied to the home, the domicile or shelter (but also, therefore, to the family, the nation, and the state). Hospitality is related to power or mastery over the home in that it always takes the form of the decision of inclusion and exclusion. From the beginning, then, hospitality is ethics. "Insofar as it has to do with the *ethos*," Derrida writes, "that is, the residence, one's home, the familiar place of dwelling, inasmuch as it is a manner of being there, the manner in which we relate to ourselves and to others, to others as our own or as foreigners, *ethics* is *hospitality*; ethics is so thoroughly coextensive with the experience of hospitality" (2001a, 16–17).[17] In one's own home, one must always retain the power to decide whom or what to welcome, to shelter, but also whom or what to exclude. Otherwise, one would no longer be the master of the house. One would indeed be the hostage. Consequently, the demand of hospitality, that there be a pact between citizen and foreigner in which both occupy the same space and are equal under the law, *must* be violated at the very moment of its inception or institutionalization, because the demand for the absolute equality of citizen and foreigner entails that the citizen/sovereign no longer be master of his or her house.

*As if there were sovereignty*

And yet, this is precisely what happens and precisely because ethics is hospitality. In order to be hospitable, then, one must (if one can) be at home with oneself, which, Derrida writes, "supposes a reception or inclusion of the other which one seeks to appropriate, control, and master according to different modalities of violence" (17). It could not be otherwise, for the relation to the other is the necessary effect of the line demarcating our difference from others and their equality to us. But the upshot of this relation to the other, the necessary opening to the other that constitutes culture or the *ethos* in the first place, is that sovereignty comes from the other. One's mastery—over oneself and one's home as much as over the other—comes from the other, from the guest or the foreigner. One thus comes into one's own, one enters one's own place only through the other: "It is *as if* the stranger or foreigner held the keys. . . . It's *as if* . . . the stranger . . . could save the master and liberate the power of his host" (2000b, 123). It is *as if* the foreigner frees the citizen; *as if* the guest liberates the host to his or her most proper self, to his or her mastery over the house, the nation, the state. "We thus enter from the inside: the master of the house is at home, but nonetheless he comes to enter his home through the guest—who comes from the outside. The master thus enters from the inside *as if* he came from the outside. He enters his home thanks to the visitor, by the grace of the visitor" (125).

It will be important not to lose sight of this *as if*, which opens onto metaphoricity and analogization, and thus onto the referral to exteriority in general. The *as if* signals the inscription of constitutive temporalization within the relation between host and guest, hence within the contract or promise that is the possibility of hospitality and the *huésped. On the one hand*, if the host is the host *as such* or *in itself*, then the host is sovereign, autonomous, and is therefore the absolute master over his house. The guest who comes from the outside and seeks entry to or asylum in the master's house will never be equal to the host. The host could never be obligated to the guest. As a consequence of such sovereignty, the guest would have no rights in the host's home. He or she would not be a guest, but a slave. But such accommodation would not be hospitable;

it would not be ethical. *On the other hand*, if the guest allows the host entry to his own house, the host will not have been the host; he will have been the guest. If the host becomes the host through the grace of the guest, then the host is not sovereign over either himself or his house. He is, rather, the hostage.[18]

The *as if* must be accounted for not because it is a ruse, a fiction, not because, *in fact*, the host *is* the host and the guest *is* the guest, but because were either what they *are*, they would *not* be that. To be called *hôte* or *huésped* is, after all, to be called *hôte* or *huésped*. Perhaps no one knew this better than Borges. At stake is the logic of homonymy. When Derrida explains that it is "*as if* the master, *qua master*, were the hostage" (123) and *as if* the guest were the host, the *as if* indicates the inscription of irreducible metaphoricity, infinite and unmasterable analogization, essential homonymy. One can be the host only *as if* one were the host, for *to be* the host—in the metaphysical sense of being *qua* presence—would mean to be the host through and through, absolutely, indivisibly. But to be the host unconditionally is to be the hostage.

At stake is the impossible condition of unconditionality. In order to *be* the host, in order to invite or to welcome the guest, one must *be* sovereign, absolutely sovereign, without conditions. But to be without conditions also means to be without defense, without any limits whatsoever and this means the absolute sovereign is absolutely vulnerable to the other. The host, therefore, must protect herself. She must act *as if* she were sovereign over her home by imposing limits, conditions, on the other, on the guest. This *as if* not only limits the other, however. It also conditions or limits the sovereign, the host. The sovereign, *in order to be sovereign*, limits herself, recognizing that the limits (and therefore the possibility) of sovereignty come from the other. It is only because my house is open to the other—and that I am, as a consequence, ineluctably conditioned by the other—that I *can* act and that I act. In other words, there can be no unconditional action, no autonomous or free action. There can be no unconditional action because the unconditional, the absolute sovereign, the *ipse* or the master of the house, is by definition *in itself*. Were there an absolute master of the house, such a master—ensconced in the house, doors and windows barred against intrusion, against unwanted visitors and visitations, invulnerable to the other—would have no need to act, to issue laws or edicts, to sign his name. But nor *could* such a sovereign act. Such a sovereign would have no motive, no reason, to act: nothing would come to precipitate movement, there would be no crisis of decision. But if the absolute or unconditional sovereign—and any host worthy of the name is sovereign—cannot act, then such a host is not only not sovereign, she is not a host: she is a hostage to whomever or whatever appears at the door. She is a prisoner, a hostage. Therefore, no sovereign ever *is* sovereign. Rather the sovereign acts *as if* he or she were sovereign, *as if* he or she were the master (or mistress) of the house. Such mastery is necessarily conditioned by the arrival of the other against whom or which the host acts, whether by inviting, welcoming, or sheltering the other; or by barring the door. This is the sovereign decision. It always comes from the other. The host asks the other's name, demands to see his or her or its documents, passport, signature. The sovereign draws a line, which has already been crossed and crossed out. There is always already translation and transgression and, as Derrida notes, "the resistance to translation *is* translation itself" (1995, 121; qtd in Naas 224). *Huésped* (*hôte*), which Borges knew meant both guest and host, incessantly resists translation and demands incessant translation. *Huésped* names the homonym of the political. Every decision of the political turns on the homonym *huésped/huésped*, the *hôte/hôte*, the host/guest, the citizen/foreigner, friend/enemy. Every decision *marks* and marks *out* the line, the inscription, the *graphe*, between them that institutes them.

Every action decides. Every action draws a line within which the action will have been circumscribed. No action without the *graphe xenius*. And there is no *graphe xenius* that is not already a decision. Asking for the name and thus conditioning or limiting one's hospitality to the other does not, however, violate the conditions of hospitality. On the contrary, there is no hospitality without such conditions, for were one to welcome whomever or whatever arrived at the door to one's house, one would be neither free nor responsible. There is, therefore, no sovereignty without the capacity, the power, to decide and there is no hospitality without such sovereignty. Yet, there is no sovereignty and no hospitality without the referral to the other, without the openness to the future and to what comes, which openness requires one to decide, to make the law, to sign one's name, to draw the line. As Derrida explains: "no hospitality, in the classic sense, without sovereignty of oneself over one's home, but since there is also no hospitality without finitude, sovereignty can only be exercised by filtering, choosing, and thus by excluding and doing violence" (2000b, 55).[19]

## *The time of decision*

The irreducible tension between the law of unconditional or absolute hospitality, on the one hand, and the laws of conditional hospitality, on the other hand, helps to explain why, for example, God can be neither sovereign nor hospitable. This is the case because God is posited beyond temporalization, beyond finitude. God therefore has no relation to the other. For this reason, Kant argues that God cannot be bound—by either pact or promise—to humans.[20] A covenant with God is untenable because God, according to Kant, has only rights and no obligations, and there can only be a covenant, a pact, a promise, or a prayer, so long as all parties have both rights and obligations. Borges understood this.

Because decisions take time, they *always* come too soon, too late. Were decisions not temporal, not finite, and accordingly not marked by the "to come," however, there would be no possibility of justice. This is especially important to remember when reading a story very much about a kingdom to come, but whose coming, were it to arrive, would end all coming and all distinctions. Borges's "Los teólogos [The Theologians]" concerns two defenders of the faith and refuters of heresies, Aureliano and Juan de Panonia. The question is how to decide between them, for, as Borges writes, "[T]he two men were soldiers in the same army, strove for the same prize, fought against the same Enemy, yet Aurelian wrote not a word that was not aimed, however unconfessably, at besting John [*Militaban los dos en el mismo ejército, anhelaban el mismo galardón, guerreaban contra el mismo Enemigo, pero Aureliano no escribió una palabra que inconfesablemente no propendiera a superar a Juan*]" (1996, 1.552/CF 203). The conflict between them, moreover, was invisible: "not once does the other man's name figure in the many volumes of Aurelian's work collected for posterity in Migne's *Patrology* [*no figura una sola vez el nombre del otro en los muchos volúmenes de Aureliano que atesora la* Patrología *de Migne*]" (1.552/CF 203). They are private—even secret—enemies, fighting on the same side against the same public foe. Everything hinges on the possibility of telling the difference between friend and enemy.[21] Borges frames this distinction as a problem of time.

"The Theologians" opens with the image of the Huns in the monastic library burning palimpsests and codices. The only remainder is the twelfth book of Augustine's *Civitas Dei*, *City of God*, "which says that in Athens Plato once taught that at the end of time all things will return again to where they once were—that he, in Athens, before the same circle of listeners, will one day teach that doctrine once again" (1.550/CF 201). Borges refers to Augustine's consideration—in book twelve, chapter fourteen—of "The cyclical theory of the world's history," which Augustine posits as the "physicists'" attempt to answer the question of God's belated creation of human beings. Because no matter how soon the human creature will have been created, it is always possible to ask why it was created so late: "In fact the first man himself might have asked, on the day after he was made, or even on the very day of his creation, why he had not been made sooner" (2003, 12.13/487). According to Augustine, the physicists "considered that there was only one possible and credible way of solving this difficulty; and that was by the postulate of periodic cycles" (12.14/487). Specifically, "They asserted that by those cycles all things in the universe have been continually renewed and repeated, in the same form, and there will be hereafter an unceasing sequence of ages, passing away and coming again in revolutions" (12.14/487). For Augustine, the difficulty with such periodicity—which has misled some commentators to misunderstand Ecclesiastes 1.9, namely, that there is nothing new under the sun—is its determination that "the same ages and the same temporal events recur in rotation" (12.14/488).

At this point Augustine invokes the image of the eternal return of Plato teaching in the Academy. Immediately following this image, he writes: "Heaven forbid, I repeat, that we should believe this" (12.14/488). The cyclical concept of time is impossible according to Augustine because Christ died for our sins *once and for all.* Citing Psalm 12 from the Latin translation of the Septuagint, Augustine points out that "the ungodly will walk in a circle" (12.14/489). This is not, however, because the lives of evildoers repeat themselves. This would be to misunderstand in the same way as those who expect to find Plato once again in the Academy teaching the same lessons to the same students. Rather, Augustine argues, "the way of their error, the way of false doctrine, goes around in circles"

(12.14/489). The reference to false doctrine suggests that the cyclical theory of time is heretical in that it denies the efficacy of Christ's crucifixion and resurrection, that he will have put an end to death once and for all.

"The Theologians" takes up the heresy of the doctrine of cyclical time, but not before a curious remark that refers back to Augustine's warning against the danger of understanding. Aureliano "knew that in theology there is no novelty without danger; then he reflected that the notion of cyclical time was too strange [*demasiado disímil*], too shocking, for the danger to be very serious. (The heresies we ought to fear are those that can be confused with orthodoxy.)" (Borges 1996, 1.550/CF 201). In principle, the novel, the new, is singular. It surprises because it is unexpected, unanticipated. Such surprise threatens, hence its danger. Aureliano, however, discounts the danger of the new in relation to the more serious threat of those heresies that can be confused with orthodoxy. The danger, therefore, lies not in the singular heresy that takes orthodoxy by surprise, but rather in the heresy that can always be identified *as* orthodoxy. The heresy that orthodoxy cannot see coming, finally, is the homonymic heresy, the heresy that results in an orthodoxy in name only. It is the heresy lodged within orthodoxy itself. In other words, the danger lies in the impossibility of deciding whether orthodoxy is heresy and vice versa. It is a problem of decision, of judgment, and, since the decision of heresy also entails a sentence, it is a problem of justice.

The twelfth book of *City of God* is not entirely consumed by the heterodoxy of the theory of cyclical time. In it Augustine also considers the creation of man, but before he can assess the temporality of creation, a problem that has vexed theology from its inception inasmuch as it requires the negotiation of the impossible determination of mortality out of immortality, he turns to the ontological status of angels, which he will have brought up in book eleven, because, as he reports, "There is no absurdity or incongruity in asserting a fellowship between men and angels" (2003, 12.1/471). On Augustine's account, good and evil angels both proceed from the same nature, that of the good. Evil angels have fallen away from the good. This will be the case as well for men. The nature of angels and of men is to be good; evil is a perversion of nature. Neither angels nor men are evil by nature. Evil results from decision. Augustine writes: "The good may exist on its own, but evil cannot. The natures which have been perverted as a result of the initiative of an evil choice, are evil insofar as they are vitiated, but insofar as they are natures, they are good" (12.3/474). Accordingly, Augustine explains, "no one is punished for faults of nature but for faults of will; and even the wickedness which has become habitual . . . had its origin in an act of choice" (12.3/474). Such a choice is understood as a "turning away from him who supremely is" and a "turning toward themselves, who do not exist in that supreme degree" (12.6/477). God is good; God is one. He is absolute, supreme being. Augustine explains that the new Latin word *essentia*, from the verb *esse*, literally translates the Greek *ousia* (12.2/473). Insofar as God is the highest being, no being or existence can be contrary to God. Only nonbeing or nothing is contrary to God. It is out of nothing that God creates angels and man. The perversion of nature—which is an effect of will and, thus, an *act* of choice—tends toward diminution and destruction. Such destruction, however, does not affect God, who "is utterly incapable of any change or injury" (12.3/474). The fellowship of angels and men, which is the fellowship or bond—the stricture—of time, cannot be shared with God, for God is invulnerable to any other. God is without affection.

*City of God* XII begins with angels and the possibility of good and evil. The possibility of falling away from God's goodness opens onto the problem of time. Chapter sixteen, "Does God's eternal sovereignty imply an eternal creation for its exercise?" (12.16/490), takes up God's relation to mortals; it thus concerns the possibility of deriving mortality from immortality. In order to address the problem of God's sovereignty, Augustine returns to the concept of temporality he outlined in book eleven, chapter six: "Thus there can be no doubt that the world was not created *in* time but *with* time. An event in time happens after one time and before another, after the past and before the future. But at the time of creation there could have been no past, because there was nothing created to provide the change and movement which is the condition of time" (11.6/436). The dilemma of book twelve can be stated in the following way. On the one hand, insofar as God creates (whether man, angels, or the world) that which is created must have a determinate beginning. But if God is eternally sovereign, prior to creation over whom or what did he exercise this sovereignty, for sovereignty is nothing if there is no one or nothing subject to it? Indeed, the modifier "prior" is already problematic in that eternity sustains no such division between before and after. On the other hand, if God's sovereignty is coeval with the creatures God creates, then these creatures are necessarily co-eternal, but this would establish them as equal to God; for if these creatures are co-eternal with God, they are necessarily no less immune to change and no less invulnerable to the other than is God. Under such circumstances it should be obvious that God would no longer be sovereign in any simple way.

Augustine's solution to the aporia is initially outlined in book eleven, chapter six: "If we are right in finding the distinction between eternity and time in the fact that without action and change there is no time, while in eternity there is no change, who can fail to see that there would have been no time, if there had been no creation to bring movement and change, and time depends on this motion and change, and is measured by the longer and shorter intervals by which things that cannot happen simultaneously succeed one another? Since God, in whose eternity there is no change at all, is the creator and director of time, I cannot see how it can be said that he created the world after a lapse of ages, unless it is asserted that there was some creation before the world existed, whose movements would make possible the course of time" (11.6/435). Augustine's point is that there is no *prior* to creation, because this would require a *time before time.* Creation does not happen *in* time. Therefore it must happen *with* time. Or, as Augustine puts it in book twelve, chapter sixteen: "if time has not existed for all time, it would follow that there was a time when there was no time. And the most complete fool would not say that!" (12.16/491). This argument necessarily posits an absolute rupture between eternity and temporality, between absolute rest and motion or change, between immortality and mortality, between creator and created. God will have existed *eternally*, whereas whatever has been created—the world, angels, humans—will have existed only *for all time*, which is not for eternity. The meaning of *always* changes when predicated of God and of mortal beings: in the one case it means for eternity; in the other, it means for all time. God "has always existed in changeless eternity; whereas they [angels, human beings, the world] were created. But they are said to have existed always because they have existed for all time, and without them no time could exist" (12.16/492).

Insofar as Augustine's solution to the aporia of eternity and time frets the problem of the before and after of God's creation and his sovereignty over that creation, his solution begs the question of the *possibility* of God's creation. If God is changeless, immutable, how does God *decide* to create? How does God *do* anything at all? Indeed, in order for God to *act*, he will have to *decide* to act, he will have to exercise his will. Such a decision goes against God's nature, however, in that in Augustine's account the good is nature and the possibility of acting depends on a turn away from nature, from what is natural, hence it requires a turn away from the good. There is no decision that does not turn away from the good, turn away from nature, and therefore that does not turn away from God. Perversion is not the doing of evil; it is rather the possibility of acting, of deciding. For God to act, God will necessarily have to turn away from Himself, abandon Himself. The perversion of an acting and therefore sovereign God is that such a God is mortal, corrupt, evil.

Augustine's response to the question of how God's sovereignty could be eternal if "created beings did not always exist to serve him?" (12.16/493) recurs to a problematic conception of the possibility of God's decision and determination. Augustine understands that in order for God to decide, there must be movement, but he writes, "in the movement of the Creator there is no question of a past which no longer exists or a future which is yet to be" (12.16/492). It should be evident, however, that there is no decision without movement and there is no movement without a past that is no longer and a future that is not yet. The impossible thought of a movement without movement or of a movement without time, exposes Augustine to "the criticism that this [his response to the problem of the temporality of creation and God's eternal sovereignty] is an affirmation of ignorance, not the communication of knowledge" (12.16/493). Nevertheless, he considered it necessary to take up the question—"without reaching any positive conclusion" (12.16/493)—in order to demonstrate to his readers "what questions they should refrain from tackling, as dangerous, and to discourage them from thinking themselves capable of understanding everything" (12.16/493). It is important to learn this, because the thought that man can understand everything, including God's *motives*, is itself heretical. Thus, any attempt to explain the relation of mortals to the immortal must necessarily come up against this untrespassable limit.

"The Theologians" transgresses this border. It does so, moreover, in terms of the limits of temporality. Within the created world—a temporal world, a world of before and after, of succession—there can be no repetition of the same. "The Theologians" turns on the temporality of repetition, for in his treatise refuting the heresy of the *Histrioni*, Aureliano repeats the same twenty words that Juan de Panonia had employed years earlier to refute the heresy of cyclical time espoused by the *Annulari*, who were also known as the *Monotoni* and who argued "that history is a circle, and that all things that exist have existed before and will exist again" (1996, 1.550/CF 201). Like Juan de Panonia, Aureliano also attempted to refute the *Annulari*, but his argument was passed over in favor of Juan's, whose treatise "was limpid, universal; it seemed written not by a particular person, but by any man—or perhaps all men" (1.551–552/CF 203). As a result, Juan de Panonia was "entrusted with refuting the errors of the Monotoni" and it was his "argument that condemned the heresiarch Euphorbus to the stake" (1.552/CF 203). From this point forward Aureliano and Juan de Panonia engage in their invisible enmity. Everything would change with the rise and spread of the *Histrioni*—also known as the *Speculari*, *Abysmali*, the *Simulacra*, and, by John of Damascus, as the "*Forms*"—, whose emblems were the mirror and the obolus.

The *Histrioni* effectively pervert the Augustinian doctrine of the two cities in that they contend that "the earth influences heaven" (1.553/CF 204), which means the temporal world influences the eternal kingdom, mortality contaminates immortality. In Heideggerian terms, the ontic corrupts the ontological, beings ruin Being. This perversion is legible, for instance, in a belief that indicates the possible influence of the earlier *Monotoni* (*Annulari*) on the *Histrioni*; namely, that "They imagined that every man is two men, and that the real one is the *other* one, the one in heaven. They also imagined that our acts cast an inverted reflection, so that if we are awake, the other man is asleep; if we fornicate, the other man is chaste; if we steal, the other man is generous. When we die, they believed, we shall join him and *be* him" (1.553/CF 205). This is the logic of homonymy. Heaven *is* hell. The histrionic heretics were not, however, of only one mind: "The heretics of Aureliano's diocese were not those who claimed that every act is reflected in heaven but rather those who claimed that time does not tolerate repetitions" (1.554/CF 205). This is one of Borges's preferred leitmotifs, one that he repeats. In "A New Refutation of Time," for instance, he asks, "Is not one single repeated terminal point enough to disrupt and confound the series in time?" (2.141/SNF 323). The *Histrioni* are the opposite of the *Monotoni* or *Annulari*, who argued that history—that every event, whatever is or happens—repeats itself, will always already have repeated itself and will repeat itself again. This opposition is belied, however, by the suggestion that the *Annulari* influenced the *Histrioni*.

The *Annulari* argue that there is never a first time. The *Histrioni* argue that there is only ever the first time since time itself cannot support repetition. Aureliano reports this aspect of the sect of *Histrioni* heretics in his diocese to the authorities in Rome: "He wrote a few paragraphs; when he tried to write the horrible thesis that no two moments are the same, his pen halted. He could not find the necessary words; the admonitions of the new doctrine were too affected and metaphorical to be transcribed. . . . Then suddenly a sentence of twenty words came to his spirit. With joy he wrote it on the page; immediately afterward, he was disturbed by the sense that it was someone else's" (1.554/CF 206). The next day Aureliano discovers the origin of the sentence: "he had read it many years ago in the *Adversus Annulares*, composed by John of Pannonia" (1.554/CF 206). This scene recalls "Pierre Menard, Author of the *Quijote*" in that Aureliano neither copies nor cites the text of Juan de Panonia. He writes the twenty words as if for the first time. It is only *after* writing them that he senses and then discovers they have another origin, another history. Upon discovering that the twenty words formed part of Juan de Panonia's treatise, Aureliano "was torn by uncertainty. To alter or omit the words was to weaken the force of the statement; to let them stand was to plagiarize a man he detested; to indicate the source was to denounce him" (1.554/CF 206). What the twenty words were does not matter. Rather, the fact that they repeat themselves, that they came to Aureliano as if for the first time and thus singularly and yet were repeated, effectively disavows their efficaciousness in answering the heresy of the *Annulari*. Further, that the same twenty words that refute the *Annulari* also characterize the *Histrioni* means that these apparently opposite heretical positions are not simply opposed. On the contrary, *both* positions are impossible. The *exact* repetition of events is as impossible as the absolute singularity of every—or any—*historical* event. Time must tolerate repetition, but repetition, because it is repeatable, hence temporal, is never absolute. The twenty words Aureliano repeats from Juan de Panonia's treatise are identical, for sure, but they are not simply or unequivocally the same. In one instance these words refute the theory of cyclical time and thus refute the notion of repetition. In the other instance, these same words refute the theory that time cannot sustain repetition.

Contrary to the narrator's argument, it is not simply a question of the different contexts in which the twenty words are repeated, as if contexts were discrete, as if the one did not influence the other: "The accused [Juan de Panonia] would not retract; time and again he repeated that to deny his proposition was to fall into the pestilential heresy of the Monotoni. He did not realize . . . that to speak of the Monotoni was to speak of a thing now forgotten" (1.554/CF 206). In short, what concerns the church at this particular moment, *now*, is the heresy of the *Histrioni*. The fact that the espousal of the uniqueness or singularity of God's redemption, the impossibility of repetition, refuted the *Annulari* (the *Monotoni*) no longer matters, for such a refutation in this context, supports the present heresy.

Aureliano "was torn by uncertainty" once he realized that Juan de Panonia's refutation of the *Annulari* effectively committed him to the heresy of the *Histrioni*. Not knowing whether to excise the sentence or to denounce Juan for his retroactive heresy, "He pleaded for divine aid" (1.554/CF 206). God's messenger, an angel, comes to him: "Toward the coming of the second twilight, his guardian angel suggested a middle way [*le dictó una solución intermedia*]" (1.554/CF 206). This angelic suggestion is not exactly divine intervention. In Augustine, angels are also created, they are temporal entities, which means they are mortal *even if they never die*. Angels can always *turn away* from God. Indeed, in order to decide—and angels must decide—they must always already have turned away from nature; they cannot *not* pervert themselves by *turning toward* themselves. The condition of possibility of decision is the perversion of temporality.

Aureliano follows this angelic advice: he "kept the words, but set this disclaimer before it: *That which the Heresiarchs howl today, to the confusion of the faith, was said during this century, with more levity than blameworthiness, by a most learned doctor of the church*" (1.554/CF 206).

Juan de Panonia is burned at the stake "under the midday sun" (1.555/CF 207). Noon marks and marks out the site of the sun's return or turning to itself. Noon indicates the closing of the ring at the site of the ring's opening, its impossible absolution or annulment. What goes around comes around, but the circle, the turn or tour, can never be closed on itself. Repetition is a necessary possibility and, at the same time, which is never the same time, such circularity depends on a singularity that cannot be calculated in itself or as such. Noon is only ever speculative, specular, simulacral, the reflection of a reflection, always only a shadow in anticipation of itself, *as if* it ever arrived, *as if* it already arrived. It is always before noon, after noon.[22] Upon Juan de Panonia's immolation, Aureliano felt "what a man cured of an incurable disease that had become a part of his life might feel" (1.555/CF 207). From here to his end, his life comes to him as the repetition of a life already lived. Finally, "at high noon, a lightening bolt set the trees afire, and Aureliano died as John had" (1.555/CF 207).

This is not the end of the story, however. According to the narrator, the end of the story "can only be told in metaphors, since it takes place in the kingdom of heaven, where time does not exist" (1.555/CF 207). We are doubly removed from eternity. Borges never retreats from his insistence on the successivity of language. But if language is constitutively successive, then it is marked by an essential divisibility or displacement. Language is referral and therefore the deferral of meaning. Consequently, if it is meaningful or communicative, it is so via analogization or metaphorization. Nothing happens or passes that is not marked or remarked *as* something. The *as* is essential to appearing and to existence. It is essential to Being as the condition of possibility of meaning. This is the case for whatever happens (*pasa*, *sucede*) whenever and wherever it happens, if it ever does. And, according to Borges, nothing happens—*nada pasa*—in the "kingdom of heaven," because there is no time. "One might say that Aureliano spoke with God and found that God takes so little interest in religious differences that he took him for John of Pannonia. That, however, would be to impute confusion to the divine intelligence. It is more correct to say that in Paradise, Aurelian discovered that in the eyes of the unfathomable deity, he and John of Pannonia (the orthodox and the heretic, the abominator and the abominated, the accuser and the victim) were a single person" (1.555–556/CF 207). God cannot tell the difference between them. He cannot decide. He has no time for such distinctions.

Nevertheless it would be a mistake to think that "The Theologians" advocates such indistinction, as if Aureliano and Juan de Panonia were the same. The point is that justice, responsibility, decision are *mortal* concerns. They are possible only insofar as we are finite beings. There is no final justice, no last day of judgment; there is no possibility of God's determination of the saved and the damned. This does not mean that there is no difference between accuser and accused, between victimizer and victim. According to the logic of homonymy, it means there is no *essential* difference between them and this means the responsibility for making the decision belongs to mortals. It is a mortal decision. It falls to us, *here and now*, to decide. Yet, because there is no *telos*, no moment of absolute calculation, because the "here and now" must be different from itself, no judgment, no decision, is ever final. This is necessarily the case because without temporalization, which means without the opening to whatever or whoever comes, there is neither the need for nor the possibility of decision. Because nothing affects God, God cannot decide. He has no need to decide, but nor could He decide were He to need to do so. God's absolute and eternal sovereignty is also, therefore, absolute and eternal condemnation: God is effectively damned, condemned to the kingdom, which is also the prison, in the sky. Absolutely sovereign, He is also absolutely irrelevant. Perhaps this explains why an angel—a necessarily fallen angel—gives Aureliano advice: God has nothing to say. He can never help anyone decide.

Because God has nothing to say to us, because He cannot ever be obliged to us, we cannot want to be friends with God. Because God cannot be affected, He can have no relation to us. He will never do anything for us. As "The Theologians" makes clear, God cannot tell His friends from His enemies. It makes no difference to Him. They are all one. No doubt this is why Derrida asserts, "*One cannot, therefore, want God for a friend*" (1997, 223). This is so because God is too distant from us, cutoff: "No friendship with God is possible because this absence and this separation also signify the absence of common measure for a proportional equality between God and me" (223). The lack of a common measure between God and mortals means God is infinitely removed from mortal beings and from friendship. As Derrida remarks, God has no need for a friend in that He only thinks about Himself, which means, finally, God "could not care less about friendship because [He] could not care less about the other" (223). Analyzing precisely these passages of Derrida, Hägglund concludes, "A perfect friendship would destroy the possibility of friendship, since there can be no friendship without mortality" (112).[23]

The only possibility of friendship, then, is between mortals. Friendship is mortal, which means that we can only be friends in a world of affection, in a world in which others affect us, in which we are vulnerable to others. Such affection is necessarily temporal and, as such, it is necessarily exposed to an uncertain future. The implications of this uncertainty are severe, for the lack of any security means all decisions are provisional. Augustine recognized this in *City of God*: "no one can love a human friend with loyalty, if he knows that in the future he will be his enemy" (12.21/499). This is the aporia of friendship. Friendship thus requires that we decide, *here and now*, who is and who is not a friend. But because friendship is mortal and thus exposed to an uncertain future, *here and now*, no one—no subject—will ever be able to decide, *once and for all*, on the friend. The possibility of friendship depends therefore on the impossibility of deciding.

### *On the impossibility of the present*

There is perhaps no more suggestive attempt to think through the implications of the impossibility of decision than Borges's "El jardín de senderos que se bifurcan [The Garden of Forking Paths]." Set during World War I, a Western conflict, the protagonists of "The Garden of Forking Paths" come from the West's margins. Yu Tsun, Chinese, formerly a professor of English in Tsingtao, is now a spy for a Germany he despises, driven to prove himself against his German superior's low estimation of his race: "I did not do it for Germany. What do I care for a barbaric country that has obligated me to the abjection of being a spy. . . . No, I did it because I felt that the Leader had little regard for the people of my race" (1996, 1.473/CF 120–121). His pursuer, Richard Madden, Irish (thus an English colonial subject) and accused of treason, works to protect England from enemies of the state. There is, then, opposition *within* and *between* the West, the ends of either "side" carried out and attained by each side's other, by each side's enemy. At the same time, the relation of the Occident to its general other, the Orient, is exposed in the play between sinologist Stephen Albert and Yu Tsun: the English friend of the East—a sinophile—killed by an anglophile from the East. The question of the difference between friend and enemy, victim and victimizer, is suspended over the entire narrative.

In "The Garden of Forking Paths" Borges poses a rather simple problem: how to tell a secret in public?[24] How can one man (Yu Tsun) shout over the din of war such that he is heard by his own private antagonist (his German supervisor) but not be overheard by the public enemy (England)? How to keep a secret while telling it? The realization that a gunshot can be heard at a great distance leads him to the home of the sinologist Stephen Albert. "The Garden of Forking Paths" turns on the relation between Yu Tsun and Stephen Albert, on the decision—*here and now*—of hospitality, of amity and enmity, of knowing who the other *is*. It is Albert who solves the puzzle of Yu Tsun's notorious ancestor, Ts'ui Pên, who retired from an illustrious life in order to dedicate thirteen years to what had been understood as two separate projects: an infinite labyrinth and a novel. Upon his death the labyrinth was never found and the novel was deemed incomprehensible. Albert recognizes that the novel is the labyrinth and that the key to the riddle of its incomprehensibility is time: "In all fictions, each time a man meets diverse alternatives, he chooses one and eliminates the others; in the work of the virtually impossible-to-disentangle Ts'ui Pên, the character chooses—simultaneously—all of them. *He creates*, thereby, several futures, several times, which themselves proliferate and fork" (1.477/CF 125). Every decision, *here and now*, does not limit or exclude possible futures; on the contrary, every decision results in every possible effect, every possible future, but always in the present. What appears to be at stake is the infinite divisibility of time, which effectively multiplies infinitely the present. The present divides in itself, ruining every decision in advance. In "La Lotería en Babilonia [The Lottery in Babylon]," Borges aptly characterizes the consequences of the infinite divisibility of time and, therefore, of the present as "incalculable" (1.458/CF 103). The present names the plurality of unpredictable singular presents.

In "The Garden of Forking Paths," all possible consequences of the present decision play themselves out *in the present*. It is this plurality of presents that Yu Tsun experiences: "From that moment, I felt all about me and within my obscure body an invisible, intangible pullulation—not that of the divergent, parallel, and finally coalescing armies, but an agitation more inaccessible, more inward than that, yet one those armies somehow prefigured" (1.478/CF 126). The narrator feels the plurality of presents taking place *simultaneously*, each time at this time, *here and now*. According to Yu Tsun, the *here and now*, the present, is the time in which whatever happens takes place: "Then I reflected that all things happen to oneself, and happen precisely, precisely now. Centuries and centuries, yet events occur only in the present; innumerable men in the air, on the land and sea, yet everything that truly happens, happens to me" (1.472/CF 120).

In "La escritura del dios [The Writing of the God]," Borges makes a very different assertion. Explaining that he can only see "At the shadowless hour [midday]" when a small door is opened above the prisoners, the narrator (Tzinacán himself) notes the rest of his time is spent in darkness and *memory*: "Driven by the inevitability of doing *something*, of somehow filling time, I tried, in my darkness, to remember everything I knew" (1.596/CF 250). There are two things to remark in this passage. First, to do something, to act, is *inevitable*. We cannot not do something. Second, for something to *happen in the present*, which is to say, to act in the present, which is the only time to act, there must be memory. Acting in the present is remembering. The present—the time in which Tzinacán can see, the time, then, of sense perception—is shadowless. There is no trace of time *in the present*. The present leaves no trace because the present is not. Time *passes* and only because it passes does something—anything—*happen*. The happening or passing of the event—of whatever or whoever happens—can only ever be remembered. In other words, whatever happens is only ever *as if* it were *present*. The infinite divisibility of the present in "The Garden of Forking Paths" has the effect of ruining the present as the "in itself" or the "as such" of time, as the *now* in which everything happens to me. Nothing happens *now*. The present, the *here and now*, is not. Insofar as it incalculably divides, the exposure or openness to the other is irreducible. In Borges's terms, the coming of the other *here and now* is *implacable*: "Madden was implacable. Better said, he was obliged to be implacable"; "It seemed incredible to me that this day, without premonitions or symbols, would be the day of my implacable death" (1.472/CF 119). The implacable cannot be mitigated or put off; it cannot be deferred. Rather, the implacable puts off the here and now, the present. What is implacable is not what *is*, but what *comes*. The implacable names deferral.

The simultaneity—the "at the same time"—of these presents within a present that cannot be unified *as such* ex-poses the present. The other selves that haunt Yu Tsun in the present include his "own" self in its *coming to* itself, in its ex-position, its constitutive being-outside-itself: "I felt again that pullulation I have mentioned. I sensed that the dew-drenched garden that surrounded the house was saturated, infinitely, with invisible persons. Those persons were Albert and myself—secret, busily at work, multiform—in other dimensions of time" (1.479/CF 127). In every case, in every present, it becomes a question of hospitality. One will have to decide how to respond to the other: "That fabric of times that approach one another, fork, are snipped off, or are simply unknown for centuries, contains *all* possibilities. In most of those times, we do not exist; in some, you exist but I do not; in others, I do and you do not; in others still, we both do. In this one, which the favouring hand of chance has dealt me, you have come to my home; in another, when you come through my garden you find me dead; in another, I say these same words, but I am an error, a ghost" (1.479/CF 127). As is so often the case in Borges, it comes down to the relation between necessity and chance, between the ineluctable necessity of every circumstance and condition dictated by the totality of all possible presents, on the one hand; and, on the other hand, the chance of their singular coming together *here and now*.

It is important to understand the conception of time articulated in "The Garden of Forking Paths." At the moment of decision, if *all* possible futures play themselves out, *here and now*, then all *possible* futures are in fact necessary. One implication of this is that the future, because it is present, is no longer undetermined or incalculable. Since all possible futures present themselves, the future is absolutely calculable, which would suggest that chance plays no part. Yu Tsun's arrival at Stephen Albert's door is simply one of the calculable number of possibilities, all present, consequent upon a certain decision. This explains why the children Yu Tsun encounters on the way to Stephen Albert's house know where he is going; this is why Stephen Albert expects Yu Tsun without having invited him.

The concept of time outlined in "The Garden of Forking Paths" in fact abolishes time, and with it, all responsibility and the possibility of justice. A person makes a decision. In most narratives, the decision—which is only possible and necessary because what comes is unknowable and incalculable—excludes or forecloses all outcomes but one. "The Garden of Forking Paths," however, admits *every possible* outcome: "In all fictions, each time a man meets diverse alternatives, he chooses one and eliminates the others; in the work of the virtually impossible-to-disentangle Ts'ui Pên, the character chooses—simultaneously—all of them. He creates, thereby, 'several futures,' several *times*, which themselves proliferate and fork" (1.477/CF 125). Yu Tsun arrives at Stephen Albert's door. This arrival opens onto every *possible* determination, including the most and the least hospitable. Stephen Albert himself may not be home; Stephen Albert may not recognize or admit Yu Tsun; he may be his enemy; and so on. The only criterion for this plurality of presents is their possibility. Whatever is possible happens, according to the logic of Ts'ui Pên's infinite labyrinth, *here and now*. This means that the possible is an effect or determination of the present. And this means there is no future in Ts'ui Pên's novel. The labyrinth is the absolute present. It is the Aleph.

The figure of a temporality conceived as simultaneity would be, as the narrator of "The Garden of Forking Paths" calls Ts'ui Pên's novel, "an irresolute [*indeciso*] heap" (1.476/CF 124). Why an indecisive or undecided heap? Because if time were simply or absolutely simultaneous, there would be neither past nor future: everything would *be* at once, but nothing could ever *happen* (*suceder*, *pasar*, *arriver*). This includes the "decision" invoked in Ts'ui Pên's labyrinthine novel. A decision is only a decision if it *decides*, if it makes a difference. But a decision such as the one described in "The Garden of Forking Paths," because it opens onto *every* possibility, decides nothing and is therefore not a decision. Everything is possible insofar as everything *is*, but nothing happens. In the strict sense, there is no decision without the temporal difference that necessarily excludes possibilities, that inscribes irreducible difference between past and future, between the *no longer* and the *not yet*. The decision, then, is what happens. But, again, nothing could ever happen in the absolute present of the labyrinth described in "The Garden of Forking Paths." Consequently, in "The Garden of Forking Paths" everything is possible *except the decision*. The decision is impossible.

Having heard Stephen Albert's litany of the possible futures of their encounter, Yu Tsun suggests one constant: "In all . . . I am grateful for and venerate, your re-creation of the garden of Ts'ui Pên" (1.479/CF 127). But Stephen Albert knows otherwise: "Not in all. . . . Time forks, perpetually, into countless futures. In one of them, I am your enemy"

(1.479/CF 127). At this moment Yu Tsun feels for the second time the preponderance of persons around him. He responds, "The future already exists . . . but I am your friend" (1.479/CF 127). In "The Garden of Forking Paths" the future always already exists. It is the present; it is what is possible. When Stephen Albert turns away, Yu Tsun shoots him in the back.

Between friends, there is the murder that proves one's fidelity to the enemy. Yu Tsun communicates the name of the city to be bombed in the name of the friend. "The Garden of Forking Paths" articulates the play of friendship and enmity, the alliances and antagonisms that cannot, finally, be deciphered or detained. Friendships between enemies (the colonized, dispossessed Irish allied with the colonizer; the devalued Chinese working for the Germans, who, in 1941, the year the story was first published, will have allied themselves with Japan, China's invader and oppressor); enmity between friends (the lover of Chinese, the decipherer of *The Garden of Forking Paths*, killed by his friend, the anglophile Chinese ancestor of Ts'ui Pên). How to tell friends from enemies, friendship from enmity? What is the difference between them? Or is it not the case that at the very heart of friendship lies enmity, in the heart of the friend beats the heart of the enemy?

## *The friend and enemy I am to myself*

There is no evidence that Borges read Carl Schmitt, for whom the friend/enemy distinction was the essence of the political. It is nonetheless obvious that in the early 1940s the friend/enemy distinction preoccupied Borges and did so in the precise terms in which Schmitt formulated the problem: "[T]he political does not reside in the battle itself . . . but in . . . being able to distinguish correctly the real friend and the real enemy" (37). Borges's overdetermination of the complex national and ethnic identities and allegiances of Yu Tsun and Richard Madden worries the distinction between friend and enemy and signals what Schmitt also stresses: the decision of the friend and the enemy is always contingent, never once and for all. Borges further complicates the problem of the decision in "Tema del traidor y del héroe [Theme of the Traitor and the Hero]" and "El milagro secreto [The Secret Miracle]," both published in *Ficciones* (1944), in which he pressures the epistemological and ontological certainty of the difference between friends and enemies. In "Theme of the Traitor and the Hero," just as in "The Garden of Forking Paths," he thematizes Ireland's oppressed condition: "The action takes place in an oppressed yet stubborn country. . . . Let's say . . . Ireland; let's say 1824" (1996, 1.496/CF 143). Despite locating the story's action in the early nineteenth century, Borges foregrounds the narrator's historical moment in the first paragraph: 3 January 1944, the height of World War II, some six months prior to the Allied invasion. All of Europe is in some respect occupied. "The Secret Miracle," however, is set on the eve of World War II, 14 March 1939. Its protagonist is a Jewish author living in Prague, Jaromir Hladík, who is captured by the Nazis and condemned to die on 29 March at 9:00 a.m. One of Hladík's works is an unfinished play, *Los enemigos*. The epigraph to "The Secret Milagro" is taken from the Koran. It tells the story of how God makes someone die for one hundred years and when God then revives this man and asks him how long he had been dead, he responds: "a day or part of a day" (1.508/CF 157; Koran 2.269). This is the story Borges tells in "The Secret Miracle": the night before he is to be executed, Hladík asks God for a reprieve of one year in order to finish his incomplete play. God grants him this wish; he finishes *Los enemigos*; he is executed on 29 March at 9:02 a.m. *Los enemigos*, moreover, has a temporal structure not unlike that of Ts'ui Pên's *Garden of Forking Paths*, but in this case, as in "The Theologians," the relations are between "secret enemies."

"Theme of the Traitor and the Hero" is no less temporally labyrinthine except that its labyrinth is "a secret form of time" (1.497/CF 144) and is constituted through various repetitions that are constitutive of the possibility of history. Here, repetition instances the invention of history in and as literature: "He is saved from those circular labyrinths by a curious discovery, a discovery which, however, will plunge him deep into other, yet more tangled and heterogeneous mazes: it seems that certain words spoken by a beggar who spoke with Fergus Kilpatrick on the day of his death had been prefigured by Shakespeare, in *Macbeth*. That history might have copied history is sufficiently astonishing; that history should copy *literature* is inconceivable" (1.497/CF 144). On the one hand, "Theme" concerns the representation of history, specifically, that history is always already inscribed within the structure of iterability or of citationality. It is possible that literature is the name par excellence for this differantial and aporetic structure of citation. On the other hand, "Theme of the Traitor and the Hero" also troubles the sovereign political decision—the decision of the friend and the enemy—by reinscribing it as a hetero-auto-nomous decision. The decision of oneself, of one's identity and property, is always already jeopardized, ruined. The sovereign decision of oneself always passes through the other; it always passes through a necessary undecidability.

The story's narrator, Ryan, is the great-grandson of its protagonist, Fergus Kilpatrick, who was both a heroic conspirator against the oppressive English and, at the same time, a traitor to the Irish cause. As the "secret and glorious captain of conspirators" (1.496/CF 143), Kilpatrick assigned his oldest friend, James Alexander Nolan, the task of discovering the traitor. Borges writes: "Nolan carried out his mission. He announced to the gathered comrades that the traitor was Kilpatrick himself. He proved the truth of his accusation beyond the shadow of a doubt, and the men at the council that night condemned their leader to death. The leader signed his own death sentence, but he pleaded that his punishment not harm the cause" (1.497–8/CF 145). At one and the same time, Kilpatrick is an Irish hero and a loyal British subject and thus a traitor to the cause of Irish home rule. He is simultaneously friend and enemy. He is a homonym.

The difficulty that "Theme of the Traitor and the Hero" makes palpable is, precisely, how to decide on which side to locate Fergus Kilpatrick, and no less so, how does Fergus Kilpatrick decide who or what he is, where to locate himself, given that what he is called upon to decide is undecidable. This decision is impossible not because one does not desire to decide, not because one is passive or reticent, but because the decision is never simply one's own, which means the decision is never *simple*.[25] The decision comes from the other, from the future. Without this exposure to the future, there would be neither the need nor the chance for a decision. Indeed, because every decision must be calculated with the future, and the future, *qua* monstrous, cannot be determined, the decision necessarily calculates with the incalculable.[26] It is precisely the impossibility of deciding—despite the necessity to decide and to take responsibility for decisions that are never *simply* one's own—that leads Derrida, following Kierkegaard, to write that "The instant of decision is a madness" (2002a, 255).

The burden of any reading of "Theme of the Traitor and the Hero," "The Secret Miracle," and "The Garden of Forking Paths," therefore, is not to arrive at a moment of absolute undecidability, as if Borges hoped to realize a permanent stasis or incapacity to act as a politics. On the contrary, if one thing is certain about these texts it is not only that decisions are made, but that they *must* be made, that they are necessary. It is impossible not to decide. Yu Tsun murders Stephen Albert; Hladík is executed at 9:02 a.m.; Nolan identifies the traitor; Fergus Kilpatrick signs his own death warrant and remains both a hero and a traitor to the cause. The difficulty is to think the finitude that makes it possible—hence, necessary—for one to be both friend and enemy *at the same time*. This is, finally, what is at stake in the notion of the public enemy, *hostis*. For *hostis* means both host and enemy. In order to decide between friends and enemies, one must already have reduced the temporality that inscribes friend *and* enemy *within* the concept of the friend *and* enemy. One must reduce the irreducible play of the homonym. One has to presuppose a position of stability, of security and invulnerability, a position not yet marked by the friend/enemy complex in order to determine *from the start* that there are friends and enemies, and that *hostis* is simply the enemy.[27]

Borges, however, makes no such decision. In *Signs of Borges*, Sylvia Molloy reads "The Garden of Forking Paths" as an allegory of the relation between reading and death. She contends that Borges outlines the limits of any reading grounded in epistemological certitude. She writes: "Stephen Albert is so sure of his successful reading of Ts'ui Pên's labyrinth, in which he knows that Yu Tsun will be his enemy, that he disregards . . . the exact moment and nature of the act of reading: a confrontation, forever in the present, with a mobile text based on other mobile texts, never congealing"; thus, she concludes, "Turning his back on Yu Tsun, [Stephen] Albert reduces his careful deciphering of Ts'ui Pên's labyrinth to one of its many possible situations, which he unwittingly provokes and fixes with his own death" (35). This reading misstates the temporal problem: the confrontation can never happen in the present insofar as the present, if there is one, is a vanishing limit that displaces the possibility of being (in) itself. The mobile text that will not congeal to which Molloy refers is the impossible possibility of the present. It is the cite or site, but never the sight *qua* perception, of the confrontation.

The certainty of the decision that distinguishes friends from enemies is the transcendental illusion of the togetherness of time, the fiction of time's transcendental unity. But according to Borges, the impossible simultaneity of "each time" authorizes readers *neither* to do nothing at all *nor* to do anything at all. On the contrary, in every instant there must be the impossible decision that exposes the present and its totality of possibilities to the future of impossibility. In other words, the singular decision necessarily calculates with the incalculable. As a consequence, although the decision is always made in specific circumstances, in a specific context, because the *here and now* is infinitely divisible, these circumstances are always incalculably open to the other, to the future, to what or whoever comes. Were this not the case, no decision would be necessary—but nor could any decision ever be made, happen. Such exposure *decides* the decision *and* the one who makes it. The sovereign is subject to the decision, to its infinite exposure to the future. There is no decision, no sovereignty, without such exposure; yet, such exposure makes the decision and sovereignty impossible.

In "The Garden of Forking Paths" Borges insists on the decision. Without the decision, there would be nothing but an irresolute heap, *un acervo indeciso*, an undecidable jumble. Nevertheless, within the temporal logic of Ts'ui Pên's novel, *The Garden of Forking Paths*, the decision makes no difference. Death makes no difference: "a hero dies in one chapter and, in the succeeding chapter, he lives." If everything happens in the present, *simultaneously*, then effectively nothing happens, nothing comes and nothing passes, nothing makes any difference. Nothing is lost and nothing is gained. There are no consequences and thus there is no responsibility. There is no justice and, despite the story's insistence on political identification, no politics either, no friends, no enemies. The privilege of the present in which every possibility actualizes itself in spite of the decision that necessarily makes a difference forecloses the possibility of mourning, of loss, of responsibility. This is so because in an absolute present there would be no possibility of either loss or gain and thus no difference between mourning and celebration, no difference between life and death. There would be neither despair nor hope, because there would be no difference between them.[28] But this is not the world Borges proposes.

"The Garden of Forking Paths" concludes with Richard Madden's arrest of Yu Tsun, the report of the success of Yu Tsun's mission, the communication of the proper name "Albert" to his German superiors, and the notice of Yu Tsun's condemnation. His last words, "He does not know (no one can know) my endless contrition, and my weariness [*No sabe (nadie puede saber) mi innumerable contrición y cansancio*]" (1.480/CF 128). The decision to murder Stephen Albert sentences Yu Tsun to infinite contrition, but it does not banish him to the nightmare of Ts'ui Pên's novel, because within the absolute present outlined in Ts'ui Pên's *The Garden of Forking Paths* endless or innumerable contrition would be impossible. Contrition would be only *one* possibility and since *all* possibilities take place in the absolute present, the possible possibilities of contrition cannot be endless or without number. Even were there only one instance in which Yu Tsun did not feel contrite, the possibilities of contrition would necessarily be limited, hence neither endless nor innumerable. And since, according to the logic of simultaneity and absolution described in the novel, in at least one possible present Stephen Albert's murder will not have been actualized, it must also be possible that Yu Tsun will *not* be contrite in every possible present. Innumerable or endless contrition is only possible if the decision to murder Stephen Albert makes a difference. Indeed, to the extent contrition indicates responsibility or an irrevocable sentiment, it is only infinite if it affects every possible present and it can do so only if the decision, *here and now*, makes a difference. And the decision can make a difference only if it is always exposed beyond the horizon of the present. In short, the impossibility of the decision—namely, that a decision cannot be calculated or determined, programmed, in advance, that it must make a difference and therefore necessarily exclude or foreclose possibilities—makes possible and necessary Yu Tsun's infinite contrition. In the present of Ts'ui Pên's *The Garden of Forking Paths*, there is no time for decision, but the decision plays its part nonetheless. In so doing, it shatters the horizon of the present. It inscribes temporal difference as the impossible condition of possibility of simultaneity and the present. The absolute hospitality of the absolute present—a present that welcomes and shelters whatever or whoever *is* simultaneously and without any discrimination—is impossible because it is conditioned, necessarily and irrevocably, by the impossible decision.

The structure of homonymy—the undecidability of essence or *ousia*—ruins in advance any and every decision. All *possible* decisions are *im*possible. Only because Being is essentially equivocal, homonymic, and thus impossible in itself, is it possible but also necessary to decide. This is not what Heidegger calls "the quiet force of the possible," which is always thought on the basis of the present and presence.[29] It is rather what might be called the force of the impossible and the impossibility of force.[30] No force is ever secure in itself, sovereign, such that it can decide while exempting or excepting itself from the force of the decision. This force is nothing. It is the temporalization—or the metaphorization, the irreducible analogization, the infinite homonymy—that destroys every possibility of being. Whatever is, then, is *in name only*. There is only metaphoricity without essence, without ground. The world is *hrönir*, *kenningar*. As in "La busca de Averroës [Averroës' Search]," there is only ever the translation of translation, and thus the impossibility of distinguishing tragedy from comedy, but also friend from enemy, as if either one were ever *present*. As if the language of God were possible.

# 5

# Idiocy, the Name of God

The previous chapters have demonstrated Borges's preoccupation for what he called the contradiction of the time that passes and the identity that endures. The Introduction argued that Borges's principal concern is already legible in Aristotle's understanding of time and identity and that the "contradiction" stems from what Martin Hägglund calls the philosophical problem of the synthesis of succession. In rearticulating the relation of time to identity, it was possible to rethink the relation of the accidental to the necessary, of the singular to the universal, of literature to philosophy. In Chapters 2 and 3 attention to this contradiction made it possible to foment Borgesian "deconstructions" of Humean empiricism and Kantian transcendentalism, that is, on the one hand, to read in Hume the necessarily transcendental moment of "belief," a belief that could never be determined empirically; and, on the other hand, to read in Kant the necessary instance of a monogrammaticality that could never be comprehended or accounted for transcendentally. In both Hume and Kant, the imagination plays the decisive part in that, in its capacity as automatic translating machine, it is, to quote Rodolphe Gasché, "the operator of différance." Chapter 4 pursued the implications of the first three chapters through the problem of metaphor, analogy, and homonymy. The temporal structure of infinite referral and deferral or, more simply, infinite homonymy, led to the conclusion that Being is *in name only* (*homonumus*), hence accidental. This had implications for how to understand Borges's conception of the present and possibility, as well as for his understanding of the structure of decision, which, in Borges, is always ruined by undecidability. This chapter extends the implications of the notion of translation (displacement, metaphoricity or constitutive homonymy, originary technicity) developed throughout the previous chapters to Borges's consideration of the name of God. At stake in the infinite referral and deferral of translation is the impossibility of the name (and) of God. In taking up the necessary temporalization of God's self-nomination—whether in Christianity, Islam, or Judaism—God's idiocy is revealed as the only possible revelation.

## *The spacing of the aleph*

Two moments in "El Aleph" provide the points of departure. The first is Borges's recognition of the impossibility of narrating the Aleph, of describing it, without, at the same time and in the very narrative that describes it, destroying its effect: "I come now to the ineffable center of my tale; it is here that a writer's hopelessness begins. Every language is an alphabet of symbols the employment of which assumes a past shared by its interlocutors. How can one transmit to others the infinite Aleph, which my timorous memory can scarcely contain?" (1996, 1.624/CF 282). Borges suggests that language works as a device for communication only insofar as its conventionality—the implicit agreement of all interlocutors that words mean or refer to the same things, that is, to the same other words—depends on a shared past, on a common inheritance or tradition. Consequently, the language I use cannot be singularly my own. An idiolect, a strictly private language, is impossible. To the extent Borges accepts this premise, he effectively acknowledges that not only Carlos Argentino Daneri's words are insubstantial—"his vapid chatter [*sus palabras insustanciales*]" (1.624/CF 282)—but that all words are, because the dream of a substantial word is the dream of the end of language in that a substantial word would be a word that does not refer, not even to itself. The dream of a substantial word would be the dream of the absolute reduction of the difference between words and things. It would be, in short, the proper name of God; it would be the very name of indifference.[1] The "shared past" to which Borges refers and upon which language depends is not, however, a shared past *experience*, but, rather, it is the shared *a priori* convention of language. There is no community without this convention. This shared convention instances the possibility of language *qua* instrument of communication, but does so at the cost of the articulation of anyone's singular experience. It is precisely the singularity of experience that cannot be said, expressed, and thus communicated, shared. Or rather the conventionality of language means that my own experience is always already referred to another. My experience is always the experience of the other.[2]

The relation to the other is constitutive of life. We need only recall Borges's "Funes the Memorious" to understand the limitations of a life determined as absolute self-presence. Such a life is congested. It is immobile. Indeed, an absolutely full life is cast in bronze, always already entombed, monumental. We should recall that Funes passes his life lying in state, literally on his deathbed. "The Aleph" points in the direction of a necessary forgetting as well: "Does the Aleph exist, within the heart of a stone? Did I see it when I saw all things, and then forget it? Our minds are permeable to forgetfulness; I myself am distorting [*falseando*] and losing, through the tragic erosion of the years, the features of Beatriz" (1.627/CF 286). Here, at the conclusion of the 1943 *Posdata*, Borges laments the loss of the memory of his beloved. Earlier, however, at the conclusion of "The Aleph," he tells a different story: "Out in the street, on the steps of the Constitución Station, in the subway, all the faces seemed familiar. I feared there was nothing that had the power to surprise or astonish me anymore, I feared that I would never again be without a sense of *déjà vu* [*la impresión de volver*]. Fortunately, after a few unsleeping nights, forgetfulness began to work in me" (1.626/CF 284). We will recall that, according to Borges's account of Funes's inability to think because of his inability to discriminate and thus to abstract and generalize, the condition of possibility of remembering is forgetting. That Borges would both celebrate and lament the necessity of forgetting is understandable, because forgetting is the impossible condition of possibility for loving another. For example, Borges is able to love Beatriz Viterbo only insofar as he is capable of discrimination and decision. Loving Beatriz means forgetting everyone else; it means choosing Beatriz. Nevertheless, the possibility of Borges's love for Beatriz is also the impossibility of loving her, because the forgetting constitutive of such love necessarily makes possible the forgetting of Beatriz. Borges notes as much in "The Theologians" when he explains, "There are those who seek the love of a woman in order to forget her, in order not to think of her any more [*para olvidarse de ella, para no pensar más en ella*]" (1.551/CF 202). It is always possible to forget the one we love; it is always possible to forget that we love the one we love. This is the promise of love, both its chance and its threat.

In "The Aleph," Borges confronts the irreducible problem of narrating—which depends on forgetting—absolute plenitude, *pleroma*, or full presence. Moreover, and importantly, in "The Aleph" he names the constitutive impossibility of narrating absolute presence and thus of experiencing the presence of the present. He calls this impossibility literature: "Perhaps the gods would not deny me the discovery of an equivalent image, but then this report would be polluted with literature, with falseness" (1.624/CF 282). The possibility of an image equivalent to the Aleph requires recourse to literature. Yet, because literature is fundamentally temporal, successive (like all language), it necessarily falsifies and thus corrupts the Aleph, which is simultaneous. The possibility of representing the Aleph, which is all that can ever be done, is its impossibility. Borges writes: "[T]he central problem—the enumeration, even partial enumeration, of infinity—is irresolvable. In that unbounded moment [*En ese instante gigantesco*], I saw millions of delightful and horrible acts; none amazed me so much as the fact that all occupied the same point, without superposition and without transparency. What my eyes saw was *simultaneous*; what I shall write is *successive*, because language is successive" (1.624–25/CF 282–83). The truth of the Aleph or the Aleph *qua* truth depends on its capacity never to lose anything. The truth, then, is the self-presence of the present. Within the Aleph, there is neither past nor future: everything is present, which means there is neither space nor time. Hence, *within the Aleph*, truth is eternal.

The first point of departure is the impossibility of narrating the Aleph, which, *qua* absolute, simultaneously contains all that ever was, is, or will be. It is impossible to narrate the Aleph without falsifying it, that is, without fictionalizing it, without consigning it to literature. The second point of departure, however, displaces the first point, and does so because it is *a second point*, a second *infinite* point: "I believe that there is (or was) another Alelph; I believe that the Aleph of Calle Garay was a *false* Aleph" (1.627/CF 285). Borges is not describing the scene in which within the Aleph of Calle Garay is represented the Aleph of Calle Garay and then within that representation there is the representation of the representation. This would be the abyssal structure of *mise en abyme*, which, according to Rodolphe Gasché, "is too representational. It belongs, as does spurious infinity [which Hegel contrasts to true or positive infinity and which Derrida rethinks as structural infinity], to the realm of *Vorstellung* and imagination" (1994, 138). "In other words," Gasché explains, the abyssal structure of *mise en abyme*—as it is outlined, for example, in "The Aleph"—is "an essentially empirical concept" (138) that remains determined in terms of a representation itself determined in relation to the possibility of a totality, namely, the sum total of the abyssal representations which must remain, within the horizon of the abyssal structure, a necessary possibility for thought. Nevertheless, in the suggestion of the possibility of *another* Aleph, that is, of a second point that includes all points, what cannot be represented is the *spacing* of the two points—the two infinite points, each necessarily displacing the other, thus limiting or conditioning the other—that displaces and exceeds the truth, *qua* representation or *adequatio*, of the other. Another name for this displacement or necessary reference to the other, according to Borges, is literature. This means that the determination that the Aleph of Calle Garay is false is *also* false; that is, that assertion, too, is literary.

The nonrepresentational *spacing* essential to the possibility of the two Alephs as either true or false corrupts in every instance the perspective or the point of view from which such a determination could be made. Because there must be a place in and from which to perceive the Aleph, which place, however, is always already displaced by the possibility of another Aleph, it follows that there is no one Aleph if there are not (at least) two. Literature—i.e., constitutive falseness—signifies the impossible possibility of the Aleph in that it names and instances the spacing of *two* points of departure and infinitude, *two* points of absolute plenitude or presence, and thus the impossibility of either one being present as such or in and to itself *alone*. Such spacing opens onto a structural infinity. The spacing of the two Alephs, however, cannot be determined because it is never simply present within either the empirical (negative) or transcendental (positive) infinity of either one of the Alephs.[3]

It is clear, then, that in "The Aleph," Borges yet once more frets the aporetic relation of space and time. On the one hand, pure space, pure simultaneity, would be the end of time, but also of space. On the other hand, pure time, pure succession, would be the end of space, but also of time. When Borges writes that "an Alelph is one of the points in space that contain all points" and that it is "the place where, without admixture or confusion, all the places of the world, seen from every angle, coexist" (1.623/CF 280, 281), he defines the Aleph as absolute or pure space.[4] But when he writes that the Aleph is "that unbounded moment [*ese instante gigantesco*]" (1.625/CF 283), he defines it as absolute or pure time. "The Aleph"'s two epigraphs, however, indicate the problem of thinking space without time and time without space.

The epigraph from Shakespeare's *Hamlet*—"O God, I could be bounded in a nutshell, and count myself a king of infinite space" (2.2.254–6)—is unthinkable without recourse to succession, to time, in that what is at stake is the infinitely successive division of space. What is required to think the infinite division of space is, in fact, one division *after* another *ad infinitum*. Hamlet's understanding that he could be confined within a nutshell and yet imagine himself king of infinite space can only be thought according to the *temporal* logic of the infinite divisibility of space. The epigraph from *Leviathan* reveals Hobbes's negative assessment of the idea of the absolute *here and now*, thus of absolute time: "But they will teach us, that Eternity is the Standing still of the Present Time, a *Nunc-stans* (as the Schools call it;) which neither they, nor any else understand, no more than they would a *Hic-stans* for an infinite greatnesse of Place" (466–67). Hobbes's discussion of the inconceivability of either an absolute place (*Hic-stans*) or an absolute present (*Nunc-stans*) occurs within his discussion of the attributes of God and, as a consequence, makes clear that the problem of thinking either pure space or pure time is a theological problem. The name for the figure of the inconceivability of pure space and pure time is God: "the Name of God is used, not to make us conceive him; (for he is Incomprehensible; and his greatnesse, and power are unconceivable;) but that we may honour him" (23). God is a metaphor for what we cannot think. God is a cipher, a limit concept. The name of God is the metaphor to end all metaphors.

### *Decaying sense*

In Hobbes it is necessary to understand that every idea is empirically determined as sense, which is, he writes, a "*seeming*, or *fancy*" (*Leviathan* 14) that results from the impression on our bodily organs of objects outside us. Insofar as sense is nothing more than the register of this impression in us, it concerns appearances ("seeming," "fancy") and is thus related to the imagination, which Hobbes writes, "is nothing but *decaying sense*" (15). Borges is perhaps nowhere more aware that sense only ever decays than in the first story collected in *El aleph*, "El inmortal [The Immortal]," the theme of which, Borges explained in the Afterword to the same collection, is "an ethics of immortality" or "the effect that immortality would have on humankind" (1996, 1.629/CF 287). Comparing himself to the so-called Troglodyte, who, it turns out, is one of the immortals, the narrator observes: "I reflected that our perceptions were identical but that Argos combined them differently than I, constructed from them different objects; I reflected that perhaps for him there were no objects, but rather a constant, dizzying play of swift impressions. I imagined a world without memory, without time; I considered the possibility of a language that had no nouns [*un lenguaje que ignorara los sustantivos*], a language of impersonal verbs or indeclinable adjectives [*de indeclinables epítetos*]" (1.539/CF 189). This last recalls "Tlön, Uqbar, Orbis Tertius," where Borges discusses the possibility of a culture whose language would be without substantives. In "The Immortal," however, such a language follows from the lack of temporal synthesis and the concomitant absence of any objects, for without temporal synthesis nothing ever appears to be or to objectify itself.

If, as Hobbes argues, all of our ideas are empirically grounded in sense impressions and if all sense impressions are constitutively decaying, then the Hobbesian world must be unstable. In "The Immortal" Borges proposes the limit of a language grounded on sense impressions without necessary temporal synthesis: such a language would be incapable of objectifying or substantiating the world. Hobbes, too, understood the threat that a world of sense posed to cognition. The inconstancy of fleeting impressions results in Hobbes's concern for metaphor, which is, by definition, substitution, displacement, translation. According to Hobbes, metaphorical language is necessarily false because such a language can never be referred back to an original, hence stable perception or experience. Contrary to the representation within the Aleph, which contains the totality of "universal space [*espacio cósmico*] . . . with no diminution in size" (1.625/CF 283), Hobbesian imagination, because it is *decaying* sense, cannot fail to falsify that which it represents. The structure of *decay*—which is an effect of temporal succession and thus of substitution—is of interest in that it is determinative of the possibility of God and of the name of God.

*Stuttering in Hebrew and Arabic, in Kabbalah and Islam*

In chapter thirty-six of *Leviathan*, in which Hobbes considers the word of God and of the prophets, he writes, "that God saith to *Moses* concerning *Aaron, He shall be thy Spokes-man to the People; and he shall be to thee a mouth, and thou shalt be to him the stead of God*" (290). Aaron speaks for Moses; Moses stands in for God. There is already, from the start, the double mediation, the double withdrawal of God from Egypt: in standing-in for God, Moses nonetheless cannot present himself—cannot make himself present, whether as Moses or God—either to himself or to another. He can present himself *here and now* only in the voice and in the place of another. Self-presentation is always *auto-hetero-*(*re*)-presentation, the representation of the self in and by another. Substitution—which means falsification, literature—marks and marks out self-presentation: Moses in the place of—*as*—God; Aaron in the place of—*as*—Moses. It is worth wondering whether the aporia of the promise of a spokesman is not precisely what Borges had in mind in "Theme of the Traitor and the Hero" when he wrote of Fergus Kilpatrick that he was "[l]ike Moses, who from the land of Moab glimpsed yet could not reach the promised land [*divisó y no pudo pisar la tierra prometida*]" (1.496/CF 143). Like Moses, like God, Kilpatrick can never present himself simply, in himself. He is not wherever he is. Thus Moses, the slow, hesitant speaker, takes God's place, telling Aaron what to say. The beginning is marked by a remarkable stutter[5]: unable to speak for himself, God sends Moses, who cannot speak for himself, and is thus substituted for by Aaron. In order to get the word out, there must be the possibility of substitution, repetition, citation. The word of God is only the word of God in and through another. In the beginning, the Word (*Logos*) is doubly displaced in order that God take place. But it is more than this, for Aaron does not take Moses's place: he is his mouth. Aaron is *diminished* at the same time that God and Moses speak through the mouth of another: their mouth, which is already shared, is the mouth of another. My mouth is the mouth of another. In whose mouth will God say his name? In whose mouth is the Word (of God)?

The structure of substitution calls for (at least) two remarks. *First,* this "stuttering" at the origin is not only part and parcel of the Judeo-Christian tradition. It also informs the other Abrahamic religion, Islam. The Qur'an begins without *saying* anything: "*Alif Lâm Mîm,*" which three letters "are one of the miracles of the Qur'an" (2). One of several different *Al-Muqatta'at* that mark the opening of twenty-nine of the Qur'an's one hundred fourteen sûrahs, *Alif Lâm Mîm* is not a phrase, but only the articulation of three sounds. It has been speculated that the various *Al-Muqatta'at* indicate the names of God, but N. J. Dawood remarks: "The fact is that no one knows what they stand for. Traditional commentators dismiss them by saying, 'God alone knows what He means by these letters' " (4).[6] In short, they are meaningless articulations that on at least twenty-nine occasions precede the meaning of the Qur'an. The first such *Al-Muqatta'at* is *Alif Lâm Mîm. Alif* is both the first sound of the Qur'an and the first letter of the Arabic alphabet. Its numerical value, like that of the Greek *alpha,* is one. Consequently, *Alif* is the sign and the sound of one, of univocity and unicity. Before one begins to recite the Qur'an, one necessarily—but without knowing what it means or if it means anything at all—sounds the *Alif.* The Qur'an thus begins with an insignificant stutter. God does not, therefore, reveal himself or his word to Muhammad in the first instance: in the beginning is not the word, but the repetition or recitation of that which makes no sense and yet makes all sense possible.

This is not only the case for Islam, however. In the "Postscript" to "The Aleph," dated 1 March 1943, Borges—whom George Steiner calls, along with Benjamin and Kafka, "our third modern Kabbalist" (67)—explains: " 'aleph' . . . is the name of the first letter of the alphabet of the sacred language. Its application to the disk of my tale would not appear to be accidental. In the Kabbala, that letter signifies the En Soph, the pure and unlimited godhead" (1.627/CF 285). But according to Gershom Scholem, if the *aleph* signifies the name of God, it does so only by synecdoche. In *On the Kabbalah and Its Symbolism,* Scholem explains, "In Rabbi Mendel's view not even the first two Commandments were revealed directly to the whole people of Israel. All that Israel heard was the *aleph* with which in the Hebrew text the first Commandment begins, the *aleph* of the word *anokhi,* 'I' " (1965, 30). The *aleph* does not mean "I" and surely does not in itself or by itself signify the name of God. It is the first sound, the first articulation of the possibility of

"I." The point, however, is not that all our thoughts are, as Descartes would ultimately claim, accompanied by a doubtless "I" or "I think," but that the "I" of the "I am the LORD thy God" (Exodus 20:1) depends on the *aleph*. The most meaningful articulation depends on that which means nothing at all: "To hear the *aleph*," Scholem writes, "is to hear next to nothing; it is the preparation for all audible language, but in itself conveys no determinate, specific meaning" (30).[7] Following Rabbi Mendel Torum of Rymanóv, Scholem asserts, "the actual revelation to Israel consisted only of the *aleph*," which means that in order for the revelation "to become the foundation of religious authority, it had to be translated into human language" (30). Unlike Islam, which for devotional purposes (rather than, say, educational purposes) authorizes only the recitation, repetition, without translation, of the Qur'an, Kabbalah understands that the *aleph*, which is revelation as the promise of revelation—and thus revelation as re-veiling—demands translation, interpretation, even as it recognizes that such translation or interpretation ruins revelation. In a letter to Martin Buber concerning the relation of revelation to the Law, Franz Rosenzweig explains, "Thus revelation is certainly not Law-giving. It is only this: Revelation. The primary content of revelation is revelation itself. 'He came down'—this already concludes the revelation; 'He spoke' is the beginning of interpretation, and certainly 'I am'" (118).[8] In other words, the first sound of the first word of the first commandment, "I" (*'anokhi*), already demands interpretation, which, however necessary, is nonetheless accidental to revelation as such and, therefore, corrupts it; what ought to be universal, univocal, is ruined by the singularity of its articulation.[9]

This is precisely what is at stake in Rosenzweig's double gesture: to deny revelation its status as Law-giving, then to question the limit of legitimate (thus authorized and authoritative) interpretation. Because revelation reveals only itself, because it is the *aleph*, it is nothing at all. It is the anticipation of meaning that neither means anything in itself nor provides a rule or limit for the meaning that comes to displace and ruin it. Revelation opens onto interpretation, demands it, for without such interpretation it is meaningless; yet every interpretation necessarily goes too far and jeopardizes what Rosenzweig calls revelation's "original self-interpretation" (118), which is nothing more (but also nothing less) than the *aleph*. The *aleph*, then, is *already* interpretation. In revealing itself revelation goes too far.

At issue is the impossibility of the *aleph* to mark or indicate, to sound, revelation: "But the truly divine element in this revelation, the immense *aleph*, was not in itself sufficient to express the divine message, and in itself it was more than the community could bear" (Scholem 1965, 31). The "immense *aleph*" is both *too small* for the divine message and *too large* for human understanding. Which means divine authority is an effect of prophetic—i.e., human—understanding: "Only the prophet was empowered to communicate the meaning of this inarticulate voice to the community" (31).[10] Because the *aleph*, however immense, is *too small* for the divine message, it cannot be said to contain it; at the same time, whatever the prophet hears in the *aleph*, which is *too great* for humanity to bear, necessarily diminishes the *aleph*, thereby reducing it to human intelligibility. The *aleph*, then, is untranslatable. Nonetheless, the *aleph* demands translation since it is only through translation that the message that is the *aleph* might arrive in the first place. Consequently, the *aleph* articulates the impossible condition of possibility of translation and interpretation.

*Second*, the demand for interpretation is not the effect of *human* failure or limitation, for it is not the case that God simply and fully presents Himself in the *aleph*. On the contrary, as Scholem stresses, the *aleph* is not only too large for humans, it is also too small for God. This means that God cannot *simply* say Himself in and as *aleph*. The "original self-interpretation of revelation" in and as *aleph*, hence in itself, demands interpretation. Not even God understands Himself in the articulation of the *aleph*. As a consequence, the pronunciation of the *aleph* always and only calls for another pronunciation of the *aleph*. Its inscription is always and necessarily a re-inscription. Revelation reveals the impossibility of revelation. God repeats Himself in order to constitute Himself. There is a stutter at the origin: there are always (at least) two *alephs*.

Borges's positing of two Alephs—which possibility necessarily inscribes duplication and duplicity, counterfeit, within the divine, marks the divine as an effect of essential falsification, of literature—signals this inaugural stutter and implicitly remarks the problem of origin in Jewish mysticism. Although Borges claims in a lecture on Kabbalah published in 1980 that he will "have just read" Scholem's *On the Kabbalah and Its Symbolism*, and there is no indication that he will have read Scholem's earlier *Major Trends in Jewish Mysticism* (1941), nevertheless, Virginia Gutiérrez Berner points out that Scholem's work "was one of the main sources of his knowledge of Kabbalah" (139).[11]

Whereas pre-Lurianic Kabbalah begins with divine emanation, Luria asked how a perfect being, a being absolutely in itself and thus one, could create anything at all.[12] For there to be creation, there must first be a space for creation, a space in which the unlimited divinity is not. For creation to happen, then, the unlimited and unconditional divinity must be limited, conditioned. The self-limitation of the divine is *tsimtsum* (*zimzum*), but, as Scholem explains, in Lurianic Kabbalah the self-limitation of God is not "an emanation or projection, in which God steps out of Himself, communicates or reveals Himself. On the contrary, it is a withdrawal into Himself. Instead of turning outward, He contracts His essence, which becomes more and more hidden" (Scholem 1965, 110). In effect, God puts on the veil, withdraws, and hides himself, in order that the space for creation becomes possible. A more recent commentator argues, "at the heart of Luria's teachings is the imperfection of beginning. Existence does not begin with a perfect Creator bringing into being an imperfect universe; rather, the existence of the universe is the result of an inherent flaw or crisis within the infinite Godhead, and the purpose of creation is to correct it" (Dan 74). The withdrawal of the *en sof*, which is absolutely unlimited and negative, into itself opens the space of pleroma, plenitude, within which creation takes place.

Yet, insofar as pleroma results from God's withdrawal, it provides the place for any possible determination, which means the pleroma is as much the place of evil as of good: "In the *tsimtsum* the powers of judgment, which in God's essence were united in infinite harmony with the 'roots' of all other potencies, are gathered and concentrated in a single point, namely, the primordial space, or pleroma, from which God withdraws. But the powers of stern judgment ultimately include evil" (Scholem 1965, 111). Because all judgment is conditioned by temporalization, the chance of evil cannot be circumscribed. According to Lurianic Kabbalah, creation is an effect of a crisis within the divine: God's withdrawal marks His attempt at "a gradual purification of the divine organism from the elements of evil" (111). In order to purify Himself, God absents Himself from Himself. From before the beginning, from before the unity of God, there is crisis and the crisis of and in God manifests itself, according to Scholem, as "a primordial exile or self-banishment" (111). The crisis within divinity, which can only be resolved in God's auto-exile, results in a fundamental displacement:

"Nothing remains in its proper place. Everything is somewhere else. But a being that is not in its proper place is in exile. Thus, since that primordial act, all being has been a being in exile, in need of being led back and redeemed" (112). Redemption, however, is strictly impossible since the potential for redemption depends upon judgment and judgment necessarily runs the risk of evil. Because justice never *is*, it can never ground redemption. This would include, moreover, the possibility of a redemption and restoration of God to His "proper" place. God's proper place, therefore, is improper and God's Word is always the word in exile from itself. Thus, God takes place in and as translation, *translatio*, in the literal movement from one place to another. Insofar as God takes place in exile and in translation, His Word is never properly His own.

The Word of God is sayable *in the first place* only in and through—i.e., *as*—translation: the translation from God to Moses to Aaron instances only one representation of the double displacement at and of the origin of the word (of God). At the moment of its articulation and as the condition of its possibility, the univocity of the Word is suspended in and exposed to and as translation, iteration, repetition. The Word of God, accordingly, is never single, never one, never the One: it is always more than one. Wherever and whenever translation happens, it does so always in at least two voices (*voces*), always between at least two words (*voces*), always between at least two places.

The constitutive displacement of the *aleph* opens onto the question of martyrdom. How to bear witness, either to oneself or to another? How to testify to God? How does God testify to Himself? On the one hand, testimony demands exemplarity: both the one who testifies and that to which one testifies must be unique, singular. On the other hand, testimony demands substitutability: the irreplaceable must be replaceable. As Derrida remarks, the one who testifies to his or her unique experience, testifies that any other, in his or her place, would testify to the same. This means that one can never simply be in one's own place. The unique, the singular—the unrepeatable and unsubstitutable—must be universalizable; it must be repeatable.[13] Borges elegantly and succinctly addresses the aporia of testimony and experience in the "Prologue" to *La cifra*: "There is not a single beautiful word, with the doubtful exception of *witness*, that is not an abstraction [*No hay una sola hermosa palabra, con la excepción dudosa de* testigo, *que no sea una abstracción*]" (1996,

3.290). This is Borges's attempt to *mark out* the absolute universality of language by *re*marking the necessary singularity of articulation, even if that singularity is no less necessarily abstracted, universalized, in the instant of its enunciation. How does God, for instance, testify to Himself if the *aleph*, which is the articulation of the unlimited Godhead, is always already repeated, hence repeatable as its condition of possibility and, therefore, constitutively *false*? The *aleph* marks, inscribes the most minimal instance of literature. God stutters under oath; He perjures Himself. He presents Himself as if He were not a fiction.

Moses calls God to account. In Exodus 3, Moses asks God to bear witness to Himself, to testify: he asks God his name. "But Moses said to God, 'If I come to the Israelites and say to them, "The God of your ancestors has sent me to you," and they ask me, "What is his name?"' what shall I say to them? God said to Moses, 'I AM WHO I AM [*EHYEH ASHER EHYEH*]' " (Exodus 3:13–14). In "Historia de los ecos de un nombre [A History of the Echoes of a Name]," Borges follows Martin Buber, who claims that "*Ehyeh asher ehyeh* may also be translated as *I am what I will be* [*Soy el que seré*] or by *I will be where I will be* [*Yo estaré donde yo estaré*]" (1996, 2.129/SNF 406). The editors of the *New Oxford Annotated Bible* point out that *Ehyeh asher ehyeh* also could be translated as either "I am what I am" or "I will be what I will be." Borges suggests, moreover, that "multiplied by [*por*: also "through"] human languages—*Ich bin der ich bin, Ego sum qui sum, I am that I am*—, the sententious name of God, . . . in spite of consisting of many words, is more impenetrable and more resolute [*firme*] than if it were composed of only one" (2.129/SNF 406). According to the Christian interpretation, Borges claims that the name of God, *Soy El Que Soy*, amounts to an "ontological affirmation" (2.129/SNF 406).[14] This would seem to accord with the earlier recollection that "for magical or primitive thought [*el pensamiento mágico, o primitivo*], names are not arbitrary symbols but a vital part of what they define" (2.128/SNF 405). To this statement Borges nevertheless appends a footnote: "One of the Platonic dialogues, the *Cratylus*, discusses and seems to negate a necessary connection of words and things" (2.128n1/SNF 405n1). The enigma of God's name, which Borges emphasizes by displacing it into the mouths of a Shakespearean fool (Parolles) and of a madman (Jonathan Swift), ultimately spells out the necessary idiocy of the name. Of Swift, who, according to Borges, was always fascinated by idiocy ("siempre lo fascinó la idiotez"), Borges writes: "Deafness, dizziness, fear of madness, and finally idiocy aggravated and deepened Swift's melancholy. He began to lose his memory. He didn't want to use glasses; he couldn't read, and he was incapable of writing. He prayed to God every day to send him death. And one evening, old and mad and wasted, he was heard repeating, we don't know whether in resignation or desperation or as one affirms or anchors oneself in one's own invulnerable personal essence [*o como quien se afirma y se ancla en su íntima esencia invulnerable*]: 'I am that I am, I am that I am' " (2.130/SNF 407).

His intimate and invulnerable essence is his idiocy, *idios*. What is Swift's own most essence, what is closest to him, is his name, which is also God's impenetrable name. It is a name, however, that no matter how proper, no matter how idiosyncratic and singular, cannot *not* repeat itself, and thus cannot *not* refer to itself, that is, to another. Who am I? I am who I am. In order to say his name, to *anchor* himself in himself and thus to ground himself, thereby avoiding the slippage of metaphoricity, Swift—madly, idiotically—repeats God's name as his own, repeats a name that repeats itself in order to determine the One, the absolute, the in-itself. Shakespeare, in Borges's reading of *All's Well that Ends Well*, puts in Parolles's mouth "words that reflect, as in a fallen mirror" (2.129/SNF 406), God's name, which reflects and doubles itself and in so doing reveals the impenetrability of all names, of all naming.

To read God's name therefore is to look in the mirror but to see only enigmatically, only darkly. In "El espejo de los enigmas [The Mirror of Enigmas]," which was also published in *Otras inquisiciones* (1952), Borges considers Paul's famous pronouncement, "*videmous nunc per speculum in aenigmate: tunc autem facie ad faciem. Nunc cognosco ex parte: tunc autem cognoscam sicut et cognitus sum*" (1 Corinthians 13:12; quoted in Borges 1996, 2.98/OI 125). "The Mirror of Enigmas," not unlike "History of the Echoes of a Name," chronicles the interpretation and understanding, thus the translation, of this Pauline dictum as it manifests itself in the work of Léon Bloy, who, Borges writes, agrees with Cipriano de Valera that Paul's brief text refers not to "our vision of divinity" but to "our vision in general" (2.98/OI 126). Although Bloy "did not impress upon his conjecture a definitive form [*no imprimió a su conjetura una forma definitiva*]" (2.98/OI 126), through Borges's various renderings of Bloy's references to Paul's conception of the "*per speculum*," it becomes clear that Bloy is a closet Kabbalist: "Bloy (I repeat) did nothing but apply to the whole Creation the method that the Jewish cabalists applied to the Scripture. They thought that a work dictated by the Holy Spirit was an absolute text: a text where the collaboration of chance is calculable at zero [*vale decir un texto donde la colaboración del azar es calculable en cero*]" (2.100/OI 128). The result is a world, a universe, in which everything is determined beforehand, according to an implacable logic or calculus: "Since the events related by Scripture are true (God is Truth, the Truth cannot lie, et cetera), we must admit that as men acted out those events they were blindly performing a secret drama determined and premeditated by God" (2.98/OI 125). Borges is close here to "Theme of the Traitor and the Hero," which also plays out a "secret drama" in public. But unlike in "Theme of the Traitor and the Hero," in which a literary text determines the truth of a historical event, here Borges writes that the external world "is a language that men have forgotten or that we barely decipher [*que hemos olvidado los hombres, o que deletreamos apenas*]" (2.98/OI 125).

It cannot be, however, that men have simply forgotten. The constitutive mirroring of God's name means that there will never have been a time *before* reflection, before translation and interpretation, thus before misunderstanding and confusion. The world, insofar as it is an expression of God's will, will never not have been opaque, enigmatic, obscure, not because our eyes are clouded over, but because the condition of possibility of God's self-presentation will have been referral (I am that I am, I am what I am, I will be where I will be, etc.), and withdrawal, deferral, such that He will never not have been presented obscurely, as in a mirror darkly, even to Himself, whom He will not have been able to discern, whose visage will have been illegible.

The impossibility of reading, of marking out or tracing, the outline of one's own face, of one's own life, is one of Borges's most persistent themes. " 'No man knows who he is ['*Ningún hombre sabe quién es*'], affirmed Léon Bloy. Who could have illustrated that intimate ignorance [*ignorancia íntima*] better than he? He believed himself to be a strict Catholic and he was a continuer of the cabalists, a secret brother of Swedenborg and of Blake: heresiarchs" (2.100/OI 128). Just a few years later, however, in 1960, Borges suggested that this "intimate ignorance" is absolved at the hour of our death: "A man proposes to himself the work of drawing the world [*se propone la tarea de dibujar el mundo*]. Over the years he peoples a space with images of provinces, kingdoms, mountains, bays, islands, fishes, rooms, instruments, stars, horses, and individuals. A short time before he dies, he discovers that that patient labyrinth of lines traces the image of his face [*traza la imagen de su cara*]" (2.232/CF 327). At first blush, it appears the man proposes to himself a divine labor, namely, the creation of a world. Its accomplishment, it appears, happens "poco antes de morir [a short time before he dies]." At stake is memory, for what is traced is not unlike the line, say, in Kant, or the circle from one noon to the next. Borges imagines the possibility that the various trajectories of one's life trace the image, the lines and the outline, of one's face. Thus, at the final instance, a little before one dies, the circle closes: one comes (back) to one's self.

This, however, is impossible. "Poco antes de morir"—a short time before dying—leaves open the space and the time of life. What cannot be traced and thus what can be neither experienced nor comprehended, what cannot be outlined and therefore circumscribed, what one will never be able to delineate, is one's *own* death.[15] If the circle that is one's life is to be closed at one's death, then one will never be able to close it, one will never know the image of one's face. Put simply, we are always "poco antes de morir," a little before dying. This is the definition of mortality. As a consequence, we can never know the totality of our image, of our life. We will never see "face to face," as Paul has it; or, more exactly, seeing "face to face" *is* seeing in the mirror darkly.

## *The time of confusion*

Shortly after the famous passage from 1 Corinthians that Borges frets in the work of Léon Bloy, Paul explicitly addresses the question of confusion and does so according to the logic of the fundamental distinction between speaking in tongues (*glossolalia*) and interpretation or prophecy, that is, speaking with a meaningful language (*phonē*). Near the conclusion of 1 Corinthians 14 Paul insists, "God is not a God of confusion but of peace" (1 Corinthians 14:33).[16] "Confusion" translates *akatastasias*, which might also be rendered as instability or unsettledness. Seeing in the mirror darkly is confusing, it is the Hobbesian world of decaying sense. In the intervening chapter 13, in the famous verses devoted to love, Paul articulates the condition for seeing "face to face" as a love that takes no time (*chronos*), a kairotic love or a love that happens in the moment (*kairos*) that does not pass away. In short, only the suspension of chronological time in the love of the absolute present saves us from confusion, from seeing as in a mirror darkly. Only the *kairos*, and the love that is possible in the *kairos*, makes possible the peace, the stability, of seeing "face to face." Insofar as God is love He inhabits the *kairos*. According to Paul, God is not the "author"—as the King James Version has it—of instability, which is the effect of *chronos*, but of peace. The claim that God is not the God of confusion follows the determination that "the spirits of the prophets are subject to the prophets" (1 Corinthians 14:32). Clearly Paul means that when speaking in tongues (*glossolalia*) one's spirit is no longer subject to oneself, no longer subjected: one is outside or foreign to oneself, one is therefore an *idiot* to oneself. Prophecy, however, cannot solve the problem of instability, for prophecy is itself open to endless reiterations and reinterpretations: "Let two or three prophets speak, and let the others weigh what is said [*diakrinetosan*]" (1 Corinthians 14:29), that is, two or three will speak and the others will decide, judge, distinguish. In short, they will interpret. Prophecy, which in Paul is interpretation, demands interpretation. Consequently, there is always an exposure to an outside and to outsiders, *idiōtēs*. The beginning of interpretation, of prophecy, is speaking in tongues, ecstasy, constitutive being-unsubjected-to-self of the self. But if this is the case, then God is nothing other than the God of confusion and instability.

That God is not the God of peace but of confusion and that He is so precisely in terms of language, of the one and many tongues, is clear from the Babel story in Genesis:

> And the whole earth was of one language, and of one speech. And it came to pass, as they journeyed from then east, that they found a plain in the land of Shinar; and they dwelt there. And they said one to another, Go to, let us make brick, and burn them thoroughly. And they had brick for stone, and slime had they for mortar. And they said, Go to, let us build us a city and a tower, whose top may reach unto heaven; and let us make us a name, lest we be scattered

> abroad upon the face of the whole earth. And the LORD came down to see the city and the tower, which the children of men builded. And the LORD said, Behold, the people is one, and they have all one language; and this they begin to do: and now nothing will be restrained from them, which they have imagined to do. Go to, let us go down, and there confound their language, that they may not understand one another's speech. So the LORD scattered them abroad from thence upon the face of all the earth: and they left off to build the city. There is the name of it called Babel; because the LORD did there confound the language of all the earth. (Genesis 11)[17]

What language does God speak to Himself in order to determine his action? God's potentiality is figured in the same terms as those who wish to build the city and the tower: "Go to." Moreover, although there was only one language prior to God's descent, there was already the desire to impose a name and thus to mark out or determine a legacy and an inheritance. Those who built what would become known as the tower of Babel did not undertake the task in order to know God. They did so in order to know themselves, to establish and preserve themselves as a people by making a name for themselves.[18] To make a name for themselves, they must colonize the space of the city and mark off their difference from others. They would have imposed upon themselves a name and in doing so, they would have provided both for descent and the possibility, in the same language, of dissent. God comes down and imposes his own name, Babel, which is the name of the father, but also the proper name of the city and, as well, the name of confusion.[19]

The King James Bible does not specify that God came down and consigned everyone to a different language. It indicates only that "the LORD did there confound the language of all the earth" (Genesis 11). We no longer understand ourselves, not even when we speak the same language. This is the upshot of Paul's effort to distinguish speaking in tongues from speaking with a known language, but it is also what is at issue in Borges's "The Library of Babel," when he remarks, parenthetically, "(A number *n* of the possible languages employ the same vocabulary; in some of them the symbol 'library' possesses the correct definition 'everlasting, ubiquitous system of hexagonal galleries,' while a library—the thing—is a loaf of bread or a pyramid or something else, and the six words that define it themselves have other definitions. You who read me—are you certain you understand my language?)" (1996, 1.470/CF 118). This would be the confusion, the Babel/babble, of a "single" language. It would be the necessary multiplicity of tongues within and as a single voice. Borges, moreover, repeats Paul's understanding that there are many languages but none without meaning: "For while the Library contains all verbal structures, all the variations allowed by the twenty-five orthographic symbols, it includes not a single absolute piece of nonsense [*pero no un solo disparate absoluto*]" (1.470/CF 117). Unlike Paul, however, for whom meaningful language is an effect of the *phonē*, Borges determines the limits of the library and the possibility of meaning as an effect of the written mark, the twenty-five orthographic symbols. The concluding footnote to "La biblioteca de Babel" suggests that the vast library is "useless": "strictly speaking, all that is required is *a single volume*" (1.471/CF 118). Indeed, "The Aleph" argues that a single volume is no less useless than the vast library: the *aleph* is the infinite labyrinth of languages in a single letter, in a single sound.

Paul responds to the Babel story when he writes that God is not the God of confusion, but of peace, but not all the Abrahamic religions, the so-called religions of the book, see it this way. Sûrah 10, verse 19, of the Qur'an, for instance, claims, "Mankind were but one community, then they differed, and had not it been for a Word that went forth before from your Lord, it would have been settled between them regarding what they differed." God's Word thus sustains the antagonism between Islam, Judaism, and Christianity. About this, there is no confusion.

### *Executing kairos*

The Pauline assertion that confusion results from *chronos* whereas understanding—seeing face to face—is an effect of *kairos* or the moment, is dramatized and troubled in "The Secret Miracle." Set in Prague, in March 1939, the protagonist Jerome Hladik, the author of *A Vindication of Eternity* and of the unfinished tragedy *The Enemies*, is arrested near dusk on 19 March on suspicion of being Jewish. He is condemned to death. His execution is "set for March 29, at 9:00 A. M. That delay . . . was caused by the administrative desire to work impersonally and deliberately, as vegetables do, or planets" (1.508–509/CF 158). During the ten days he awaits his death, Hladik thinks about the instant of his death, about the nature of time, and, insofar as "the problematic exercise of literature constituted the whole of his life" (1.509/CF 158), he thought about his unfinished verse drama, *The Enemies*. The play is not unlike the novel *The Garden of Forking Paths* in that "incoherences multiply; actors come back on stage who had apparently been discarded from the plot; for one instant, the man that Römerstadt killed returns" (1.510/CF 159). In order to finish the play, Hladik prays, "*If . . . I do somehow exist, if I am not one of Thy repetitions or errata, then I exist as the author of* The Enemies. *In order to complete that play, which can justify me and justify Thee as well, I need one more year. Grant me those days, you who art [Tú de quien son] the centuries and time itself*" (1.511/CF 160).

Ten minutes later Hladik is asleep; near dawn, he dreams that he is in the Clementine Library searching for God. "*God*, the librarian said, *is in one of the letters on one of the pages of one of the four hundred thousand volumes in the Clementine*" (1.511/CF 160). God is in the detail, then, but it is easy enough to read in this remark a precursor to "The Aleph" and, given the protagonist's Jewish heritage, Borges's subtle insinuation of the Kabbalistic tradition. Another patron of the Library returns what he considers a "worthless [*inútil*]" atlas. Hladik opens it "at random [*al azar*]," sees a map of India, "a dizzying page [*vertiginoso*]," and "he touched one of the tiny letters [*tocó una de las mínimas letras*]. An ubiquitous voice spoke to him: 'The time of your labor has been granted' " (1.511/CF 160). When Hladik awoke "He remembered that the dreams of men belong to God and that Maimonides had written that the words of a dream, when they are clear and distinct and one cannot see who spoke them, are holy" (1.511/CF 160). Hladik is then led from his cell and executed at the appointed hour. He dies 29 March 1939 at 9:02 a.m. "He had asked God for an entire year in which to finish his work; God in His omnipotence had granted him a year. God had performed for him a secret miracle: the German bullet would kill him, at the determined hour, but in Hladik's mind a year would pass between the order to fire and the discharge of the rifles" (1.512/CF 161–162).

"The Secret Miracle" thus concerns the synthesis of time, which it figures as precisely the "time" of salvation or as the kairotic suspension of *chronos*. *Kairos* opens up within *chronos*, suspends *chronos*, without, however, interrupting chronology[20]: "The weapons converged upon Hladik, but the men who were to kill him were immobile. The sergeant's arm seemed to freeze, eternal, in an inconclusive gesture. On one of the paving stones of the yard, a bee cast a motionless shadow. As though in a painting, the wind had died. Hladik attempted a scream, a syllable, the twisting of a hand. He realized that he was paralyzed. He could hear not the slightest murmur of the halted world. *I am in hell*, he thought, *I am dead*. Then *I am mad*, he thought. And then, *time has halted*. Then he reflected that if that were true, his thoughts would have halted as well" (1.512/CF 161). But his thought does not halt. As the narrator observes, the play is "forged in time [*urdió en el tiempo*]" (1.512/CF 162). It is documented in Hladik's memory. At issue, then, is the possibility of two times, *chronos*, the time of Hladik's execution, and *kairos*, the time of Hladik's memory, the time that suspends *chronos*. But Borges's point is that the kairological suspension of *chronos*—the time, then, that God gives to Hladik—*takes time*. The suspension of time takes time. This means that *kairos*, the due time or the appropriate time, must necessarily be subject to division. The stretching out of the instant—the secret miracle—of Hladik's memory and execution must also be corruptible. *Kairos* is *executable*. The kairological seizure of *chronos* within which Hladik finishes his play is ruined by *chronos*: Hladik is executed, his memory destroyed. Hladik is, then, one of God's repetitions, one of his *errata*. He is an accident.

## *Maimonides, the Law, and the name of God*

Borges takes the epigraph for "The Secret Miracle" from the Koran: "And God caused him to die for an hundred years, and then raised him to life. And God said, 'How long hast thou waited?' He said, 'I have waited for a day or part of a day' " (1.508/CF 157). Borges displaces this Koranic story into the context of European anti-Semitic persecution. The rare—if not unique—reference to Maimonides, which discloses almost nothing about Maimonides or his thought, is important, for Maimonides, whom Thomas Aquinas called Rabbi Moses, was a "Jewish" philosopher born in Córdoba in 1135, but who would leave al-Andalus and ultimately die in Alexandria, Egypt, in 1204. All his major works, with the exception of his *Second Law* or the *Mishneh Torah*, were written in Arabic and it is not unlikely, although by no means certain, that Maimonides himself converted from Judaism to Islam.[21] The reference to Maimonides is significant because it signals Borges's deep concern for the problem of understanding divinity or the infinite Godhead. Not unlike Paul, for instance, Maimonides was troubled by the paradoxical necessity for and impossibility of interpreting the Law. But according to Maimonides the demand for and the impossibility of interpretation results from the fundamental confusion of the Law itself. In the *Guide for the Perplexed* he gives (at least) three reasons for this constitutive confusion. It is a confusion, moreover, that necessarily manifests itself in the *Guide*.

*First*, the language of the Law, the Torah, is itself in need of interpretation. Maimonides makes this clear from the beginning. He describes his "primary object" as the explanation of "certain words occurring in the prophetic books," of which "some are homonyms, and of their several meanings the ignorant choose the wrong ones; other terms which are employed in a figurative sense are erroneously taken by such persons in their primary signification" (2). The *Guide for the Perplexed* is nothing if not a theory of reading, but it is not simply for the ignorant. On the contrary, it is also for the well informed or the educated man. Maimonides writes: "the object of this treatise is to enlighten a religious man who has been trained to believe in the truth of our holy Law, who conscientiously fulfills his moral and religious duties, and at the same time has been successful in his philosophical studies" (2). The problem the Law poses for the educated man is that a literal reading of the Law results in a misguided understanding of God and of one's relation to God. If one follows the Torah literally, one inevitably falls into anthropomorphisms or corporealisms and, consequently, into idolatry. Yet, if the educated man follows only his reason, if he relies exclusively on his training in philosophy and natural science and thus fails to adhere to the fundamental principles of the Law, he effectively abdicates his faith and becomes an outsider, an unbeliever, what Paul called an idiot. The Torah thus sustains *neither* literal *nor* figurative interpretation. The reader is obligated to decipher over and over again the limits of context in order to decide whether or not to read a word figuratively or literally.

*Second*, the difficulties for reading that the Law presents are such that the *Guide* cannot avoid reproducing them. The confusion of the

Torah is not an accident, but constitutive and, moreover, the *Guide* cannot mitigate such confusion without violating the very Law it seeks to make transparent. On this point Maimonides follows Averroës' *Tahafut al-Tahafut* (*The Incoherence of the Incoherence* or *The Destruction of Destruction*), which is a response to Ghazali's *Tahafut al Falasifa* (*The Incoherence of the Philosophers*). In chapter eleven—the same chapter to which Borges refers in "La busca de Averroës [Averroës' Search]"—Averroës argues, against Ghazali, that "not all knowledge about which the Holy Law is silent needs to be explored and explained to the masses as being, according to speculative thought, part of the dogmas of religion; for from this the greatest confusion arises. One must not speak about those things concerning which the Holy Law is silent; the masses must learn that human understanding is not sufficient to treat these problems, and must not go beyond what the teaching of the Holy Law explains in its texts, since this is teaching in which all can participate and which suffices for the attainment of their happiness. . . . So the Lord of the Holy Law instructs the masses only in so far as is needed for their acquisition of happiness" (Averroës 258). Averroës, the Islamic Aristotelian, influenced Maimonides, the Jewish Aristotelian. This would not have been lost on Borges. For his part, Maimonides explains that according to rabbinical authority, the description of the Chariot, the *Ma'aseh Mercabah*, "must not be fully expounded even in the presence of a single student, unless he be wise and able to reason for himself, and even then you should only acquaint him with the heads of the different sections of the subject" (Maimonides 2–3; qtd. from Babyl. Talm. *Hagigah*, fol. II b). Further, Maimonides notes that tradition holds that the account of Creation, the *Ma'aseh Bereshith*, "must not be expounded in the presence of two" (3) persons. How is Maimonides to observe the prohibition against dissemination in a treatise that proposes "to expound, as far as possible" (251) both the account of creation and the description of the divine chariot? Maimonides himself admits that explaining "These principles in writing . . . would be equal to expounding them unto thousands of men" (3). Maimonides can write without forsaking the Law—which dictates that the truth not be exposed or expounded—only by teaching in a way that accords with the Law that mandates *not teaching* even in the presence of one. Only in this way will Maimonides "not be in opposition to the Divine Will . . . which has withheld from the multitude the truths required for the knowledge of God, according to the words, 'The secret of the Lord is with them that fear him' (Ps. XXV.14)" (3).

*Third*, the *Guide* is methodologically impossible: "You must know," Maimonides writes, "that if a person, who has attained a certain degree of perfection wishes to impart to others, either orally or in writing, any portion of the knowledge which he has acquired of these subjects, he is utterly unable to be as systematic and explicit as he could be in a science of which the method is well known. The same difficulties which he encountered when investigating the subject for himself will attend him when endeavoring to instruct others; viz., at one time the explanation will appear lucid, at another time, obscure; this property of the subject appears to remain the same for both the advanced scholar and the beginner" (4). The implications of this admission are severe. In effect, Maimonides claims that there is nothing but the repetition of the errors and deviations that constitute the possibility of learning the Law. There is no method that would make it possible *not* to repeat such errors. The experience of learning the Law is the infinitely repeated experience of the impossibility of learning the Law. The Law of experience, then, is error, errancy. If the *Guide* leads anywhere at all, it ineluctably leads back into itself, back into the uncertainties and perplexities from which it leads us.

The confusion of the *Guide*, therefore, is neither more nor less than the confusion of the experience of the Law. To follow the Law is to be confused by the Law. God is a God of confusion. The *Guide* is the *literal* place of the experience of confusion. Insofar as there is no experience that is not marked by the experience of the Law, it follows that the *Guide* is the singular, yet infinitely repeatable, thus universal, *site/cite* of experience. Indeed, the logic of the *Guide* figures experience as citation. To bring the *Guide* into conformity with Islam and the Qur'an, thus into conformity with what was perhaps Maimonides's adopted faith, experience is perhaps best thought as *re-citation* (recitation). One can only repeat the experience—the perplexity—of trying to understand the Law of experience. The way out of perplexity is the way into perplexity. Or, as Leo Strauss put it, "The *Guide* as a whole is not merely a key to a forest, but is itself a forest" (142).

The aporia of understanding extends to the organization of the *Guide* and, further, to language more generally. On the one hand, Maimonides explains that because of the restrictions placed on expounding the Law, readers should not expect from *The Guide* more than the barest outline of the subject. He provides only the subject or chapter headings, "and even these," he notes, "have not been methodically or systematically arranged in this work, but have been, on the contrary, scattered, and are interspersed with other topics" (Maimonides 3). On the other hand, in his "Directions for the Study of this Work," Maimonides states, "Nothing of what is mentioned is out of place" (8). At one and the same time, the topics of the *Guide* are *both* scattered and interspersed with other topics *and* in their proper place such that in order to derive the most benefit from the *Guide* the chapters should be read "in connected order" (8). The *Guide* appears, then, to be accidentally arranged and in its necessary order. Nothing is in its proper place at the same time that everything is in its proper place.[22] Maimonides claims this as a compositional strategy that enables him to write the *Guide* without trespassing the Law. He explains: "My object in adopting this arrangement is that the truths should be at one time apparent, and at another time concealed" (3). The model for such structural (dis)organization or (dis)placement is the Torah. Scholem quotes Rabbi Eleazar who, commenting on Job 28:13, explains, " 'No man knoweth its [the Torah's] order. . . . The various sections of the Torah were not given in their correct order. For if they had been given in their correct order, anyone who read them would be able to wake the dead and perform miracles. For this reason the correct order and arrangement of the Torah were hidden and are known only to the Holy One' " (1965, 37). The Law exposes itself as such, but does so by hiding itself within its own self-presentation, for were it to appear as it is as such or in itself, anyone who read it would have divine power. The rules governing the presentation of the Torah are the same as those that govern the pronunciation of God's name, and for the same reason, namely, that were one to say God's name, one would have the power of creation.

Given this understanding of the structuring principle of the Torah, it is easy to understand the Kabbalistic leap that argues, "the Torah is not only made up of the names of God but is as a whole the one great Name of God" (39). At the same time and in the same place, in the word par excellence, the name, the truth is both exposed and veiled. At stake is a certain revelation or apocalypse, a re-vealing that is a re-veiling.

Insofar as the *Guide* is dedicated to reading between literal and figural meanings, insofar as it is dedicated to the labor of a certain translation, Maimonides is especially attuned to the problem of meaning and the instability of intention. His attention to the language of the Law will have prepared the ground for this warning to his readers: "I adjure any reader of my book, in the name of the Most High, not to add any explanation even to a single word; nor to explain to another any portion of it except such passages as have been fully treated of by previous theological authorities; he must not teach others anything that he has learnt from my work alone, and that has not been hitherto discussed by any of our authorities. The reader must, moreover, beware of raising objections to any of my statements because it is very probable that he may understand my words to mean the exact opposite of what I intended to say" (Maimonides 8–9). This is the library of Babel. This is Borges's labyrinth.

Although Maimonides demands a submissive reading, nonetheless it remains possible that one will understand the opposite of what was meant. This is the law of language and, consequently, the law of the *Guide* and the law of the Law. Put another way, it is always possible that in *marking* out or delimiting one's intention, in determining one's meaning, one in fact ineluctably marks *out—erases—*the limits of one's intention. Perhaps no one knows this better than Maimonides, whose *Guide* must be read as a treatise on language and the impossible possibility of ever saying what one means. This means that the place of one's intention, of one's meaning, also marks the *site/cite* of the displacement of meaning and intention. In chapter twenty-nine, Maimonides writes:

> If we hear a person speaking whose language we do not understand, we undoubtedly know that he speaks, but do not know what his words mean; it may even happen that we hear some words which mean one thing in the tongue of the speaker, and exactly the reverse in our language, and taking the words in the sense which they have in our language, we imagine that the speaker employed them in that sense. Suppose, e.g., an Arab hears of a Hebrew the *abah*, he thinks that the Hebrew relates how a man despised and refused a certain thing, whilst the Hebrew in reality says

> that the man was pleased and satisfied with it. The very same thing happens to the ordinary reader of the Prophets; some of their words he does not understand at all . . . ; in other passages he finds the opposite or the reverse of what the prophet meant. . . . Besides, it must be borne in mind that every prophet has his own peculiar diction, which is, as it were, his language, and it is in that language that the prophecy addressed to him is communicated to those who understand it. (204)

Writing in exile from al-Andalus and perhaps from Judaism as well, Maimonides's choice of interlocutors, the Arab and the Jew, is perhaps not simply fortuitous. What is compelling about this scene, which Maimonides uses to introduce the chapter on the language of the prophets, is that it effectively represents the way in which one always speaks to oneself, the way in which one always addresses oneself as an other, perhaps as the most other. To oneself and with oneself, one always speaks a private language (*idios*), a language one cannot understand and to which one comes as an idiot (*idiōtēs*), an outsider, ignorant, disbelieving, a foreigner. There is always already this division between us, this decision between me and myself, I and the other I am. I am that I am an idiot to myself. That which makes possible the unity of the I that I am is that which divides me from myself: the common language, that which passes between us without having been grounded in any atemporal unity that would found and secure meaning. In other words, what passes between us, between Arab and Jew, say, and does so without meaning or understanding, is common. It is the *aleph* of language. The private language, the absolutely singular tongue (*glossa*) or *idios* that I speak to myself is always already in common with the other (that) I am and therefore with every other. It is necessarily exposed to the other; as such it is the condition of possibility of any privacy whatsoever. There is no privacy without exposure to the other. This means that language designates the ungrounded and infinite referral that is also the deferral of any possible absolution.

Language is always already translation. Hence, the origin—which includes here both the Law and the Word—is an effect of translation understood as the structure of infinite referral to an outside.[23] Translation destines—sends—language without address.

Where does this leave Maimonides? On the one hand, every language is singular, absolutely proper and private (*idios*), idiosyncratic, thus strictly incomprehensible, unintelligible. Every language is the *aleph*. On the other hand, in order to be language, every language must be communicable, thus universalizable, common, shared. Every language is the *aleph*. The private, the singular and unique must be marked from before the beginning—as the possibility of any beginning whatsoever—by the *trans*-, by the movement of translation, which is also and ineluctably the movement of *mis*translation. Consequently, the possibility of understanding is inscribed within the necessary possibility of *mis*understanding. The univocal is the effect of the sharing out—the errancy, the equivocation or the equivocality—of language that is translation.

The difficulty of this theory of language for Maimonides, however, is that at the instant in which it opens the place for or makes an interpretation and understanding of the Law possible, it necessarily temporalizes and displaces the possibility of such a unified place, indeed, of any possible unity. In being placed or *sited*, every word, every unity is originarily exposed to *citation*, to *re-citation*. There is no first, no last word, no word beyond translation, no singular, universal word. The word is always already *cited* and *recited*, *in other words*.

It would be a mistake, therefore, to think that the *Guide for the Perplexed* only attempts to decorporealize the reading of the Law. On the contrary, such decorporealization is necessary because the interpretation of the Law that leads to corporealism jeopardizes the fundamental Jewish belief in the unity of God. Maimonides writes: "Without incorporeality there is no unity, for a corporeal thing is in the first case not simple, but composed of matter and form which are two separate things by definition, and secondly, as it has extension it is also divisible" (50).[24] To speak of God, to say God's name, to describe God, places and displaces God, *sites and cites* God. To name God puts God in His place at the same time that it displaces Him inasmuch as naming repeats, cites and recites, God. God is not, then, wherever He is *named*, wherever He is *said* to be. God is *elsewhere*, which is perhaps *nowhere*.[25] Put simply, naming God and thereby locating Him in His proper place falls under the same general rule as does the possibility of reading Maimonides's *Guide*.

The problem of corporealism thus literally extends to the name of God. "It is well known," Maimonides writes, "that all the names of God occurring in Scripture are derived from His actions, except one, namely, the Tetragrammaton. . . . This name is applied exclusively to God, and is on that account called . . . , 'The *nomen proprium*'" (89). The proper name of God is the proper name par excellence, the name by which He calls himself and through which we are called to Him: "Go and gather the elders of Israel, . . . and they shall hearken to thy voice" (*Exodus* 15:18; qtd. in Maimonides 94). And what is God's proper name? God's name, according to Maimonides, "indicates nothing but His essence" (91); it is the name that "is peculiar to Me" (*Numbers* 6:27; qtd. in Maimonides 90). The name of God derives from no other being, nor is it "positively known, the word having no additional signification" (90). It is the "distinct and exclusive designation of the Divine Being" (89). In that the name of God has no positive meaning, it shares the same essence as *alif* or *aleph*: the vocative that, in itself having no meaning, makes possible all meaning. Maimonides concludes that insofar as "Every other name of God is a derivative, only the Tetragrammaton is a real *nomen proprium*, and must not be considered from any other point of view" (91).

Considering that the *nomen proprium* conveys "the meaning of 'absolute existence'" (90), it is difficult to see how any other point of view could be taken. Absolute existence implies that there is no point of view at all. God does not have a point of view, for a point of view constitutes a determined perspective and a perspective is always necessarily limited, thus differential. Within the absolute there is neither time nor space for difference. Moreover, the unpronounceability of the name of God is no doubt fortuitous, for the Tetragrammaton is the name that cannot be spoken. It can be spelled, but without the vowels necessary for its enunciation and temporalization. Yet, the name nonetheless operates as a sign. It designates itself. It signifies itself *qua* signified. According to Maimonides, the Tetragrammaton means nothing but itself. It has no other derivations, no other significations; it is ostensibly the only word that does not point to other words in order to point to itself, which explains its absolute propriety, its absolute sovereignty. It names the absolutization of signifier and signified. This is why God need only say this one word: all of creation, all existence—including God—is contained in it. At once, immediately. Unlike other words, which are necessarily mediated by other words, by the structure of referral and thus of deferral and *différance*, this word, the name of God, which is thus *the* proper name, is all there is, was, or ever will be.

As such, however, this proper name is properly incapable of designation, for designation requires an interval of difference between that which designates and what is designated. When Moses asks God how he is to call Him in order that others will know that he has been called by God, God answers, "I am that I am," *Ehyeh asher Ehyeh*. Maimonides notes:

> The principal point in this phrase is that the same word which denotes 'existence,' *is repeated* as an attribute. The word *asher*, 'that,' . . . is an incomplete noun that must be completed by another noun; it may be considered as the subject of the predicate which follows. The first noun which is to be described is *ehyeh*; the second, by which the first is to be described, is likewise *ehyeh*, the identical word, *as if* to show that the object which is to be described and the attribute by which it is described are in this case necessarily identical. This is, therefore, the expression of the idea that God exists, but not in the ordinary sense of the term; or, *in other words*, He is the existing Being which is the existing Being, *that is to say*, the Being whose existence is absolute. (94–5, emphases added)

God's enunciation of his name results in remarkable interpretive contortions on Maimonides's part, beginning with the grammatical explanation of the function of "that." The most salient tension, however, arises in God's repetition of his name as the singular, proper and absolute name. It is not enough to say—it will never be enough to say—*I am*: even God must elaborate *in other words*, even if those other words are the same words, "I am *that* I am." That is, even God must interpret, *flesh out*, his name. At stake is the citation or recitation within the absolute that makes impossible the absolute, the One, but makes possible His name. God differs from Himself in order to be Himself in the first place. God designates Himself and in so doing *re*marks his difference from Himself. The condition of possibility of the proper name necessarily divides that name against itself in the structure of referral without reference: "I am that I am that I am . . . ," *ad infinitum*; which is another way of saying,

"I am God." Yet, insofar as God's name, "I am that I am," is a sign, and thus temporal, God—or the one who says, "I am that I am"—is mortal. In *Speech and Phenomena* Derrida remarks, "The *I am*, being experienced only as an *I am present,* itself presupposes the relationship with presence in general, with being as presence. The appearing of the *I* to itself in the *I am* is thus originally a relation with its own possible disappearance. Therefore, *I am* originally means *I am mortal.* . . . We can go even further: as a linguistic statement 'I am he who am' is the admission of a mortal" (1973, 54).[26] Indeed, as Hägglund points out, the "I am that I am" is "a name among other names and the common denominator for all names is that they spell out the mortality of whatever is named" (2008, 145).

Of course, one can always act as if God's mortality made no difference. Perhaps it is enough to say that God is an idiot. On the one hand, he speaks a private language, a language absolutely peculiar (*idios*) to himself. On the other hand, he is ignorant (*idiōtēs*) of this language, hence, foreign, an outsider, to the language he speaks. As an idiot (foreigner, stranger, outsider, unbeliever) to Himself, not even God can be said to believe in Himself.

## *The ethics of immortality, or forgetting God*

Borges took up the problem of the name of God in nearly the same terms as Maimonides. In a note to his poem "The Thing I Am," he reveals that the poem's title comes from Shakespeare's *All's Well That Ends Well.* Paroles, whom Borges identifies as a "subaltern character" (1996, 3.203), remarks, "Captain I'll be no more/ But I will eat and drink and sleep as soft/ As captain shall. Simply the thing I am/ Shall make me live." Borges then interprets less Shakespeare than his own poetic appropriation of the phrase "the thing I am": "In the penultimate verse one hears the echo of the tremendous name I Am That I Am, which in the English version reads *I am that I am* (Buber understands that it deals with an evasion [*evasiva*] by a scheming God [*del Señor urdida*] not to reveal his true and secret name to Moses). Swift, on the eve of his death, wandered insanely and alone from room to room, repeating *I am that I am.* Like the Creator, the creature is what it is, although only adjectivally" (3.203). The proper name—the noun and thus the substantive par excellence—is an adjective, an attribute, an accident. Borges undermines the substantiality of any being, not only of God (Being) but also of creatures (beings). According to Borges, creatures reveal themselves in the same way God reveals himself, by re-veiling themselves, by re-veiling the secret, the name, they cannot *not* share, but which they cannot know.

In the Kabbalistic "La muerte y la brújula [Death and the Compass]," the esoteric detective Erik Lönnrot is led to his death by the possibility of the articulation of the name of God. Ignoring the police investigation of the murder of Marcelo Yarmolinsky, which hypothesized that chance played its part and that the real object of criminal interest was not the rabbi, but the sapphires of the Tetrarch of Galilee, Lönnrot undertook the study of Yarmolinsky's biography, that is, his life *as* his writings, which included "a monograph . . . on the Tetragrammaton; another on the divine nomenclature of the Pentateuch" (1.500/CF 148). In the study of Yarmolinsky's writings Lönnrot learns of "the virtues and terrors of the Tetragrammaton, the ineffable name of God" and of "the notion that God has a secret name, which . . . contains His ninth attribute, eternity—that is, immediate knowledge—of all things that shall be, are, and have been in the universe" (1.500–501/CF 149). Lönnrot's insistence on the symmetry of the murder—a rabbi's death requiring a rabbinical explanation—and his disdain of chance ("He had virtually solved the problem; the mere circumstances, the reality (names, arrests, faces, the paperwork of trial and imprisonment), held very little interest for him now" [1.504/CF 152–153]), ultimately leads him to his death. The ideality of his solution to the murder, the perfect square, the name of God, the refusal of circumstances, of chance, results in the perfect crime: the crime in which the solution plays its part, the crime that ultimately leads the detective, the one who solves the crime, to the place of his own death. Effectively, Lönnrot plots his own murder.

Just before Lönnrot encounters Red Scharlach, however, the narrator remarks, "He was stopped by an astonished, dizzying recollection" (1.505/CF 154). This vertiginous memory is the memory of his mortality, for what astonishes him can only be the fact, the evidence, of contingency, of the accident of existence, and thus of singularity and chance—which is to say, the accidents of time—in the ideal solution to the crime. In an ideal solution to an ideal crime, time would not matter. It would play no part, for the ideal is by definition eternal. Yet, after Scharlach's men have apprehended and disarmed Lönnrot, Scharlach's first words to Lönnrot are, "You are so kind. You have saved us a night and a day" (1.505/CF 154). In an ideal "world" saving time would be impossible: one would always and only ever arrive at the appointed hour. When Lönnrot asks, "Scharlach—*you* are looking for the secret name?" (1.505/CF 154), Scharlach's answer makes clear that Lönnrot's concern for perfection, for the ideal, hence the nonaleatory, is misguided and misleading: "No . . . I am looking for something more fleeting and more perishable than that—I am looking for Erik Lönnrot" (1.505/CF 154). Scharlach then unfolds the story into which Lönnrot will have been enfolded, a story that will have depended on chance and human affectivity, on a certain madness, in which the name of God figures as only one more overdetermined site in a finite, thus mortal, fatal plan, determined on both ends by chance and finitude.

At the conclusion to "La cábala [The Kabbalah]," after repeating Scholem's claim in *On the Kabbalah and Its Symbolism* that for the Kabbalists the Torah is the name of God and that the one capable of reading that name, of pronouncing it correctly, "would be able to create a world and would also be able to create a golem, a man," Borges writes, "This world, evidently, cannot be the work of an all-powerful and just God, rather it depends on us" (3.274–75). Lönnrot will have forgotten this until just before the instant of his death.

Borges understood quite well the Judeo-Islamic-Christian hypthothesis of the name of God. In "La cábala," for example, he repeats the theory that the name of God alone is sufficient for all creation. Inasmuch as "The Aleph" names the absolute present and presence of all that was, is, and will be, it too participates in the discourse on the name of God. We could multiply the examples. More interesting, in these texts and in others, is Borges's persistent attempt to delimit the potentiality, the promise, of such a name.

Published in the collection *El aleph* in 1949, "La Escritura del Dios" must be read as another of Borges's considerations of the impossible possibility of divine utterance. But from its title the story will have given itself away: it is not "The Voice of the God," but "The Writing of the God," which already introduces a certain divine—that is, mortal—limitation. "The Writing of the God" tells the story of Tzinacán, the magician of Qaholom, and of his captivity at the hands of Pedro de Alvarado. Tzinacán shares his cell with a jaguar, which he can see only at noon, "At the shadowless hour [*En la hora sin sombra*]" (1.596/CF 250), when his jailors open a trap at the ceiling's apex in order to lower pails with water and pieces of meat. Noon is the impossible and always already vanishing instant upon which time is calculated. Noon does not appear, it leaves no trace of itself, no shadow.

Like Funes, Tzinacán lies in the dark, waiting, "in the posture of [his] death, for the end the gods have destined for [him]" (1.596/CF 250). Tzinacán lies next to Funes and he, too, thinks about language. But first he thinks about apocalypse: "One night I sensed that a precise recollection was upon me; before the traveler sees the ocean, he feels a stirring in his blood. Hours later, I began to make out the memory; it was one of the legends [*tradiciones*] of the god. On the first day of creation, foreseeing that at the end of time many disasters and calamities would befall, the god had written a magical phrase [*una sentencia mágica*], capable of warding off those evils. He wrote it in such a way that it would pass down to the farthest generations, and remain untouched by fate [*y que no la tocara el azar*]. No one knows where he wrote it, or with what letters, but we do know that it endures, a secret text, and that one of the elect shall read it. I reflected that we were, as always, at the end of time, and that it would be my fate, as the last priest of the god, to be afforded the privilege of intuiting those words [*esa escritura*]" (1.596–597/CF 251). Here is the necessary consequence of the absolutism of God's Word: if, in the Word of God, there were no difference between being and saying, if there were no *différance*, no deferral of and referral to the other, then the Word of God would have to be not only absolutely creative, but also and necessarily absolutely destructive.

Borges takes seriously the problem of the infinite convertibility of the absolute. Thus, in "The Writing of the God," insofar as God creates the world, God must necessarily foresee the end of the world and *inscribe* that end in the origin. Creation is literally a death sentence, *una sentencia*. Borges's *sentencia mágica* is a "magical phrase," as Andrew Hurley translates it, but its magic inheres in the sentence's articulation of the absolution of divinity. On the one hand, the sentence of creation is the sentence of destruction, but, on the other hand, that God would have to inscribe this sentence, to write it, and leave it to a reader to decipher and thus leave it to the future, means that writing—and thus the absence of God from Himself at the origin—is always already inscribed *within* the decision. God can only decide—whether to create or to destroy or to do both in the same sentence—if at the moment or instant of decision, He is not present to Himself at the scene of writing. But insofar as God is absent from Himself, He is not God; He is not.

"The Writing of the God," which has been translated on at least one occasion as "The Handwriting of God,"[27] thus describes a double aporia. *On the one hand*, God cannot write a sentence at all if God is absolute presence, for writing inscribes absence, death, deferral: it is the mnemotechnical device that traces what is past exposing it to the future. Insofar as God is fully present to Himself, He cannot lose anything. Writing therefore would not only be unnecessary for God, it would be impossible. Up to a point, Tzinacán understands the limit of the divine sentence:

> Gradually, I came to be tormented less by the concrete enigma which occupied my mind than by the generic enigma of a message written by a god. What sort of sentence, I asked myself, would be constructed by an absolute mind? I reflected that even in the languages of humans there is no proposition that does not imply the entire universe; to say "the jaguar" is to say all the jaguars that engendered it, the deer and turtles it has devoured, the grass that fed the deer, the earth that was mother to the grass, the sky that gave light to the earth. I reflected that in the language of a god every word would speak that infinite concatenation of events, and not implicitly but explicitly, and not linearly but instantaneously. In time, the idea of a divine utterance came to strike me as puerile, or as blasphemous. A god, I reflected, must speak but a single word, and in that word there must be *absolute plenitude*. (1.597–598/CF 252)

The limit of Tzinacán's understanding of the limit of the divine sentence is the word: God would not need an entire sentence because every single word he speaks contains everything, *la plenitud*, which Hurley translates, not incorrectly, as "*absolute plenitude*" (CF 252), complete with italics, so that no one misunderstands *in translation* what is at stake in God's enunciation. This one word would be God's name, according to Maimonides's *Guide*. We already know, however, that if God were to say anything at all, he would not even need a word, a name, to say everything: a sound, an *aleph*, *alif*, would do. Furthermore, in this understanding of the impossibility of God's sentence, Tzinacán refers to God's speech. It is always a question of what God *says* and does not need *to say*. It is a question of speech, of the voice (*voz*) and the word (*voz*). There is no mention of writing; yet, God writes and thus distances Himself from Himself. He inscribes His own mortality at the very heart of His magical sentence of absolution.

*On the other hand*, as a finite being, Tzinacán ought not to be able to read God's writing, for to read such writing would necessitate that Tzinacán be infinite. This limit is indicated when Tzinacán thinks to himself, "perhaps I had seen Qaholom's inscription thousands of times, and only failed to understand it" (1.597/CF 251). The inability to understand God's script, the inscription of God, owes itself to finitude, mortality. Were a God able to write, mortals would not be able to read it. This would have to be the case, for, as "The Writing of the God" makes clear, "a man *is*, in the long run, his circumstances" (1.598/CF 253), while the Word of God, far from being limited to circumstances, would be total, absolute, immediate: "No word uttered by a god could be less than the universe, or briefer than the sum of time" (1.598/CF 252). Time is the condition of possibility of understanding anything at all, but time also makes impossible the understanding—which is to say, the conception and the comprehension—of either absolute plenitude or absolute presence.

How, then, to read God's sentence, to hear and understand God? How to say His name? The gap between God and the human is unbridgeable. It is a suspension that cannot be spanned. Between God (absolute universality, absolute immediacy) and the human (absolute circumstantiality, absolute affectivity) there is no traffic. Borges nevertheless puts them in touch and in so doing he finitizes God.

Like "The Aleph," "The Writing of the God" ends with a scene of forgetting: "But I know that I shall never speak those words, because I no longer remember Tzinacán" (1.599/CF 253). Inasmuch as he has "glimpsed [*entrevisto*] the burning designs of the universe" (1.599/CF

253), Tzinacán "can have no thought for a man, for a man's trivial joys or calamities, though he himself be that man" (1.599/CF 253–4). At the moment Tzinacán interviews (*entrevistar*) the universe, the universal and absolute, he forgets—can no longer think of—that which makes him human, his joys, calamities, those trivialities constitutive of the human *qua* circumstance or affectivity. To forget the circumstances of his humanity means Tzinacán has, as he had hoped and suspected, become a god, but Borges is clear: the cost of such immortality is mortality, which means finitude conditions God. Borges instances God's mortality first in the necessary possibility of repetition, specifically, the iterability necessary to the possible decipherment of the Word of God; and, second, through the possibility of forgetting Tzinacán. The condition of possibility of becoming "todopoderoso"—the effect of saying the Word of God—is the *forgetting* of the human, even the human that one happens to be.

In "The Writing of the God," Borges comes to this impossible, aporetic conclusion: God must forget in order to be God. God is all powerful, omniscient, omnipresent, *and* necessarily forgetful. Inasmuch as God cannot remember the human, God is not God, not eternal, but rather temporally determined, finite, in fine, human, mortal. In forgetting the human and becoming Himself, God necessarily forgets Himself. At the very moment God calls Himself to Himself, at the very moment He calls His own name, He knows neither whom to call nor what to say. God will never be able to answer His own call. This is God's idiocy.

The implications of this forgetting are severe. Immortality costs Tzinacán his humanity and with it any ethical relation to the other. Nowhere, however, are the ethics of immortality more clearly spelled out than in Borges's "El inmortal [The Immortal]," *El aleph*'s opening story: "Taught by centuries of living, the republic of immortal men had achieved a perfection of tolerance, almost of disdain. They knew that over an infinitely long span of time, all things happen to all men. As reward for his past and future virtues, every man merited every kindness—yet also every betrayal, as reward for his past and future iniquities. . . . Viewed in that way, all our acts are just, though also unimportant" (1.540–541/CF 191). The perfection of tolerance, which results from the immortals' "notion of the world as a system of exact compensations" (1.541/CF 191), manifests itself as indifference: "In the first place, it made them immune to pity [*invulnerable a la piedad*]" (1.541/CF 191). Such indifference, moreover, is not restricted to the plight of others. It also applies to oneself: "I have mentioned the ancient quarries that dotted the countryside on the far bank of the stream; a man fell into the deepest of those pits; he could not be hurt, could not die, and yet he burned with thirst; seventy years passed before he was thrown a rope. Nor was he much interested in his own fate. His body was a submissive domestic animal; all the charity it required each month was a few hours' sleep, a little water, and a scrap of meat" (1.541/CF 192). The possibility of justice depends on temporalization. Temporalization, however, necessarily entails affectivity. There is no decision, no justice, without affection. The idea of an immortal justice, then, is absurd, precisely because, as Augustine testifies in his *Confessions*, God is "incorruptible, immune from injury, and unchangeable [*et te incorruptibilem et inviolabilem et inconmutabilem*]." Further, he remarks, "Although I did not know why and how, it was clear to me and certain that what is corruptible is inferior to that which cannot be corrupted; what is immune from injury I unhesitatingly put above that which is not immune; what suffers no change is better than that which can change" (1991, 7.1/111). Indeed, Augustine confesses, "I affirmed and firmly held divine immunity from pollution and change and the complete immutability of our God" (7.4/113). Insofar as the immortal God is incorruptible, inviolable, and immutable, He is without affect. God is absolutely unaffected. As such, He can be neither touched nor moved by the other. God literally has time neither for another nor for Himself as other. As Augustine writes, His "incorruptible and immutable will" is "sufficient to itself and in itself" (13.5/275). Hence, God is "absolute simplicity" (13.4/275).

In "The Immortal," however, Borges conceives immortality as infinite mortality. Consequently, what is at stake is not immortality, but survival. Although the immortals "delivered themselves over" to the "complex pleasure" of thought" (1996, 1.541/CF 192), "From time to time, some extraordinary stimulus might bring us back to the physical world—for example, on that dawn, the ancient elemental pleasure of rain" (1.541/CF 192). The rarity of this event notwithstanding, insofar as it indicates the immortals are affected, it gives the lie to the claim that "all Immortals were capable of perfect quietude" (1.541/CF 192). "Perfect quietude" means absolute rest. But absolute rest necessarily implies that one is absolutely immune to whatever or whoever comes. That is, to rest in perfect peace is to lie safe and sound, indemnified against any possible disturbance or threat, but also against any possible chance or hope. Nothing would happen to the immortals.[28] It is not the case, as Floyd Merrill suggests in *Unthinking Thinking*, that "If time were to stop, and if we were immortal, perhaps we could know the cumulative One and the sequential Many. But surely we would suffer the fate of Borges's Immortal, for whom there is nothing new under the sun: unadulterated tedium" (151). Were time to stop, not only could we not know anything, we could not experience anything at all, not even tedium. Tedium, too, takes time. And inasmuch as it does, it is the experience of a mortal. In short, were the immortals capable of such perfect quietude, rain would not affect them, it would not *bring them back* to the physical world. There would be no such return. In order to be affected by the rain and thus *returned to the world*, one must be mortal.

The scene of mortal affect that Borges describes does more than simply indicate the possibility of an immortal mortality or the possibility of survival. It recalls memory, which is conceivable only as the traces of what is no longer that are left for the future that destroys them. In recalling memory, the rain recalls the immortal to himself. The issue is the possibility of auto-affection and the necessary return to oneself from the other.

> Argos, his eyes fixed on the empyrean, was moaning; streams of water rolled down his face—not just rain, but also (I later learned) tears. *Argos*, I cried, *Argos!*
>
> Then, with gentle wonder, as though discovering something lost and forgotten for many years [*como si descubriera una cosa perdida y olvidada hace mucho tiempo*], Argos stammered out these words: *Argos, Ulysses' dog*. And then, without looking at me, *This dog lying on the dungheap*.
>
> . . . I asked Argos how much of the *Odyssey* he knew. He found using Greek difficult; I had to repeat the question.
>
> Very little, he replied. Less than the meagerest rhapsode. It has been eleven hundred years since I last wrote it [*que la inventé*]. (1.539–540/CF 190)

To write the *Odyssey* for the first time in eleven hundred years is to *invent* it, to discover it. It is also to remember it. But the memory of the immortal is neither immortal nor simply the immortal's. It comes from beyond the immortal and thus affects him. The immortal's memory comes from rain: it touches the immortal and moves him to tears. Importantly, the narrator cannot tell the difference between raindrops and tears. He cannot tell the difference between what comes from the outside and what comes from the inside; he cannot tell the difference between what is properly the immortal's and what is not. The limit of the proper or the prosthesis of memory is no less legible in the scene of immortal writing: "He was lying in the sand, clumsily drawing and rubbing out a row of symbols that resembled those letters in dreams that one is just on the verge of understanding when they merge and blur. At first I thought it was some sort of barbaric writing; then I realized that it was absurd to imagine that men who had never learned to speak should have invented writing [*que hombres que no llegaron a la palabra lleguen a la escritura*]. Nor did any one of the shapes resemble any other—a fact that ruled out (or made quite remote) the possibility that they were symbols. The man would draw them [*las trazaba*], look at them, and correct them. Then suddenly, as though his game irritated him, he would rub them out with his palm and forearm" (1.538/CF 189).

The iteration of memory, of writing, is the singularity of remembering, its invention. The immortal is close to Funes, close to Tzinacán, but also close to Pierre Menard in his writing, which is always a rewriting, remembering, and erasure of itself, of the traces of its elaboration. Writing is the technical device, the prosthetic, that singularizes even as it mechanizes memory and identity, the memory of identity and the identity of memory. Writing is not a matter of the word. It is a tracing, a marking; it is an erasure that leaves a trace, what Derrida calls the "arche-phenomenon of 'memory' " (1974, 70). The mechanism of memory comes from the outside, automatically, and thus finitizes immortality. The inscription of memory—and therefore of identity—is erasable, fungible. That the immortal survives—lives on—is possible only insofar as there is a memory that is not simply his. And there is no memory that is not a singular act, a promise, of writing, which is also a promise of oblivion.

# Afterword

## The Secret of Culture

> For the secret of secrecy about which we shall speak does not consist in hiding *something*, in not revealing the truth, but in respecting the absolute singularity, the infinite separation of what binds me or exposes me to the unique, to one as to the other, to *the One as to the Other*.
>
> —Jacques Derrida, "Literature in Secret"

Borges's elaboration of the name of God—across the religions of the book, Christianity, Islam, Judaism—spells out the logic of idiocy. In order to call myself, in order to name my most proper self, I must call myself in the name of the other, I must call myself from the other and thus call myself other. My singularity, the language that I speak to myself, that which is most properly my own, is necessarily foreign to me. It comes to me from the other. That which is most intimate to and in me exposes me to the outside, to the other. We are all idiots, *idiōtēs*: cut off, removed, circumcised, and circumscribed; in secret, secreted in ourselves, and secreted from ourselves; separated, held in reserve, segregated from the other, from ourselves. And this is the necessary condition of all language, of all community and communication. There is no language that does not pass between at least two; that is not structurally open to every other.[1] That which passes between me and myself passes outside of me, exposing me to every other. A private, singular language, an idiolect, is always open to every other. Such exposition is the impossible condition of privacy and, therefore, of the secret.

*On the one hand,* every language is singular, absolutely proper and private (*idios*), idiosyncratic, thus absolutely secret and untranslatable. This means that we are segregated from each other and from ourselves. As Derrida puts it, "Others are secret because they are other. I am secret, I am in secret, like any other. A singularity is of its nature in secret" (2005a, 162).[2] *On the other hand,* every language must be communicable, hence universalizable, common; consequently every language must be repeatable and translatable. *On the one hand,* there is the unconditional and absolute demand for translation. *On the other hand,* translation is necessarily impossible. This is the aporia of language: that the private, the singular and unique, must be marked, from before the beginning, by the *trans-*, by the movement of translation. Effectively, then, as Borges claims in "Averroës' Search," we are always working "from a translation of a translation" (1.582/CF 236). If the *trans-* is constitutive of the possibility of language, if there is no language without the movement of the *trans-* and thus of translation, it follows that it must be impossible to determine the original moment or first instance of translation. This must be so because, as the movement of whatever *happens,* as the possibility that something *passes,* translation cannot be detained such that it might appear as such or in itself. The appearing of translation is the constitutive displacement of translation. Translation as such or in itself does not appear; it never takes place. The language we speak is the *effect* of translation, but it is *not* translation.

Translation is the movement that makes possible the measure of the original, a movement that, as Derrida writes of the trace, "destroys its name" (1974, 80). As the "always mobile" figure "of the extreme perimeter" (Oyarzún 2009, 259) that encloses language, that marks or inscribes its limit, translation opens language simultaneously to the possibility of communication and to equivocation. Translation thus figures and disfigures language at the same time. In the same gesture it *both* makes possible *and* impossible communication and community (and thus identity). Consequently, the possibility of understanding the other and ourselves—the other ourselves—is inscribed in the possibility of misunderstanding the other (and) ourselves.

In the fifth of the *Cartesian Meditations*, Husserl explained that the other is always absolutely other: "in the case of experiencing a man: the other is himself there before us 'in person.' . . . [T]his being there in person does not keep us from admitting forthwith that, properly speaking, neither the other Ego himself, nor his subjective processes or his appearances themselves, nor anything else belonging to his own essence, becomes given in our experience originally. If it were, if what belongs to the other's own essence were directly accessible, it would be merely a moment of my own essence, and ultimately he himself and I myself would be the same" (108–9). Husserl thus affirms the transcendental necessity of the secret or of infinite separation for the possibility of phenomenology, because without a minimal difference—which, thought transcendentally, would be infinite and absolute—between self and other, a difference that ineluctably contaminates the self itself, there would be neither the necessity nor the possibility of phenomenology. In "Violence and Metaphysics," Derrida emphasizes that "Husserl's most central affirmation concerns the irreducibly mediate nature of the intentionality aiming at the other as other" (1978, 123). As Husserl recognized, such irreducible mediation is absolutely necessary, for if it were otherwise, the other that we experience would not be different from us. We would be the same. Furthermore, the consciousness of self, the experience of oneself, of the self as such would be impossible without the mediation that makes possible the awareness of oneself *as* oneself, that is, *as* the other. As a consequence of the irreducible "mediacy of intentionality" (Husserl 109), Derrida argues, "the other as transcendental other . . . can never be given to me in an original way and in person, but only through analogical appresentation" (1978, 124). Analogical appresentation does not signal an assimilative reduction of the other to the same. On the contrary, Derrida remarks that it "confirms and respects separation, the unsurpassable necessity of . . . mediation" (124). In spite of such respect and the confirmation of mediation, analogical appresentation is ambiguous because it makes possible the identification of the other *as* other. Husserlian analogical appresentation is legible in the "as," but it is always necessary to remember that the possibility of recognizing the other *as* other is its impossibility: the other is given to us only *as* the other and therefore it is *not* given to us; on the contrary, it maintains itself absolutely and infinitely segregated. Thus, the "as" obscures as much as it indicates. In the act of indicating it, the "as" obscures what Oyarzún calls the *lapsus*: "In order to dissimulate the *lapsus*, we say—we put—'as' " (2009, 258). The "as" instances the minimal structure of understanding, of language itself. It is the gesture of translation, of comparison, of analogy. It is the minimal condition of (the impossibility of) identity. The "as" inscribes and erases, at the same time, singularity, idiocy.

We exist separated, isolated, in secret, hidden *in* ourselves and hidden *from* ourselves, put on reserve from the other and from ourselves. What Husserl affirms and Derrida emphasizes is the logic of idiocy, the logic of a properness that is so proper, so intimately one's own, so secret, that it is foreign to and outside oneself. The logic of idiocy—which is the logic of singularity and of translation—names the logic of the secret.

Although it is thematized throughout the Borgesian archive, there is perhaps no text that more succinctly and more precisely exposes the logic of the secret than "El etnógrafo [The Ethnographer]," which presents a pointed critique of anthropology's investment in the other and of the representationally determined logic of the secret that organizes anthropological desire. "The Ethnographer" concerns a student whom the narrator thinks may be named Fred Murdock, about whom there is "nothing singular . . . not even that feigned singularity that is proper to the young" (2.367/CF 334). Being of an age at which he did not yet know who he was, he was ready to submit to whatever was proposed to him. In the university they advised him to study indigenous languages. "Certain esoteric rites still survived in certain tribes out West; one of his professors . . . suggested the he go live on a reservation, observe the rites, and discover the secret that the shamans revealed to the initiate [*el secreto que los brujos revelan al iniciado*]. When he came back, he would have his dissertation, and the university authorities would see that it was published" (2.367/CF 334). Murdock accepts. From the beginning he recognizes the difficulties that face him: "he would have to convince the red men to accept him as one of their own" (2.367/CF 334). Ultimately, he achieves this and, after being told to remember his dreams and after confiding them to the *sacerdote*, "the teacher at last revealed to him the tribe's secret doctrine [*revelarle su doctrina secreta*]" (2.367/CF 335). "One morning, without saying a word to anyone, Murdock left" (2.367/CF

335). Anthropology goes like that. After acquiring what they value, what they seek or desire, anthropologists go home.

What remains of the story is a conversation between Murdock and his advisor. Murdock tells him that he has learned the secret and that he has decided—resolved, *resuelto*—not to reveal it. The professor wants to know if he has sworn an oath to keep the secret. Murdock answers no, but he admits, "I learned something out there that I can't express" (2.367/CF 335). And yet the secret is not ineffable.[3] The professor asks if the problem is one of language, that perhaps English is insufficient. Murdock responds: "That's not it, sir. Now that I possess the secret, I could tell it in a hundred different and even contradictory ways" (2.367/CF 335). He adds: "And anyway, the secret is not as important as the paths that led me to it. Each person has to walk those paths himself" (2.367/CF 335). Yet, despite the need to walk those paths, Murdock is not compelled to return to live among the Indians. This is so, he says, because "What the men of the prairie taught me is good anywhere and for any circumstances" (2.367/CF 335). "The Ethnographer" concludes with the following brief biographical sketch: "Fred married, divorced, and is now one of the librarians at Yale" (2.367/CF 335).

"The Ethnographer" has largely avoided critical attention. Noting this oversight, Mabel Moraña has suggested that it would not be risking too much to say that "The Ethnographer" "is a minor text within the corpus of Borges's stories [*la cuentistica borgeana*]" (266). That the text does not figure prominently in the scholarly and critical work dedicated to Borges should not be that surprising. The bulk of the criticism written on Borges, after all, concerns a relatively small number of texts. *Kant's Dog* is no exception.[4] In *The Exhaustion of Difference*, Alberto Moreiras takes up "The Ethnographer" over the course of a few pages (226–229), but the three most extensive engagements with the story are Moraña's, Idelber Avelar's, and Kristen Mahlke's.[5]

Both Moraña and Avelar, albeit to different ends, misunderstand the secret as a content to be *either* shared *or* reserved, *both* shared *and* reserved. In this they in fact remain circumscribed by anthropological desire. For example, Moraña writes, "the story does not deny the possibility of intercultural knowledge. But it aborts, through recourse to the secret, its decipherment and dissemination" and she concludes, "the most important thing is the existence and announcement of the secret—that 'differential remainder' ['*resto diferencial*'] between the I and the others—not its revelation" (Moraña 267). In Moraña's account, this "differential remainder" must be thought on the basis of a reserved content. Writing of contemporary anthropological practice, she notes that anthropology agrees on "the partial and provisional character of all knowledge, in which is always conserved an obscure zone—a 'differential remainder'—that assures the power of the other precisely through the ellipses and reticence of her communications. Accordingly, the fragmentation of the message maintains discrete spaces of uncolonized meaning, chances of autonomy, intimacy or purity [*espacios discretos, de sentido no colonizado, resquicios de autonomía, intimidad o pureza*]" (273). On the one hand, Moraña testifies that the secret can be shared inasmuch as she acknowledges that intercultural knowledge is possible, which means we can pass our secrets across the borders or limits of cultures; thus, the secret both exists and can be announced. On the other hand, despite its existence and its announcement, the secret *ought not* be deciphered or disseminated; it *ought not* be revealed. Effectively, Moraña argues along the following lines: we know there is a difference between us, but this difference does not keep us from understanding one another. Indeed, perhaps precisely because this "differential remainder" or remnant does not impede our communication and understanding, we ought to resist interpreting it or sharing it or even, finally, revealing it—and this in order to assure the salvation of the other. In other words, the *resto diferencial* makes a *meaningful* difference between us: it marks the asymmetry of intercultural relations.[6]

Avelar highlights the same asymmetry and remarks, "it seems fairly obvious that the story is talking about ethics" (56). Nevertheless, he adds, "the fascination provoked by the story derives from its leaving unanswered the question that could make the text reducible to an ethical imperative" (55). That question is the following: "Did Murdock return because he could now live, *in the United States*, according to the principles learned among the indigenous (thus carrying and caring for the seeds of their teaching), or did he choose the detached-from-experience job of librarian at an elite university as the sign of a recoil, a refusal that ultimately canceled out the very lessons learned on the journey?" (55–56).

Two observations are worth noting about Avelar's question. *First,* Avelar assumes that the secret provides "principles" for living. It makes some sense to assume this, since Murdock also suggests this is the case. The problem is that such a principle, in order to be useful *in any place and any circumstance*, would have to be universal. Such a principle would have to be purely formal, empty of any positive content, which means it could not be cultural in the strict sense and thus Murdock could have "learned" it anywhere and anytime. Rather, he could not have "learned" it at all, since a universal ethical imperative must be *a priori*, otherwise, it could have no claim to universality.

*Second,* Avelar makes an unnecessary assumption about the experience of a librarian, whether at an elite university or not, as if nothing happens in the library. Given that for Borges the library is another name for the universe, and as "The Library of Babel" demonstrates, nothing happens anywhere else. In other words, although Avelar sees in these two possibilities the aporia of undecidability, there is in fact nothing to decide between them. If what Murdock learned amounts to a universal principle, it must of necessity be just as applicable in the library as anywhere else. Murdock himself claims nothing less.

On the one hand, then, the secret Murdock learns is *not* what Moraña calls the *resto diferencial* in that the secret makes no *cultural* difference. On the other hand, if the secret has the content suggested by Avelar's two ostensibly opposed possibilities, then far from signaling cultural asymmetry, the secret, *qua* transcendental principle, operates as the cultural leveler. Further, the rift Avelar stresses between experience and narrative—which is to say, between the value of the path Murdock took to the secret and the writing of the dissertation—is also untenable. One must only consider the quality of nostalgia Murdock feels to know that the condition of possibility of experience is mediation, hence, narrative: "In the city, he felt nostalgic for those first evenings on the prairie when, long ago, he had felt nostalgic for the city" (2.367/CF 335). Murdock feels nothing immediately: the nostalgia he experiences upon return from the *pradera* is the nostalgia of the nostalgia of the city. In short, his experience of the city upon his return is mediated through and as his nostalgia for the city, a nostalgia he felt in the *pradera*. There is no direct experience of the present object: experience is always the experience of what is not. Borges's rendering of Murdock's experience in terms of a doubly displaced nostalgia organizes experience according to the logic of mourning. Experience is only ever the nostalgia—the memory—of the nostalgia of what will never have been present as such or in itself. But the structure of mourning—the structure of experience—does not leave the subject in place to mourn the loss of what is not present, *here and now*, as if the subject were not itself marked and ruined by this very structure. The poem "Nostalgia del presente [Nostalgia for the Present]," which takes place in the interval of the repeated phrase, "En aquel preciso momento [At that very instant]" (3.315/SP 447), underscores that for Borges the present is divided from itself such that experience—even the experience of the present—always comes too late. Experience is mourning. The subject is constituted in and as this belatedness. There is no subject before mourning. The subject and the world the subject inhabits, its horizon, become possible only insofar as there is mourning, which is not.[7] As a consequence, it would be a mistake to follow Avelar in his reading of Murdock's decision to cease taking notes while living amongst the Indians as a decision in favor of direct experience. There will never have been such experience.

"The Ethnographer"'s importance lies precisely in what Moraña and Avelar note but nonetheless overlook: namely, Murdock's conflicting statements concerning the secret. *First*, Murdock claims that he has learned something that he cannot say ("aprendí algo que no puedo decir"). *Second*, he confesses that "Now that I possess the secret, I could tell it in a hundred different and even contradictory ways" (2.367/CF 335). How are these statements to be read? On the one hand, Murdock cannot tell the secret. He cannot say it. Moreover he has *resolved* not to say it. On the other hand, inasmuch as he could enunciate the secret in one hundred different ways and even contradictorily, it is easy to see that he cannot *not* tell the secret. Consequently and contradictorily, Murdock cannot tell the secret and he cannot *not* tell it. And not only Murdock, but the Indians as well. In order to keep the secret—in order to maintain cultural integrity, cultural identity *and* difference—the Indians tell it to Murdock, who will have been *initiated* into their community, who will have become one of them. Subsequently, Murdock *resolves* to keep it. According to Moraña, it is finally an ethical imperative that *we* keep the other's secrets. But in this primal scene of anthropology, to whom does the secret belong? To anthropology (to *us*) or to the Indians (to *them*)? Are *we* among *us* or among *them*?

The secret *belongs* to no one. A secret does not belong, which is why a secret can be told, shared, *and* kept. It is why a secret can be appropriated and deployed against others. If Murdock can pronounce the secret in one hundred different and contradictory ways, it stands to reason that the Indians can as well. Thus the Indians are neither more nor less capable of keeping or telling the secret than is Murdock. But if it is impossible *not* to tell the secret in keeping it and if in telling the secret we nonetheless keep it, then what is the secret and what does the secret do?

It is important to stress what Borges in fact only implies: It is impossible *not* to repeat—to tell (for telling a secret always repeats the secret)—the secret. No matter what Murdock or, for that matter, the *sacerdote* who tells him the secret decides, one affirms the secret by telling it and by keeping it. This means that one never simply decides to tell or keep the secret. The decision is not simply one's own. Consequently, the necessary repetition of the secret is not subjectively determined. It is an effect neither of the will nor of desire. Murdock's resolve not to tell the secret cannot keep him from doing so. The secret is, strictly speaking, *foreign* to the one who keeps and tells it. It is technical through and through. It is a prosthesis *internal* to the subject insofar as the subject cannot simply decide to set the secret aside. In other words, the secret is so secret, it is so properly the subject's own, that the subject cannot know it (and therefore can never know if the secret has been told or not); the secret is so far inside the subject, it is so *absolutely* secret, that it is *outside* the subject, beyond the subject. No subject ever confesses his or her *own* secret. What one confesses is always of another; my confession comes from the other. The secret thus turns the subject inside out. The secret constitutes the subject from *beyond* the subject, from *beyond* the subject *inside* the subject. The secret *decides* the subject, *exposes* the subject to an inside that is nonetheless *foreign* to and thus *outside* the subject. In short, the secret is both necessary and accidental to the subject and to culture. There is no culture without a secret. The secret is necessary to culture. But nor is there any culture that cannot *not* tell the secret regardless of its resolve to keep the secret, indeed, precisely as its resolve to keep the secret.

"The Ethnographer" tells and keeps an absolute and universal secret that "works" (*vale*) in every circumstance and every place. For this to be so, the secret must be absolutely translatable. Consequently, it must be articulated—beyond any possible intention or resolution—in every singular enunciation. The secret must be irreducibly singular. Accordingly, in every singular instance, the secret promises the other and promises to the other.

What is the first thing you say when you have a secret? You ask *yourself* and then you ask your *friend*, "can you keep a secret?" And you promise yourself and the other that you can, which means you promise yourself and the other to the future. The secret exposes us to the future. In order to keep the secret, you tell it. You share it. This is the law of the secret. As such, the secret must be affirmed. It is impossible *not* to keep and to tell the secret. Without the secret as the law of the absolute exposure to the other, there is no culture. Without the secret there is no chance to determine that which ought *not* to be shared or that which identifies us *against* them. At the same time, however, the secret also makes it possible for cultural practices to be imitated, repeated across cultural borders, thus affording the chance and the threat of Murdock's initiation into Indian culture. The chance of Murdock's initiation into Indian culture is precisely the possibility of saving Indian culture by transmitting it. It is the chance of inheritance and legacy; the chance that this particular culture will pass from one to the other, that it will be passed on. The threat of his initiation is precisely the possibility of losing Indian culture by giving it away. In passing on Indian culture, it is always possible that it will pass away.

Because the secret exposes us—promises us—to the other, culture is impossible. There is only the promise of culture. The logic of the secret contaminates culture as the possibility of culture. It follows that it is impossible to save this or that culture, to keep it unscathed, to protect or preserve it. It is always possible—hence necessary—to lose cultures. Indeed, whether we archive the secrets of the other, saving them *and* telling them by opening them to the other, to anthropology, for instance, which has always been after the other's secrets[8]; or, alternatively, whether we decide not to tell their secrets, thereby deciding to leave the other alone, that is, to put the other on the reservation in an ostensibly sealed, closed, archive, thus saving the other from contact with us; regardless, the decision to *save* other cultures—*by whatever method*—ineluctably *destroys* them.

Because the secret names the unconditional exposure to the singular other, we tell and keep secrets *both* from each other *and* from ourselves. We protect ourselves and others from ourselves and others. And with good reason: one of Murdock's elders was killed in the border antagonisms between the Indians and the dominant culture. Culture wars fought over the secret at the edges of the reservation. It is at this border, at the impossible limit of telling and keeping the secret of and from the other, of and from oneself, and of and from oneself as the other oneself, that culture happens *in* and *as* the secret, that culture both necessarily secrets itself (segregates and separates itself) and ineluctably secretes itself (shares and empties itself).

The logic of the secret—that it is both necessary and accidental—follows from the logic of translation (thus from the logic of impossibility) that *Kant's Dog* has traced both in Borges and in the text of philosophy more generally. The secret is necessary because without it there is no difference, no singularity; there is neither subject nor culture. But the secret is also accidental in that it happens—if it ever does—arbitrarily, without regard to subjective or objective determination. Both the subject and culture are effects of the secret, which means they are only ever promised. It is as if there were a subject, as if there were culture, as if there were the decision to tell or to keep the secret. It is only as if there were a secret.

The secret names the relation between the "as" (philosophy, necessity) and the "if" (literature, accidentality). It names the relation between the present of the "as" (of sense and the understanding, of truth) and the future of the "if" (of the imagination, of error) that comes, *here and now*, to destroy it. The "as if" names the act—the temporalization and thus the promise—of translation. And this means that the "as if" destroys—even as it makes possible their institution—both literature and philosophy. As if there were literature, as if there were philosophy. As if there were Borges.

# Notes

## *Introduction: Philosophy, Literature, and the Accidents of Translation*

1. See Gingerich for a discussion of Borges's own dismissal of his investment in philosophy.

2. Merrell quotes Borges from his preface to Ronald Christ's *The Narrow Act* (1969). It should be noted that Merrell goes on to explore in detail Borges's relation to mathematics, post-Einsteinian physics, and language philosophy. Ivan Almeida explains what philosophy is for Borges: "What Borges and Schopenhauer understand by philosophy is a conceptual or figuruative work of inflection calculated from human perplexities until they have found in it their precise intonation [*Lo que Borges y Schopenhauer entienden por filosofía es un trabajo conceptual o figurativa, de impostación calculada de las perplejidades humanas hasta que hayan encontrado en el su entonación justa*]" (Almeida 109). On this account, philosophy is a question of (conceptual or figurative) *tone*. It is a question of *accent*, then.

3. Almeida writes: "appreciation of a philosophical doctrine is, for Borges, a function of the virtualities of fiction that this doctrine offers him [*la apreciación de una doctrina filosófica es, para Borges, una función de las virtualidades de ficción que ésta le ofrece*]"; see Almeida 113.

4. Balderston quotes from Cordua (1988), 637. A longer, version of Cordua's 1988 essay appears under the title "La imaginería metafísica de Borges" in Cordua (1997), 115–33.

5. The work/text distinction corresponds to the tenor/vehicle distinction. The "text" is the material medium—"a group of entities used as signs" (Gracia 87)—or the vehicle that conveys meaning; the "work" is a specific meaning, thus tenor, of the text. There is no text without meaning, but there are cases in which the meaning does not meet criteria sufficient to determine it as a work. According to Gracia, "the cat is on the mat" is

meaningful, but it is not a work; *Don Quixote*, however, "is both a text and a work" (87).

6. Korsmeyer's remark that Kant's "numbingly clumsy writing" warrants "accolades . . . for advancing German as a philosophical language" (Korsmeyer 4) signals her contention that Kant made possible the philosophical determination of German as a universal language, as the language of philosophical expression. But, as we've already seen, if Kant's philosophical prose affects German, it must be conceded that philosophy has a relation to the idiom in which it is conceived. That is, the ideas of philosophy are bound to the language in which they are expressed.

7. Borges's "Autobiography" was first published in *The New Yorker* in collaboration with Norman Thomas di Giovanni. Borges dictated his "life" in English. The Spanish is a translation. Here and throughout, I refer to and translate from the translation. On Borges's relation to German and to German philosophy, see Chapter 3, "Kant's Dog."

8. Heidegger writes: "We can recognize that all translations must be an interpreting. Yet at the same time, the reverse is also true: every interpretation . . . is a translating. In that case, translating does not only move between two different languages, but there is a translating within one and the same language" (1996b, 62).

9. Here and throughout, the Greek text of Aristotle is taken from the Loeb Classical Library editions of Aristotle.

10. Brogan writes: "*Kata sumbebēkos* is the opposite of and that which is not *kath'hauto*. . . . *To sumbebēkos* is that which belongs to and is present along with that which shows itself as such. The accidental is that which is present 'under' an *archē*. The 'accidental' is governed by an *archē* that is outside itself. That which is the same can never simply belong together with itself in the way of *sumbebēkos*. Its unity—the being-together of itself—is not of the sort that one could say it just happens to be together. The law of non-contradiction says that it is impossible for a being that has *phusis* as its way of being to appear in the way 'properties' come and go in beings. It is possible for accidents not to be present. Therefore they are not necessary. That which is not necessary cannot be of itself. . . . That which shows itself as itself has the kind of presencing Aristotle calls *ousia*. This enduring presencing of the same is a unity that excludes that kind of appearing that can never hold itself in its being" (74–75).

11. On chance and necessity in Borges, see Merrell 1998 and Cámpora 2011. It is important to bear in mind that Merrell's understanding of "chance" (as probability, predictability, over the time of a negative infin-

ity, which becomes necessity when viewed from the totality of a positive infinity) is not "accidentality," which is unpredictable. Cámpora reads an implicit dialogue between Borges and Aristotle, one that plays itself out between Aristotle's *Poetics* and Borges's "El impostor inverosímil Tom Castro." Augusto Ponzio declares suggestively that "The *other* is the starting point of literary writing" (173).

12. This will be pursued in more detail in Chapter 4, "Decisions of Hospitality."

13. In *Tercer espacio: Literatura y duelo en América Latina*, after citing a passage from Xosé Luis Méndez Ferrín's "Liño" in the context of a discussion of the "third language/tongue as alienating space [*tercera lengua como espacio alienatorio*]," Alberto Moreiras concludes, "Hence, its impossibility of translating and its absolute need for translation [*De ahí su imposibilidad de traducir y su necesidad absoluta de traducción*]" (36–7). Moreiras's determination of the absolute need for and the impossibility of translation is correct, but in *Tercer espacio* he does not explain why a precise understanding of temporalization or *spacing* necessarily results in the aporetic logic of translation and, further, how the logic of translation necessarily troubles both empiricist and transcendental philosophies (something *Kant's Dog* does in its first three chapters). On the necessity of translation and the necessary kinship and diversification of languages, see Claro 2009a, *passim*, but perhaps especially 129–30.

14. See Balderston 1993, 1–17, but perhaps especially 1–4, where he cites himself as a proponent of the "irrealist" theory of Borges's *ficciones*. As Gingerich points out, Ana María Barrenechea is credited with first proposing this reading of Borges. Balderston acknowledges that the title of her book, *La expresión de la irrealidad en la obra de Jorge Luis Borges* (1957) signals "the hallmark of Borges criticism" (1).

15. Nevertheless, one would have to acknowledge that "graphology" as a science of the singular is impossible for the reasons Derrida gives; see Derrida 1974, 74–93.

16. The logic here described, which is the logic of the trace or what Martin Hägglund calls the "trace structure of time" (2008, *passim*), will be further explicated in Chapter 1, "Time: For Borges."

17. Without engaging in this critique here, it seems to me that the idea of a total library, one without any relation to an outside, would parallel Giorgio Agamben's understanding of a language that presupposes only itself and thus absolves itself of the relation to the other. See Agamben 1999, 27–47.

## *Chapter 1: Time: For Borges*

1. William Egginton also refers to this anecdote at the outset of a discussion of time in Borges, Derrida, and Heidegger; see Egginton 107.

2. Martin Hägglund notes that "the difference of time could not even be marked without a synthesis that relates the past to the future and thus posits an identity over time" (2008, 17).

3. It should be pointed out, however, that he does so in order to argue, no doubt ironically, that there is no time.

4. This double relation of the "now" to time is at the heart of Derrida's reading of Aristotle's *Physics* IV. Derrida's reading of the "now," which follows Aristotle's analogy of the point and the line, but also his attempt to think the "now" arithmetically—as numbered number rather than as numbering number—concludes in the following way: "The now, therefore is 1) a constitutive part of time and a number foreign to time; 2) a constitutive part of time and an accidental part of time. It can be considered *as such* or *as such*" (1982, 61/71).

5. The Wicksteed and Cornford translation reads: "For nothing which is finite and divisible is bounded by a single limit" (Aristotle 1957, 218a23/375).

6. There is perhaps no more poignant example and explanation of this than Derrida's observation in his last interview: "The trace I leave signifies to me at once my death, either to come or already come upon me, and the hope that this trace survives me. This is not a striving for immortality; it's something structural. I leave a piece of paper behind, I go away, I die: it is impossible to escape this structure, it is the unchanging form of my life. Each time I let something go, each time some trace leaves me, 'proceeds' from me, unable to be reappropriated, I live my death in writing. It's the ultimate test: one expropriates oneself without knowing exactly who is being entrusted with what is left behind. Who is going to inherit, and how? Will there even be any heirs?" This is the structure of the promise, which necessarily promises the future as both chance and threat. See Derrida 2007b, 32–33.

7. See also Hägglund 2009, where he further develops the logic of survival in relation to the structure of desire.

8. See also Derrida 1974, where he writes, "Without a retention within the minimal unit of temporal experience, without a trace retaining the other as other in the same, no difference would do its work and no meaning would appear" (62); see also 66–67.

9. In a recent essay responding to John Caputo, Hägglund explains that temporal succession must not be thought in terms of the chronological movement from past to present to future, but rather as the deferral that characterizes temporalization in general. See Hägglund 2011.

10. In *Sense and Sensibility*, Aristotle asks whether or not there can be an imperceptible time. His answer is no: it is not "conceivable that any portion of time should be imperceptible, or that any should be unnoticeable; the truth being that it is possible to perceive every instant of time" (1984, 448a25–26/1.711). The reason why an imperceptible time must be impossible has less to do with what we sense than with the possibility of sense in general and in particular with the sense of our existence: "For if it is impossible that a person should, while perceiving himself or anything else in a continuous time, be at any instant unaware of his own existence, and if there is in the time-continuum a time so small as to be absolutely imperceptible, then it is clear that a person, during such time, be unaware of his own existence, as well as of his seeing and perceiving" (448a26–30/1.711). What do we sense when we sense? We sense our own existence, we sense our being, we sense ourselves sensing, which is not the same as the infinite regress of seeing ourselves seeing ourselves seeing, *ad infinitum*. According to Daniel Heller-Roazen, "the refutation of the hypothesis of imperceptible time in the *De sensu* reveals an aspect of the Peripatetic doctrine that would not have been easily anticipated. It is clear that the newly formulated principle does not merely state, in the terms of the *De anima*, that sensation occurs in the present; it also does not simply add to that classic proposition the thesis according to which the time of perception, in its structural continuity, cannot admit of a lapse undetectable by the sensing faculties. Aristotle now says more. He indicates that the act of *aisthesis* reveals to the sensing being a thing far more fundamental than any perceptual quality, organ, or medium: the bare fact, namely, 'that he exists' (*hoti estin*)" (2007, 60). The importance of this cannot be overstated. For Aristotle, the most fundamental self-awareness, the awareness that one exists, is not intellectual; it is not a function of reason. It is rather aesthetic, sensible. Moreover, it is also clear that in order to be aware of—to perceive—our existence, we must be sensible (to and of ourselves) *here and now*, in the present. There can be no doubt that it is precisely because of this understanding of what is at stake in sensibility—namely, the sensibility of existence—that Aristotle conceives and so thoroughly delimits the temporal horizon of sense as the indivisible *now*. The awareness of the fact of our being depends on it. Perception, as Heller-Roazen puts it,

"unavoidably implies a fact of being: that the sensing animal exists" (62). And whatever exists apparently does so in the present.

11. Derrida explains: "Without reducing the abyss which may indeed separate retention from re-presentation, without hiding the fact that the problem of their relationship is none other than that of the history of 'life' and of life's becoming conscious, we should be able to say a priori that their common root—the possibility of re-petition in its most general form, that is, the constitution of a trace in the most universal sense—is a possibility which not only must inhabit the pure actuality of the now but must constitute it through the very movement of differance it introduces" (1973, 67). In *Writing and Difference*, Derrida makes the same point: "No doubt life protects itself by repetition, trace, *différance* (deferral). But we must be wary of this formulation: there is no life present *at first* which would *then* come to protect, postpone, or reserve itself in *différance*. The latter constitutes the essence of life. Or rather: as *différance* is not an essence, as it is not anything, it *is not* life, if Being is determined as *ousia*, presence, essence/existence, substance or subject. Life must be thought of as trace before Being may be determined as presence. This is the only condition on which we can say that life *is* death, that repetition and the beyond of the pleasure principle are native and congenital to that which they transgress" (1978, 203).

12. Both Henry Chadwick and William Watts translate Augustine's *distentio* by "stretch." For example: "Suppose I am about to recite a psalm which I know. Before I begin, my expectation is directed towards the whole. But when I have begun, the verses from it which I take into the past become the object of my memory. The life of this act is stretched [*distenditur*] in two ways, into my memory because of the words I have already said and into my expectation because of those I am about to say. But my attention [*attentio*] is on what is present: by that the future is transferred to become the past. As the action advances further and further, the shorter the expectation and the longer the memory, until all expectation is consumed, the entire action is finished, and it has passed into the memory." See Augustine 1991, XI.38/243. Unless otherwise noted all further page references will be to this edition and made to book and paragraph, followed by the page number. For the Latin, see Augustine 2000.

13. For two recent attempts to account for time in Borges via Heidegger's understanding of the "ecstatic stretching along" of Dasein, see Egginton 2007, 106–138; and Ziarek. Heidegger's most extensive discussion of the ecstatic unity of time as stretched out, stretching along is found in Heidegger 1988, 227–74.

14. Heidegger quotes from Augustine's *Confessions* at the precise moment in *Being and Time* in which he takes up the "genesis of the vulgar concept of time" (385/420). For Heidegger, the relevant passage is the following: "That is why I have come to think that time is simply a distention [*quam distentionem*]. But of what sort of thing is it a distention? I do not know, but it would be surprising if it is not that of the mind itself [*si non ipsius animi*]" (Augustine 1991, XI.26/240).

15. I borrow the image of the rubber band from Martin Hägglund, who, in spring 2003, when the University at Buffalo's Philosophical Reading Group was reading *Being and Time*, used this image to demonstrate the way Heidegger's conception of the Moment was extended and thus another name for presence. In *The Philosopher's Desire*, Egginton, who also participated in the reading group and who also thanks Hägglund for the metaphor, rejects it as an inappropriate characterization of the notion of "ecstatic unity": "This stretching along, however, does not merely replace one presence with another one, a point with a rubber band, as it were" (2007, 137). On the contrary, Egginton writes: "Dasein's totality, its unity, is nothing other than the inclusion in itself of its constitutive nothingness, its gaps, its death, its thrownness, its oblivion—its own impossibility as possibility. It is nothing other than the fact that there is nothing else to ground it than the not that it always also is" (137). Egginton then cites Heidegger: "Yet the time that has gaps in it does not go to pieces in this lack of togetherness, but is a mode of temporality that is always already disclosed and ecstatically *stretched along*" (Heidegger 1996a, 376/410). Importantly, however, Egginton describes the "ecstatic unity" of time as "a having been that is also and *inseparably* a now and a going-to-be" (2007, 127, emphasis added). Where are the "gaps" within an *inseparable*—hence *indivisible*—having-been, now, and a going-to-be? If the past, present, and future are inseparable, how are they to be distinguished? Are they not, in fact, simply one, hence simply present? Of the determination of time according to a logic of the passage from what has been to what will be, Hägglund writes: "[T]he movement of temporalization cannot be understood in terms of a presence that emerges from a past presence and is overtaken by a future presence. The 'past' cannot refer to what *has been* present, since any past was itself divided from its beginning. Likewise the 'future' cannot refer to what *will be* present, but designates a relentless displacement inherent in everything that happens" (2008, 17). The limitation of Egginton's interpretation of Heidegger is repeated in Krzysztof Ziarek's "The 'Fiction' of Possibility." Ziarek also homogenizes past, present, and future according to the metaphor of the stretching along of Dasein's temporality. Following a quotation from Borges's "Funes el memorioso,"

he affirms: "If we continued with this way of thinking, we would arrive at a picture of time in 'Funes' where time would be a labyrinth of the co-existence of the past and the present, with the past not so much absent from the present as present within it precisely as its past. This is why the past in 'Funes' is not really past but, rather, is woven into the present as its having-been, as one might put it paraphrasing Heidegger. The past is always in the mode of 'perfectum,' as having been extended into the present, and thus also as belonging to and existing within the present" (2009, 85).

16. It is worth pointing out that Derrida rejects this solution. "It is not a matter," Derrida writes, "of complicating the structure of time while conserving its homogeneity and its fundamental successivity, by demonstrating for example that the past present and the future present constitute originarily, by dividing it, the form of the living present" (1974, 67). If the present is divided by retention and protention, where retention and protention are conceived on the basis of the present (whether as a past-now and a future-now or as the unity of past, present, and future), then the present continues to determine time. Moreover, if the present organizes time, it necessarily precludes the possibility of what Freud calls "deferred effects." According to Derrida, the "linear, objective, and mundane model" of time takes the following form and has the following implications: "*Now* B would be as such constituted by the retention of *Now* A and the protention of *Now* C; in spite of the play that would follow from it, from the fact that each one of the three *Now-s* reproduces that structure in itself, this model of successivity would prohibit a *Now* X from taking the place of *Now* A, for example, and would prohibit that, by a delay that is inadmissible to consciousness, an experience be determined, in its very present, by a present which would not have preceded it immediately but would be considerably 'anterior' to it. It is the problem of the deferred effect (*Nachträglichkeit*) of which Freud speaks" (67). Repression—which must be thought as the return of the repressed—would be excluded. Indeed, if the past and the future are conceived as parts of the present, no memory could ever surprise us. It is not that we would see everything coming, but, in that the past and the future would be comprehended in and as the present, nothing would come. Not even ghosts.

17. *Historia de la eternidad* was first published in 1936.

18. Hägglund writes that the affirmation of survival "is not a matter of a choice that some people make and others do not: it is unconditional because everyone, *without exception*, is engaged by it. Whatever one may want or whatever one may do, one has to affirm the time of survival, since it opens the possibility to live on—and thus to want something or to do

something—in the first place" (2008, 2). On the unconditional affirmation of survival, see also Hägglund 2008, 129–31.

19. In *Specters of Marx*, Derrida suggests that the ghost "will not be thought so long as one relies on the simple (ideal, mechanical, or dialectical) opposition of the real presence of the real present or the living present to its ghostly simulacrum, the opposition of the effective or the actual . . . to the non-effective, inactual, which is also to say, as long as one relies on a general temporality or an historical temporality made up of the *successive* linking of presents identical to themselves and contemporary with themselves" (Derrida 1994, 70).

## *Chapter 2: Belief, in Translation*

1. George Steiner used this phrase as the epigraph to *After Babel.* Steiner's translation reads, "No problem is as completely concordant with literature and with the modest mystery of literature as is the problem posed by translation"; see Steiner. More recently, Sergio Waisman uses this text as an epigraph to the Introduction to *Borges and Translation: The Irreverence of the Periphery* (2005). Although Waisman claims that "[a] translation is always and quite significantly an interpretation of the text in question" (219n1), his only interpretation of this passage from Borges is his translation of it. In a sense, then, for Waisman, translation exhausts the interpretation of this brief text.

2. See Balderston 1993, Chapter 2, for a discussion of the connection between Borges's Menard and Valéry.

3. See Jenckes 2007, 107–108, for a discussion of these same pages. Jenckes writes: "In full Benjaminian fashion a few years avant la lettre, Borges argues that translation is not exempt from this 'olvido' or 'sombra' " (108).

4. The translation is from Waisman 57–8.

5. Derrida remarks that "one of the limits of theories of translation" is that "all too often they treat the passing from one language to another and do not sufficiently consider the possibility for languages to be implicated more than two in a text. How is a text written in several languages at a time to be translated? How is the effect of plurality to be 'rendered'? And what of translating with several languages at a time, will that be called translating?"; see Derrida 1985a, 171.

6. The Spanish *problema*, like the English *problem*, derives from the Greek προβλημα meaning anything projecting, a headland, a promontory; anything put before one, a fence, barrier, screen; a defense against something; but also that which is proposed, a task.

7. One would have to interrogate here the value of the "good": only a good text—a good film—is definitive, unchanging, despite its repetitions. Only the "good," then, is uncorrupted by repetition, which would include translation.

8. Borges's most detailed and intensive engagement with these philosophical texts is "Nueva refutación del tiempo" (1996, 2.135–149). The archive of Borges criticism is littered with references to Borges's interest in Hume, but for an accounting of Borges's citations of Hume and his relation to idealism more generally, see Martín 2000, 2002.

9. In what is known as the Hanover manuscript of the *Rules for the Direction of the Mind*, Descartes both posited this possibility and, in a marginal note, rejected it. "But if someone at some time has seen the primary colours, though not the secondary or mixed colours, then by means of a deduction of sorts it is possible for him to form images even of those he has not seen, in virtue of their similarity to those he has seen" (1985, 56–57). In the marginal note, however, Descartes objected: "This example is not absolutely true, but I did not have a better one for explicating what is true" (57n1). This assertion and the note that objects to it succinctly articulate the necessity and impossibility of analogy. In order to conceive of that of which we have no experience, we make an analogy that depends on similarity or likeness; yet, insofar as there is only likeness (that is, insofar as what is experienced and what is derived from that experience are nonetheless *not* the same), the analogy is both impossible and necessary. It is possible because it is impossible. On the problem of analogy, see Chapter 4, below.

10. Jenckes points out that, "even this 'casi perfecta disgregación' . . . conceals a structure of containment, which is the successive conception of time" (2007, 118). But Borges's analysis of the implications of the successive conception of time in fact follows Hume's own analysis of the metaphor of the stage. The "I" that Borges seeks to dismiss as "causal and temporal" (Jenckes 2007, 118), is merely indexical, deictic; it is not psychological.

11. "Cada momento que vivimos existe, no su imaginario conjunto" (2.140/SNF 322).

12. I borrow this phrase from Pablo Oyarzún who called writing a "posthumous act" during a session of the seminar on "Literature and Skepticism" that he held in the Department of Comparative Literature, University at Buffalo, 6–28 April 2010.

13. And if it is a "possibility," it must be accounted for philosophically as necessity. Such "degeneration," then, is necessary. Although I will not pursue this here, in Hume, this "degeneration" also names the condition of possibility of community and communication. There is no communi-

cation, hence no coming together, without the constitutive possibility of the degeneration of impressions to ideas (and the regeneration of ideas to impressions).

14. On Borges's relation to literal translation, Waisman writes: "Literal translations, for Borges, derive their value only from the contrasts in language that they present with contemporary usage. Although they might be interesting, literal translations are something of an oxymoron for Borges. As he states in 'Las dos maneras de traducir,' claims to literalness always make a liar of the translator. . . . In addition, by saying that all of the Homeric versions, except the most literal ones, are in a way faithful to the poet's intention, Borges reiterates his belief that translation is not necessarily accompanied by loss" (Waisman 56).

15. Waisman remarks—and he cites Steiner as authoritative source (1975, 275)—"Fidelity . . . is the basic underlying question in just about every theory of translation and remains a major issue in translation studies today" (42). Barbara Johnson points out that fidelity "to the text has meant faithfulness to the semantic tenor with as little interference as possible from the constraints of the vehicle. Translation, in other words, has always been the translation of *meaning*" (145).

16. Ricardo Piglia claims that for Borges classic texts occur by chance, by miracle; see Piglia 24.

17. See Balderston 2000, 163–165. While Balderston correctly notes that "Borges modifica nuestra idea de los cánones literarios," this modification cannot rest solely upon "La noción, defendida de manera tan apasionada en 'Sobre los clásicos,' de que no se trata sólo de una relectura sino de una relectura variada" (164, 165). By itself, this is a traditional conception of the literary canon, according to which the possibility of repeated but variable readings of the canonical texts depends upon the belief—the act of faith—that the canonical texts inherently warrant and sustain repeated readings. It is this conception of the canon that makes possible, authorizes, every generation's retranslation of the classics. It is this understanding of the classics that makes possible Pierre Menard's *Quijote*. In other words, although Balderston argues that "Borges se declara en contra de una noción atemporal del clásico y del canon" (164), in fact, the determination that classic texts sustain repeated (and necessarily different) interpretations and translations testifies to their presumed atemporality: the canonical texts, in this view, have purchase *in every context*. In other words, context makes no difference to them as such. The necessary challenge to the idea of the classics requires another understanding of their temporality, one that is not limited simply to the fact of their constitutive openness to recontextualization.

It is also worth noting that Pierre Menard's writing, for the first time, *Don Quijote* in large measure depended on his belief that the *Quijote*, unlike, say, the poetry of Edgar Alan Poe, was contingent, circumstantial, unnecessary. Thus he considered himself capable of premeditating its writing without falling into tautology.

18. Walter Benjamin sees things differently; he writes in "The Task of the Translator" that "[a] real translation is transparent; it does not cover the original, does not block its light, but allows the pure language . . . to shine upon the original all the more fully" (1996, 260). On Borges, Benjamin, translation, and the impossibility of one language, see Rosman. On the relation between Borges and Benjamin more generally, see Jenckes.

19. On the impossible possibility of speaking one language, see Derrida 1998; on the same issue, see Gasché 2006, 40–44; and 1985, 110–114. Augusto Ponzio remarks, "To perceive the extraneousness of one's own language as though it were a foreign language, or better to recognize it as belonging to others, as other, is to realize that we are not the owners of our own language and places the writer in the same position as translator" (172). Although this sounds convincing, Ponzio goes on to claim that "[w]hat the translator and writer have in common is the fact that neither of them use language directly, neither speak in their own name"; and he concludes, "Whoever presents himself with his own, direct word is a journalist, literary critic, expert in a given discipline, or whatever, but not a *writer*. A writer cannot say anything in his own name" (173). Ponzio's privileging of the writer as having a unique ontological status makes clear that Ponzio does not understand the necessary accidentality of the name as such. The condition of possibility of saying anything in one's own name is that the name is never simply one's own; no name names anyone any more than it names anyone else. What makes it possible for a name to name "whatever" is precisely its incapacity to name anything whatsoever.

20. Derrida explains conditional and unconditional hospitality in terms of such heterogeneity and indissociability in *Of Hospitality*: "This conflict does not oppose a law to a nature or an empirical fact. It marks the collision between two laws, at the frontier between two regimes of law, both of them non-empirical. The antinomy of hospitality irreconcilably opposes *The* law, in its universal singularity, to a plurality that is not only a dispersal (laws in the plural), but a structured multiplicity, determined by a process of division and differentiation. . . . These two regimes of law, of *the* law and the laws, are thus both contradictory, antinomic, and inseparable. They both imply and exclude each other simultaneously. They incorporate one another at the moment of excluding one another" (79–81). See Derrida and Anne Dufourmantelle.

21. Block de Behar refers to Blanchot (1959) and Steiner (1975).

22. Roberto González Echevarría also notes this etymological connection; see González Echevarría 67.

23. Block de Behar here paraphrases from Derrida 1981, 328. For an explanation of what Derrida means by "text," see Gasché 1986, 281–82.

24. Gasché writes: "But this exemplary function of the name of God also demonstrates, in an exemplary fashion, that the dream of full presence is not possible without the trace. For what is the trace but the minimal reference to an Other without which no God can come into His own, and which, on this account, always makes God differ from Himself. In this sense God is necessarily an effect of the trace, of a structure that retains the Other as Other in the full plenitude of a self-present entity" (1994b, 161). It follows that insofar as the trace inscribes the relation to the Other or to exteriority in general, it necessarily also exposes the full-plenitude of God to alterity and alteration. On the name of God, see Chapter 5, below.

25. Derrida writes: "Now it happens, I would say in effect, that this graphic difference (*a* instead of *e*), this marked difference between two apparently vocal notations, between two vowels, remains purely graphic: it is read, or it is written, but it cannot be heard. It cannot be apprehended in speech, and we will see why it also bypasses the order of apprehension in general. It is offered by a mute mark, by a tacit monument, I would even say by a pyramid, thinking not only of the form of the letter, when it is printed as a capital, but also of the text in Hegel's *Encyclopedia* in which the body of the sign is compared to the Egyptian Pyramid. The *a* of *différance*, thus, is not heard; it remains silent, secret and discreet as a tomb: *oikesis*. And thereby let us anticipate the delineation of a site, the familial residence and tomb of the proper in which is produced, by *différance*, the *economy of death*. This stone [*pierre*]—provided that one knows how to decipher its inscription—is not far from announcing the death of the tyrant" (1982, 3–4). On the economy of death and the dead time at the heart of the present, see Derrida 1974, 68–69.

26. For a more detailed discussion of the trace, see the Introduction to this volume.

27. Patricio Marchant writes that the critical error of most readers of "Pierre Menard" is "to attribute to Menard the *conclusions* to which the narrator of Borges's text arrives [*atribuir a Menard las conclusiones a las que llega el narrador del texto de Borges*]" (347).

28. In his contextual reading of "Pierre Menard" Balderston also participates in this strategy; see Balderston 1993, 18–38. So too does Gregg Lambert. Like Block de Behar, Lambert insists that "Menard's process . . . is neither translation nor copying," but he admits that Cervantes's and Menard's

*Quijotes* "*on first inspection* are exactly identical" (79, emphasis added). "*Upon first glance*," Lambert argues, "both versions appear identical; however, Menard's version highlights the importance of history as the mother of truth. In other words, in Menard's version history is identified not with what happened, but rather with what we judge to have happened. As a result of this change of emphasis, the difference between Menard's passage and that of Cervantes is profound; they don't say the same thing!" (80, emphasis added). Although he works to different ends than does Petrilli (or Balderston for that matter), Lambert nonetheless employs the same strategy: ultimately, the difference between Menard and Cervantes is contextually determined, which means that for Lambert, time is essentially historical. The fact of the two texts' strict identity, on which the narrator of "Pierre Menard" insists and which both Petrilli and Lambert acknowledge, goes virtually unnoticed in their readings insofar as both are concerned with time *qua* history, *qua* contextual determination. They do not ask what makes such repetition possible. They do not ask what makes possible the determination of contextual or historical authority, that is, what makes possible such authorization and such attribution.

## *Chapter 3: Kant's Dog*

1. In his Introduction to the English edition of Cassirer's classic study, Stephan Körner writes, "A person's form of life is his manner of dealing with the world in which he finds himself, not the sum of his mannerisms and trivial habits. There is for example, as Cassirer shows, a deep similarity between the form of life of a Kant, by whose daily habits the citizens of Königsberg were able to set their watches, and the form of life of a Rousseau, who threw away his watch so that he would 'no longer find it necessary to know what time of day it is' " (Cassirer 1981, xv–xvi; Körner cites Cassirer's *Rousseau, Kant and Goethe* [1945]). For a discussion of Kant's social habits and their relation to his philosophy, see Clark.

2. Heidegger writes: "The Schematism chapter is not 'confused,' but rather is constructed in an incomparably lucid way. The Schematism chapter is not 'confusing,' but leads with an unheard-of certainty into the core of the whole problematic of the *Critique of Pure Reason*" (1997, 80). Heidegger follows Kant's own assessment of the schematism chapter. In the notes to their translation of the *Critique of Pure Reason*, Paul Guyer and Allen Wood refer to "a late note in which Kant holds the chapter on schematism 'for one of the most important' " (Kant 1998, 728n51).

3. For a remarkably suggestive paragraph dedicated to "Funes el memorioso," see Cascardi 113.

4. Borges writes: "Hay una sentencia muy linda de San Agustín, que dice: *Non in tempore, sed cum tempore Deus creavit caela et terram* (es decir: No en el tiempo, sino con tiempo, Dios creó los cielos y la tierra)" (1996, 4.202).

5. The translation of "*todos los cristianos*" as "every man" runs the risk of displacing a subtle critique of the onto-theological tradition. Borges refers to *recordar* (to remember) as the *verbo sagrado*, which can be translated as either the sacred verb or the sacred word. Moreover, he asserts that only one man can be said to have a memory worthy of such a determination, all (other) Christians—in the translation this becomes every man—have fallible, defective memories marked by the effects of time. First, there is the subtle critique of Christian universality, to which Borges, a devotee of Jewish and Islamic cultures, would never subscribe. Second, there is the suggestion—to which we will return in later chapters—that, on the one hand, God is mortal; and, on the other hand, that God is constitutively incapable of judgment, that is, of decision and thus of knowing at all.

6. Borges interprets "Funes el memorioso" in Borges and Ferrari, 264.

7. Adolfo Bioy Casares cites a lecture Borges gave on 10 September 1949 in which Borges recounts that Goethe "confesses that he tried reading Kant but that after only a few pages of the *Critique of Pure Reason* he understood that the book, although admirable, would not help him [*no lo mejoraba*: would not improve him] and he stopped reading" (43). For an account of why it should not matter that Kant be read in any language other than German, and why Borges perhaps should only be read in Spanish, see Gracia and the Introduction to this volume.

8. On Borges's relation to German, see Rodríguez Monegal 134–36.

9. Among these texts must be counted the following which were published in *Sur*: "Una pedagogía del odio" (May 1937), "Una exposición afligente" (October 1938), "Ensayo de imparcialidad" (October 1939), "1941" (December 1941), "Anotación al 23 agosto 1944" (October 1944), and "Nota sobre la paz" (July 1945). Publications in other magazines include "Definición de germanófilo" (*El Hogar*, December 1940) and "Dos libros de este tiempo" (*La Nación*, December 1941). It is also worth considering other texts as belonging to Borges's particular concern for the politics of German culture during this period. "Yo, judío" (*Megáfono*, April 1934), for example, is Borges's affirmation—in response to a claim in *Crisol* (Crucible), an Argentine fascist publication, that Borges had "maliciously hidden" his

Jewish ancestry—of this ancestry and precisely in the name of his maternal heritage, Acevedo. His review of Louis Untermeyer's biography of Heinrich Heine, published in *El Hogar*, 5 August 1938, perhaps also should be read in this context. On this matter, see Gómez López-Quiñones.

10. In a paper delivered at the 2007 Latin American Studies Association meeting in Montreal, Quebec, Canada, Alberto Moreiras drew my attention to this paragraph, and to "Guayaquil" more generally.

11. For examples of this language see Heidegger 1992, 167; and 1993b, 29–39.

12. Borges writes: "El carácter del hombre y sus variaciones son el tema de la novela de nuestro tiempo; la lírica es la complaciente magnificación de venturas o desventuras amorosas; las filosofías de Heidegger y de Jaspers hacen de cada uno de nosotros el interesante interlocutor de un diálogo secreto y continuo con la nada o con la divinidad; estas disciplinas, que formalmente pueden ser admirables, fomentan esa ilusión del yo que el *Vedanta* reprueba como error capital. Suelen jugar a la desesperación y a la angustia, pero en el fondo halagan la vanidad; son, en tal sentido, inmorales" (2.127/OI 166).

13. All references will be to this edition. The A/B pagination indicates the first (A) and second (B) editions and correspond to the Akademie edition of Kant's works.

14. Kant came to the problem or solution of schematism rather late in the development of the first *Critique*. Its first mention is not until 1778–79. Guyer and Wood explain: "This late origin of the concept is consistent with the absence of any separation between the tasks of a transcendental deduction and of a theory of principles of judgment in the reflections of the mid-1770s . . . ; only once the two tasks had been separated would it have been necessary to invent the bridge between them, and so the final form of the 'Transcendental Analytic,' in which the 'Schematism' forms a bridge between the 'Analytic of Concepts' and 'Analytic of Principles' ('Doctrine of Judgment'), though it is formally the first chapter of the latter, does not appear to have taken shape in Kant's mind before 1778" (Kant 1998, 728n51).

15. Compare with Borges's assertion in the lecture "El tiempo": "The eternal is the world of archetypes. In the eternal, for example, there is no triangle. There is a single triangle, which is neither equalateral nor isoceles nor escalene. That triangle is the three things at once and none of them. The fact that that triangle is inconceivable is of no importance: that triangle exists [*Lo eterno es el mundo de los arquetipos. En lo eterno, por ejemplo, no hay triángulo. Hay un solo triángulo, que no es ni equilátero, ni isosceles, ni escaleno. Ese triángulo es las tres cosas a la vez y ninguna de ellas. El hecho*

*de que ese triángulo sea inconcebible no importa nada: ese triángulo existe*]" (1996, 4.204).

16. See also Locke 3.5, §4/429.

17. There is a parallel operation determinative of the train of sensations, namely, the moment of what Kant called *empirical apperception*, specifically, the moment of "attention," which enables the synthesis of sensation to be comprehended in the first place and to be comprehended as an idea. Sensations that are not synthesized as ideas—sensations, then, to which the mind does not pay attention—are, Locke claims, entirely missed: "How often may a Man observe in himself, that whilst his Mind is intently employ'd in the contemplation of some Objects; and curiously surveying some *Ideas* that are there, it takes no notice of impressions of sounding Bodies, made upon the Organ of Hearing, with the same alteration, that uses to be for the producing the *Idea* of a Sound? A sufficient impulse there may be on the organ; but it not reaching the observation of the Mind, there follows no perception: And though the motion, that uses to produce the *Idea* of Sound, be made in the Ear, yet no sound is heard. Want of Sensation in this case, is not through any defect in the Organ, or that the Man's Ears are less affected, than at other times, when he does hear: but that which uses to produce the *Idea*, though conveyed in by the usual Organ, not being taken notice of in the Understanding, and so imprinting no *Idea* on the Mind, there follows no Sensation. *So that where-ever there is Sense, or Perception, there some* Idea *is actually produced, and present in the Understanding*" (2.9, §4/144). This is the condition of possibility of experience, but it is clear that at the moment there is perception (i.e., attention, hence an *idea*), there is number *qua* the idea of unity, and thus the train of ideas has already started, already left the station.

18. In *The Life of the Mind*, in the section devoted to "Language and Metaphor," Hannah Arendt refers to Kant's understanding of transcendental schematism in drawing out the differences between civilizations in which "the written sign rather than the spoken word is decisive," such as Chinese civilization, and those in which speech is decisive, such as Western civilization. Kant's conception of transcendental schematism, she writes, "clarifies one of the basic assumptions of all Western thinking, namely that our mind's faculty to deal with invisibles is needed even for ordinary sense experience, for us to recognize a dog as dog no matter in what form the four-footed animal may present itself" (100–101). I thank Rodolphe Gasché for drawing my attention to Arendt's reference to schematism in Kant.

19. Kant explains: "Wherever our representations may arise, whether through the influence of external things or as the effect of inner causes,

whether they have originated *a priori* or empirically as appearances—as modifications of the mind they nevertheless belong to inner sense, and as such all of our cognitions are in the end subjected to the formal condition of inner sense, namely time, as that in which they must all be ordered, connected, and brought into relations. This is a general remark on which one must ground everything that follows" (228; A98–99).

20. Writing on Hegel's semiology, Derrida notes that in Kant, "the movement of the transcendental imagination is the movement of temporalization" (1982, 79).

21. According to Kant, "To be rich and original in ideas is not as necessary for the sake of beauty as is the suitability of the imagination in its freedom to the lawfulness of the understanding. For all the richness of the former produces, in its lawless freedom, nothing but nonsense; the power of judgment, however, is the faculty for bringing it [the imagination, genius] in line with the understanding" (2000, 197/5:319).

22. Kant writes: "[I]f anything must be sacrificed in the conflict of the two properties [genius and taste] in one product, it must rather be on the side of genius: and the power of judgment, which in matters of beautiful art makes its pronouncements on the basis of its own principles, will sooner permit damage to the freedom and richness of the imagination than to the understanding" (2000, 197/5:319–320).

23. See Menninghaus 1–2 and 15–31.

24. It is important to remember that what Kant calls "productive imagination" in the *Anthropology* corresponds to what he calls "reproductive imagination" in the *Critique of Pure Reason.*

25. See Derrida 1988, 48.

26. Heidegger's reading of the schema in terms of the schema-image notwithstanding; see Heidegger 1997, 65–80 and 121–136.

27. The schematism of transcendental imagination, however, fails to account for the necessary synthesis of the manifold in sensibility, which in the *Critique of Pure Reason* Kant accounts for under the heading, "synthesis of apprehension in sensibility." Kant remarks on this synthesis, which is no doubt schematic in its structure, in the *Critique of Judgment*: "The universal communicability of the sensation (of satisfaction or dissatisfaction), and indeed one that occurs without concepts, the unanimity, so far as possible, of all times and peoples about this feeling in the representation of certain objects: although weak and hardly sufficient for conjecture, this is the empirical criterion of the derivation of a taste, confirmed by examples, from the common ground, deeply buried in all human beings, of unanimity in the judging of forms under which objects are given to them" (2000, 116/5:231–232). See Japaridze, 69–71.

28. I have argued elsewhere that transcendental schematism has a necessarily empirical, thus material, support. In other words, the *marking* essential to empirical imagination is also and necessarily at work in transcendental imagination. See D. E. Johnson 2004.

29. What is in play in this remarkable passage is the relation of understanding to misunderstanding and, more generally, of reason to unreason. The fact that such misattribution—the impossibility of understanding oneself or one's intention—is owed to the imagination in its marking or designating operation means that the imagination, and specifically in its capacity to sign, always brings reason in touch with unreason. Already in Descartes' *Discourse on the Method* writing's complication of intention—and thus of knowing what one thinks—becomes legible in that Descartes confesses that the attempt to write, to put on paper, ideas that at the time of their conception seemed true, corrupts his thought and makes it appear false. It would be easy enough to show that the effects of writing already inform—and thus deform—thought in its conception. See Descartes 144–45. On the relation of reason to unreason, see Borges's 1939 essay, "Avatares de la tortuga," which takes up Zeno of Elea's paradox of motion and philosophy's multiple attempts to solve it. First, Borges allows that we should admit "lo que todos los idealistas admiten: el carácter alucinatorio del mundo. Hagamos lo que ningún idealista ha hecho: busquemos irrealidades que confirmen ese carácter. Las hallaremos, creo, en las antinomias de Kant y en la dialéctica de Zenón" (1996, 1.258/OI 114). Second, he agrees with Novalis's assertion that we have taken our phantasms as autonomous beings. Finally, he concludes, "Nosotros (la indivisa divinidad que opera en nosotros) hemos soñado el mundo. Lo hemos soñado resistente, misterioso, visible, ubicuo en el espacio y firme en el tiempo; pero hemos consentido en su arquitectura tenues y eternos intersticios de sinrazón para saber que es falso" (1.258/OI 115). Borges treads Kantian ground here. The indivisible divinity operating inside us is reason and perhaps more specifically Kant's placement of the principle of noncontradiction as the foundation of the entire Kantian edifice. Yet, although Borges grants the indivisible divinity that determines the structure, it is nonetheless a divinity marked by its own corruption: the ground is always already fissured. The principle of reason, in short, is from the very beginning marked, on the inside, in its very foundation, by madness, by *sinrazón*. This madness is the "concepto que es el corruptor y el desatinador" (1996, 1.254/OI 109) of all the other concepts. It is the concept of infinity, but this infinity is not positive infinity, which would be God, the indivisible divinity grounding the house of reason. On the contrary, this is negative infinity, the infinite regress that does not come to a halt at the bottom, the ground, of reason, but that absolutely—infinitely—finitizes

reason. Madness, then, does not attack reason from the outside; it does not befall reason as a guest or stranger foreign to reason. Madness is always already at home in the house of reason; indeed, there could be no home of and for reason without this constitutive *sinrazón*. On the principle of noncontradiction in Kant, see Hägglund 2008, 20–25. On the difference between positive and negative infinity, see Hägglund 2008, 92–94 and 166–69; and Gasché 1994, 129–49.

30. See Hägglund 2008, 22–23.

31. "Heap" and "Haufen" both derive from the Old High German *houf.*

32. For the second example, see Aristotle 1984, 1084b21/2.1714.

33. On Borges's reading of Schopenhauer, see Gingerich and Almeida.

34. On Locke and language, see Bennington. Bennington refers to Borges's "Funes" (125) in order to set up a reading of Locke on language. Although his discussion of "Funes" is rather brief, it is nonetheless quite suggestive. In *Signs of Borges* Sylvia Molloy remarks that his attempt to construct a rigorously particular language can only be "sustained by Funes's attention" and that the words of such a language "finally make sense only to him. Indeed, all that holds them together . . . is Funes himself" (118). On Molloy's account, the singularity of Funes's language, grounded as it is only in Funes himself, explains "the narrator's inability to *reproduce*" it (118). This is no doubt correct, but Molloy fails to read the maximal effect of Funes's empiricism: namely, the impossibility of any irreducible "himself" that could function as a point of reference. There is no unity of consciousness that guarantees to Funes an "I" that grounds the selfsameness of perception and cognition. This is so because temporality makes impossible the "as such" or the "in itself" of any concept, including the concept of identity. There is always only the possibility of conceptualization, which is another way to say that the concept is impossible. The concept "dog," therefore, can never be self-identical, unique or self-same. That it cannot be is an effect of temporalization or spacing.

35. "The Analytical Language of John Wilkins" was first published in *La Nación* in 1942. Beatriz Sarlo inexplicably refers to John Wilkins as an "invented character in one of Borges's fictional essays" (69). He was anything but invented.

36. For a reading of the Chinese encyclopedia as it figures at the outset of Foucault's *Les mots et les choses*, see Wicks.

37. On this problem, see Bennington 132–33.

38. See "Historia de los ecos de un nombre [A History of the Echoes of a Name" (2.128–131/SNF 405–408), in which Borges takes up the "I am that I am," concluding with Swift's mad and incessant repetition of

the phrase. See, too, Oyarzún's remarkable reading of this locution, which concludes with Borges's reading of Swift's pronunciation of his name (2009, 70–98). See Chapter 5, below, for an extended reading of Borges's concern for the name of God.

39. Derrida concludes *Speech and Phenomena* by claiming that "New names indeed will have to be used if we are to conceive as 'normal' and preprimordial what Husserl believed he could isolate as a particular and accidental experience, something dependent and secondary—that is, the indefinite drift of signs, as errance and change of scene (*Verwanderlung*), linking re-presentations (*Vergegenwärtigungen*) one to another without beginning or end. There never was any 'perception'; and 'presentation' is a representation of the representation that yearns for itself therein as for its own birth or its death" (1973, 103). On Derrida's deconstruction of perception and the living present in Husserl, see Hägglund 2008, 64–75. Hägglund writes: "What Derrida wants to demonstrate is rather that the structure of re-presentation is the condition for the identity of the self from the first inception. The subject can never be given in an autonomous presentation but is constituted by relating to itself as an other. As I will attempt to demonstrate, this conclusion necessarily follows if one thinks time as irreducible on every level of constitution. The subject is always already divided by what Derrida calls 'the movement of transcendental temporalization' (*SP*, 68/76), which does not allow anything to repose *in itself*' (65). In "Signature Event Context," Derrida calls the gesture of exclusion "typical of the philosophical tradition" and notes, "It consists in recognizing that the possibility of the negative . . . is certainly a structural possibility, that failure is an essential risk in the operations under consideration; and then, with an almost *immediately simultaneous* gesture made in the name of a kind of ideal regulation, an exclusion of this risk as an accidental, exterior one that teaches us nothing . . ." (1982, 323).

40. This is apparent in the *Critique of Pure Reason* where Kant takes up the paralogisms of pure reason. Here Kant defines transcendental apperception as the "I think," which is the "concept" that is "the vehicle of all concepts whatever, and hence also of transcendental concepts" (1998, 411; A341/B399). Accordingly, the "I think" or transcendental apperception "is thus always comprehended among" all other concepts. Nevertheless, Kant asserts, "it can have no special title, because it serves only to introduce all thinking as belonging to consciousness" (411–12; A341–2/B399–400). Now, the paralogism of pure reason concerns the dialectically sophistical assertion of the absolute unity of the subject as an objective *reality*, that is, as an object of cognition. For this to be the case, the "I think" alone,

without any admixture of empirical attributes, would have to ground a purely rational psychology. That is, we would have to be able to say something about the "I think," even if only that the "I think" exists as the unity of consciousness. We would have to be able to cognize it. But in order to cognize the "I think," it must leave a trace and thus must be limited by space and time. Kant says that this is not possible, for it would open onto an infinite regress. The "I" that is an object of cognition, is called the "soul" (Kant's quotation marks, see 412; A342/B400). But this is also problematic, for the "I" as an object of inner sense must be *apparent* to consciousness, for sensibility provides representations to the understanding via the imagination. Consciousness must be able to see itself insofar as it, the self, is an object of cognitions and is therefore necessarily determined temporally. According to Kant, consciousness can only *not* see itself in and as its unity in transcendental apperception: in seeing myself as an object of inner sense, I cannot see myself as the "I think" that accompanies all possibility of seeing myself without being seen. But if this is the case, why does schematism, which Kant will have said is hidden in the depths of the human soul, remain hidden? Indeed, in Kant's account, the imagination is a fundamental faculty of the soul, which ought to mean that the imagination is available in and to inner sense; yet we know that the imagination is never present to itself, but rather always distracted from any possible "itself." In other words, there is a double displacement at work. On the one hand, in order to speak of transcendental apperception, the "I think," one necessarily posits it as an object of cognition and thus displaces it into the horizon of inner sense, where it nonetheless cannot be found without jeopardizing the unity of consciousness. On the other hand, in order that there be the possibility of determining a self as an object of inner sense, to know something about the self, the self must nevertheless be grounded in a displacement, the constitutive displacement of the imagination that makes possible any cognition whatsoever, but which nevertheless cannot "itself" take place outside time and space. This fundamental problem also inscribes itself in the tension between, on the one hand, Kant's determination that all perception is spatially/temporally determined and, on the other hand, his occasional insistence on the possibility of *immediate* perception. For just one example, compare 512; A493/B521 (where perception is delimited as constitutively temporal) to 425; A367, where Kant writes, "We can rightly assert that only what is in ourselves can be *immediately perceived*, and that my own existence alone could be the object of a mere perception" (emphasis added). What is only in us can undoubtedly be perceived, but only via the mediation of inner sense, hence, as temporal and thus not as immediately given.

*Chapter 4: Decisions of Hospitality*

1. I thank Juli Highfill both for bringing this essay to my attention and for providing me with a copy.

2. For a lucid account of Aristotle's *Rhetoric* and particularly of the "fragility" of its taking place between sophistry ("charlatanería") and knowledge ("ciencia"), see Gasché 2010, 59–100.

3. Shaun Irlam reminded me of this passage from the *Poetics*. On two occasions, once in Salvador de Bahía, Brazil (31 May 2007), and again at the Universidad de la Habana, in Havana, Cuba (4 June 2007), in a paper devoted to metaphoricity in the Caribbean, Shaun referred to this passage. My reading of it here owes much to those occasions. For a discussion of the relation between Aristotle's *Rhetoric* and his *Poetics* and the place of metaphor in each, see Ricoeur, 9–43. For an account of Borges's engagement with Aristotle's *Poetics*, in order to investigate his relation to "theory" more generally, see Balderston 2000, 151–170. Balderston points out that Borges refers to the *Poetics* only twice: once in "La busca de Averroës" and again in "El pudor de la historia" (152).

4. George Kennedy translates this sentence as "Of the four kinds of metaphor, those by analogy are most well liked"; see Aristotle 1991.

5. Hugh Tredennick translates *homonumos* as "merely a common epithet"; see Aristotle 1933, 1003a33.

6. Cook and Tredennick translate this first sentence in the following way: "Things are equivocally named, when they have the name only in common, the definition (or statement of essence) corresponding with the name being different." See Aristotle 1938. E. M. Edghill translates the first sentence of *Categories* thusly: "Things are said to be named 'equivocally' when, though they have a common name, the definition corresponding with the name differs for each." See Aristotle 1941. The translation of *homonumos* as "equivocal" is the legacy of medieval scholasticism.

7. The phrase can also be translated as "to produce a good metaphor is to see a likeness." This alternate translation is Alan Bass's translation of Budé's French translation of the Greek original. See Derrida 1982, 237.

8. See Derrida 1974, 89 and 106–118.

9. In 1952, the same year as the publication of the second "Metaphor" essay, Borges published a series of essays on language in Argentina with José Edmundo Clemente entitled *El lenguaje de Buenos Aires* and in which Borges expresses disdain for the so called "riqueza del español," which he claims "es el otro nombre eufemístico de su muerte" (19). The symptom of this death is the proliferation of synonyms: "La sinonimia perfecta es lo que ellos [los académicos] quieren, el sermón hispánico. El máximo desfile

verbal, aunque de fantasmas o de ausentes o de difuntos. La falta de expresión nada importa: lo que importa son los arreos, galas y riquezas del español, por otro nombre el fraude. La sueñera mental y la concepción acústica del estilo son las que fomentan sinónimos: palabras que sin la incomodidad de cambiar de idea, cambian de ruido" (19–20).

10. "Irreducible analogy" is Michael Naas's phrase. In *Derrida from Now On*, in an important chapter entitled "Analogy and Anagram: Deconstruction as the Deconstruction of the as," Naas takes up Derrida's persistent targeting of what Naas calls "[t]he sovereign reign of analogy" (38). Naas argues that "For Derrida, in 'Plato's Pharmacy,' Platonism is an enormous system of hierarchically ordered oppositions sustained by the structure of *analogy*, that is, by a network of seemingly *reducible analogies*, what we might call *mere analogies*, which would seem to point back to an essential meaning that precedes, exceeds, and governs them" (43). Naas's reading of Derrida—which extends from "Plato's Pharmacy" to Derrida's "Khora" and *Rogues*—makes clear however that "Analogy as a structure of resemblance—that is, of resemblances that can never be reduced to a common *meaning*—now appears to have been made possible by an irreducible anagram that at once opens up and undercuts every *as such*, *as if*, and *as*. Anagrammaticality would thus be the condition of possibility and impossibility of all analogy" (45). Irreducible anagrammaticality thus names what Derrida calls, "the irreducibility of structure and relation, of proportionality, of analogy" (Derrida 1981, 159; qtd in Naas 45). For Naas, importantly, what he calls "irreducible analogy" is "the anagram" (61), that is, like the anagram, such irreducible analogy is marked by writing, difference, nonbeing, temporalization or *spacing*, contingency or chance. The interest of the present chapter is to read, in a rather limited way, what Naas calls "irreducible analogy" as the necessary effect of what Aristotle calls homonymy.

11. On Giorgio Agamben's reading of this same problem, see D. E. Johnson 2007.

12. I am following Rodolphe Gasché's account both of Heidegger and of Derrida's reading of him. Gasché writes: "[T]he generalized analogism that I have pointed out must serve to account for at least two things: The first is the fundamental analogism in metaphysics which, under the form of the analogy of being, secures the univocality and the proper name of Being through an idealization and a simultaneous destruction of analogy by casting metaphor against metaphor in a war of language against itself, in short through the metaphysical *Aufhebung* of analogy, metaphor, and all other rhetorical figures. . . . And the second is the irradicably analogical nature of the proper name of Being and the irreducible plurality—Nothingness—

that separates the different senses of Being and haunts Being's proper name precisely insofar as it is a proper name" (1986, 305).

13. In April 2010, at the concluding session of the University at Buffalo's Philosophical Reading Group, Andrew J. Mitchell discussed Heidegger's concept of essence and the possibility that, through a reading of the *Contributions*, Heidegger may in fact avoid the critique Derrida levies in *Of Spirit* (1989) that Heidegger cannot think contamination and thus Being remains pure, uncorrupted by the ontic metaphor. Mitchell's presentation was largely based on his essay (see Mitchell 2008). During the question and answer period following Mitchell's presentation, Paula Cucurella Lavín asked whether Mitchell's understanding of a constitutively contaminated Being—which in his reading is neither inside nor outside beings but is rather the limit of beings—permitted the possibility that beings might contaminate Being, for without this possibility Being remains *proper to itself*, thus pure. Cucurella Lavín's question points in the direction of the critique I have attempted to elaborate here, where Being ultimately is a homonym, thus unessential, accidental.

14. Entries are from the *Diccionario de la lengua española de la Real Academia Española*.

15. Emile Benveniste, *Problems in General Linguistics*, trans. Mary Elizabeth Meek (Coral Gables, FL: University of Miami Press, 1971); subsequent citations to this edition and given in the text.

16. Benveniste reconstructs the etymology of "*hospitalité*" from a chain that includes *hôte, hostis, hospes, hosti-pet-s*; *-pet-, pot-, potis, pósis, despótes*; *-pt*, whence come *-pte*, and perhaps *i-pse*. Hospitality is from the start bound up with the host and the guest, with the enemy, the stranger, and the hostage, but also with the possibility of power, with sovereignty over one's home, one's clan. It is always marked by exchange, by inclusion and exclusion.

17. For readings of hospitality in Derrida, see Gasché 2009, 334–38; Hägglund 2008, 103–106; and Naas 18–37.

18. Derrida writes: "It's *as if* the master, *qua* master, were prisoner of his place and his power, of his ipseity, of his subjectivity (his subjectivity is hostage). So it is indeed the master, the one who invites, the inviting host, who becomes the hostage—and who really always has been. And the guest, the invited hostage, becomes the one who invites, the master of the host. The guest becomes the host's host. The guest (*hôte*) becomes the host (*hôte*) of the host (*hôte*)" (2000b, 123–125).

19. Hägglund writes: "We can thus understand why Derrida says that unconditional hospitality is at once indissociable from *and* heterogeneous to conditional hospitality. On the one hand, unconditional hospitality is

*indissociable* from conditional hospitality, since it is the exposure to the visitation of others that makes it necessary to establish conditions of hospitality, to regulate who is allowed to enter. On the other hand, unconditional hospitality is *heterogeneous* to conditional hospitality, since no regulation finally can master the exposure to the visitation of others. Even the most securely guarded borders may be transgressed or compromised from within. Otherwise there would be no need for protection in the first place. In effect, all limitations of hospitality are at the same time exposed to what they seek to exclude, haunted by those who—rightly or not—question the legitimacy of the determined restrictions" (2008, 104). See Hägglund 2008, 29–30, for an analysis of Derrida's dissociation of unconditionality and sovereignty.

20. See Kant 1996, 33.

21. On the political and the friend/enemy distinction, see Schmitt. On Schmitt and the decision of the political, see Derrida 1997, 75–170.

22. On the impossible possibility of noon, see Derrida 1985b, 1–38; and Gasché 1981.

23. In a brief text that Derrida cites in *Politics of Friendship*, Pierre Aubenque remarks, "at the limit, perfect friendship destroys itself [*à la limite, l'amitié parfaite se détruit elle-même*]" (Aubenque 180).

24. On the logic of the secret, see the Afterword to this volume, but also see Derrida 2008, 119–58; 1995b, 3–31; Kronick 1–30, 157–75; and Oyarzún R. 2011.

25. Stories like "Theme of the Traitor and the Hero" and "The Garden of Forking Paths" force readers to think the possibility of what Derrida calls "The paradox without paradox" of the decision: "the responsible decision must be this impossible possibility of a 'passive' decision, a decision of the other-in-me who will not acquit me of any freedom or responsibility" (2002b, 357). What Derrida means by the passive decision, however, is not that the subject is passive before the other. On the contrary, his conception of the passive decision means that the decision is not of the order of the present in that it takes time. Martin Hägglund observes, "Even the most active and sovereign decision is passive, for the same reason that even the most immediate auto-affection is inhabited by a hetero-affection. Whoever makes a decision is passively affected by his own decision because the decision *takes time* and has effects that cannot finally be mastered by the one who makes the decision. This condition of the event is the possibility for everything good and everything bad, since without it nothing could happen" (2008, 184).

26. In *Politics of Friendship*, for example, Derrida writes, "the instant of decision must remain heterogeneous to all knowledge as such, to all theo-

retical or reportive determination, even if it may and must be preceded by all possible science and conscience. The latter are unable to determine the leap of decision without transforming it into the irresponsible application of a programme, hence without depriving it of what makes it a sovereign and free decision—in a word, of what makes it a decision, if there is one" (219). And, in *A Taste for the Secret,* he further explains, "A decision has to be prepared by reflection and knowledge, but the moment of the decision, and thus the moment of responsibility, supposes a rupture with knowledge, and therefore an opening to the incalculable—a sort of 'passive' decision. In other words, one cannot rationally distribute the part that is calculable and the part that is incalculable. One has to calculate as far as possible, but the incalculable happens: it is the other, and singularity, and chance, without one's being able to do one's part; the parting between reason and its other, the calculable and the incalculable, the necessary and the aleatory, is without example; it does not obey a logic of distinction, it is not a parting with two parts" (Derrida and Ferraris 61).

27. See Hägglund's analysis of Derrida's deconstruction of Schmitt's reliance upon the notion of indivisible sovereignty in order to anchor the decision of exception (2008, 178–184).

28. Derrida explains: "[I]f one could *count* on what is coming, hope would be but the calculation of a program. One would have the prospect but one would [no] longer wait for anything or anyone" (1994, 169).

29. Stambaugh renders this as "the silent power of the possible"; see Heidegger 1996a, 360/394. For a reading of "The Garden of Forking Paths" and the notion of the "quiet force of the possible," see Ziarek 76–77.

30. Here it would be necessary to follow closely Derrida's discussion of *dúnamis* in his remarkable essay on Louis Marin, "By Force of Mourning"; see Derrida 2001c, 142–64, perhaps especially 146–48.

## *Chapter 5: Idiocy, the Name of God*

1. In *Of Grammatology,* Derrida explains, "Only infinite being can reduce the difference in presence. In that sense, the name of God . . . is the name of indifference itself" (1974, 71). At the site in which language and being coincide without remainder, at that site and in that instant, language comes to its end in that it no longer refers; it simply is. This would be the word of words or the name of names, the unique word, the unique name. Such a word or name would not simply forget the difference between Being and beings, for example, it would obliterate that difference altogether. Forgetting would no longer be possible, but nor would remembering. There

would no longer be becoming or potency, but only absolute being or actuality, absolute presence. It is precisely this dream of a substantial word—of a word absolutely indemnified against homonymy—that, according to Derrida, haunts Heidegger's project and that surfaces as what Derrida calls "Heideggerian *hope*" (1982, 27), which manifests itself in Heidegger as the hope that language would find "a single word, the unique word" of Being (Heidegger, 1975, 52). At stake here is the difference between Heideggerian onto-theology and Derridean deconstruction, for insofar as Heidegger hopes for the possibility of finding the unique name of Being, Being remains thought as presence and as the presence of the present, as ineffable, perhaps, but only because language, which houses Being, in and through which Being speaks, has not yet found the proper word for and proper name of Being. Derrida, *contra* Heidegger, explains that " 'Older' than Being itself, such a *différance* has no name in our language. But we 'already know' that if it is unnameable, it is not provisionally so, not because our language has not yet found or received this *name*, or because we would have to seek it in another language, outside the finite system of our own. It is rather because there is no *name* for it at all, not even the name of essence or of Being, not even that of '*différance*,' which is not a name, which is not a pure nominal unity, and unceasingly dislocates itself in a chain of differing and deferring substitutions" (1982, 26).

2. Derrida writes, "The coming of the event is what cannot and should not be prevented; it is another name for the future itself. This does not mean that it is good—good in itself—for everything or anything to arrive; it is not that one should give up trying to prevent certain things from coming to pass (without which there would be no decision, no responsibility, ethics, or politics). But one should only ever oppose events that one thinks will block the future or that bring death with them: events that would put an end to the possibility of the event, to the affirmative opening to the coming of the other" (2002b, 94). Elsewhere Derrida is more succinct: "The event is another name for that which, in the thing that happens, we can neither reduce nor deny (or simply deny). It is another name for experience itself, which is always experience of the other" (Derrida and Stiegler 11).

3. The problem of the totality of the Aleph and the displacement of that totality—whether empirically or transcendentally determined—in the suggestion of a second Aleph, which suggestion is necessarily false, that is, literary or literature, opens onto the problem of the world that Sol Peláez broaches in her impeccably argued "On the World: 'My Desperation as a Writer.' "

4. On Borges's notion of the Aleph as a "space-time singularity" and especially a "naked singularity," see Merrell 145–154.

5. For a reading of Moses's stutter, see Shell 102–136. Shell writes: "God as ventriloquist needed a spokesman because He was unable to speak directly to the people. We will see that the dummy Moses, whom He called on to speak for Him, was both too much and too little like God to do the job. We will also see, though, that the most important aspect of the job seemed to require that the Hebrews' monotheistic legislator and alphabetical scribe be a stutterer" (107).

6. For an explanation of the *Al-Muqatta'at*, see Ahmed 1996.

7. In a note Scholem refers to Moses Maimonides's discussion of the difference between Moses's experience of revelation and that of all other Israelites. See Scholem, 30n1; and Maimonides 221–23. On the way Greek incorporated the semitic *alef*, see Claro 2009b, 358–64.

8. Scholem cites this letter at 30–31n3.

9. Andrés Claro organizes the different relationships to writing in "Greek" and "Hebrew" thought along the following lines: "Hay en el pensamiento hebreo de la escritura una tendencia que cuestiona los supuestos de la ontología griega, desde el instante mismo en que se levanta en defensa de la contingencia y particularidad del significante frente a la necesidad y universalidad del significado" (2009b, 357).

10. *Zohar, The Book of Enlightenment* claims that "All of Israel saw the letters/ flying through space in every direction,/ engraving themselves on the tablets of stone" (120). Since Kabbalah understands the *aleph* to be the "spiritual root of all other letters" (Scholem 30), there is no necessary disagreement on this point between Maimonides's teaching and Kabbalah. Indeed, insofar as "All of Israel" saw only the letters, what was needed was interpretation. Kabbalah rests on the principle that the words of the Torah constitute the Torah's garment and not the Torah itself. Hence, to understand—that is, to see—the Torah, one must remove the garment, lift the veil that covers its divinity; to do so requires an attention not to the words but to the letter: to know the spirit, one must go through the letter in order to go beyond it. And the letter of letters is *aleph*. In the "Foreword" to his translation and heavily edited edition of *Zohar*, Daniel C. Matt writes, "The teachings of Kabbalah are profound and powerful. One who hopes to enter and emerge in peace must be careful, persevering, and receptive. Follow the words to what lies beyond and within. Open the gates of imagination. Let Zohar *alef* the Ineffable" (xvi). See *Zohar, The Book of Enlightenment*.

11. Borges writes, "Las leyendas del golem han sido hermosamente aprovechadas por Gershom Scholem en su libro *El simbolismo de la cábala*, que acabo de leer [The legends of the golem have been beautifully appropriated by Gershom Scholem in his book *On the Kabbalah and Its Symbolism*,

which I have just read]" (1996, 3.274); he goes on to say, however, that Scholem's is one of the clearest books on the subject. Gutiérrez Berner also points out that those aspects of Kabbalah that Borges appears to valorize are those that Scholem discounts as not actually part of Kaballah (139–40).

12. On creation in Pre-Lurianic Kabbalah, see also Scholem 1941, 260–68.

13. See Derrida 2000a, 40–43.

14. Kate Jenckes writes: "The Christian tradition interprets God's statement as an affirmation of his existence: God is what he is, there is no explanation necessary, nothing that exceeds or escapes the direct predicate God = God or Yo = Yo. He is what he is, he is that which *is*" (126).

15. For a discussion of the impossibility of experiencing one's own death, see Derrida 1993.

16. All quotations from Paul's letters are from Meeks.

17. I quote from Robert Alter's translation published as *The Five Books of Moses*.

18. In fact, they succeed: Robert Alter points out that *shem* means "name" and it is from the lineage of Shem that Abraham will descend. See *The Five Books of Moses*.

19. See Derrida 1985a, 165–175. See also Alter's commentary on this chapter of Genesis in *The Five Books of Moses*.

20. This is Giorgio Agamben's definition of *kairos*, which he deploys in his reading of Paul's Letter to the Romans. Agamben follows the definition of *kairos* he finds in the *Corpus Hippocraticum*: "*chronos* is that in which there is *kairos*, and *kairos* is that in which there is little *chronos*" (2005, 68–69). He thus concludes: "*Kairos* . . . does not have another time at its disposal; in other words, what we take hold of when we seize *kairos* is not another time, but a contracted and abridged *chronos*" (69). Moreover, according to Agamben, "That messianic 'healing' happens in *kairos* is evident, but this *kairos* is nothing more than seized *chronos*" (69). It is clear, then, that *chronos* is the time that cannot seize itself, the time that remains unfulfilled in itself. As such, *chronos* must be thought as infinite succession or infinite divisibility. As infinite divisibility, as Aristotle argues, no part of *chronos is* (*Physics* 218b). This definition of *chronos* is at the heart of the determination that there cannot be any pure perception or presentation. This explains why, for Agamben, *chronos* is the time of representation. Agamben's project is to rethink the synthesis of time against what he considers the perpetual deferral of *chronos*, toward the restoration of the value of presence, which will always be for Agamben messianic presence, in and through *kairos*. "Messianic presence [*parousia*] lies beside itself, since, without ever coinciding

with a chronological instant, and without ever adding itself onto it, it seizes hold of this instant and brings it forth to fulfillment. . . . The Messiah has already arrived, the messianic event has already happened, but its presence contains within itself another time, which stretches its *parousia*, not in order to defer it, but, on the contrary, to make it graspable" (2005, 71). *Kairos* stretches *chronos*. It suspends and spans it or contracts and abridges it. This "stretching" refers obliquely to Heidegger and it imports all the problems already identified in that gesture. For a reading of Agamben that spells out in more detail the implications of his understanding of time, see D. E. Johnson 2007.

21. In the Introduction to his translation of the *Guide*, M. Friedländer rejects the idea that Maimonides converted. Taking as fundamental to his argument two statements of Maimonides, he writes: "From these two statements it may be inferred that in times of persecution Maimonides and his family did not seek to protect their lives and property by dissimulation. They submitted to the troubles of exile in order that they might remain faithful to their religion" (Maimonides xviii). Despite Maimonides's own writing on "involuntary apostasy," Friedländer claims, "A critical examination of these documents compels us to reject their evidence as inadmissible" (xviii). María Rosa Menocal, however, takes those documents seriously and concludes, "a fundamental part of Maimonides's public makeup and profile was his attack against the concept of Jewish martyrs. Many religious leaders encouraged voluntary martyrdom as preferable to conversion, but Maimonides vehemently disagreed and mounted an open defense of dissembled conversion in order for Jews to survive during times of religious persecution" (210). Furthermore, she notes Maimonides "has nearly everything in common with the Muslim who was his fellow Cordoban and fellow Aristotelian" (211), that is, Averroës. See Menocal 208–13. For his part, Leo Strauss explains, "One begins to understand the *Guide* once one sees that it is not a philosophic book—a book written by a philosopher for philosophers—but a Jewish book: a book written by a Jew for Jews. Its first premise is the old Jewish premise that being a Jew and being a philosopher are two incompatible things" (142). There is no question in Strauss of Maimonides's possible apostasy.

22. See Anidjar 11–12.

23. Translation is marked by the logic of the trace, which, Gasché explains, "is a structure of referral to Other (in general), its referrals refer to other referrals without decidable destination, the latter remaining unsaturated" (1994, 162).

24. Strauss confirms: "The necessity to refute 'corporealism' (the belief that God is corporeal) does not merely arise from the fact that corporealism

is demonstrably untrue: corporealism is dangerous because it endangers the belief shared by all Jews in God's unity" (149).

25. Writing of Saint Paul's Epistle to the Philippians, Derrida remarks: "The disciples are asked to work toward their salvation not in the presence (*parousia*) but in the absence (*apousia*) of the master" (2008, 57), and, further, "If Paul says 'adieu' and absents himself as he asks them to obey, in fact ordering them to obey . . . it is because God is absent, hidden and silent, separate, secret, at the moment he has to be obeyed" (58).

26. In "God, For Example," Gasché points to this passage and explains, "this exemplary function of the name of God also demonstrates, in an exemplary fashion, that the dream of full presence is not possible without the trace. For what is the trace but the minimal reference to an Other without which no God can come into His own, and which, on this account, always makes God differ from Himself? In this sense God is necessarily the effect of the trace" (1994, 161).

27. See Borges 1981, 235–38.

28. In *Rogues*, Derrida explains that "with absolute immunity, nothing would ever happen or arrive; we would no longer wait, await, or expect, no longer expect one another, or expect any event" (2005b, 152). Nothing would happen.

## *Afterword: The Secret of Culture*

1. Derrida writes, "It is, finally, to the extent that talking always involves two, at least two (at least in the 'at least' of this 'at least two,' the structure of which is indestructible even when it enters into the composition of vast polylogues of 2 + n voices), to the extent, then, that *there is dialogue*, there can be lie and inviolate secret" (1991, 151).

2. Gasché points out that "One of Derrida's undeniable accomplishments is to have consistently taken into account the logical and conceptual fact that a strict concept of the other implies irreducible strangeness. Another is *stricto sensu* an other only if absolutely singular and foreign. Derrida has, therefore, at all moments in dealing with an other who or which is other to and from myself, inscribed the place—be it an empty place or seat like the one reserved for Elijah at the dinner table during the seder—of an otherness beyond the other who as *my* other is always already determined from my perspective, hence made predictable and identifiable. To hold open this space for an other to come—an other singular enough to be an other and hence noncategorizable in terms of the other of myself—is an exigency of thought, a necessity demanded by the thought of the other itself" (2009, 328).

3. Nor is it a question of an unfulfillable potentiality of language to tell the secret. Kate Jenckes writes: "The 'secret sense' is something that is intrinsic to language, something that potentially can be revealed and yet is never completely revealed. It is something that always remains within the folds of language" (114). This understanding of the secret operates according to the metaphysical opposition of passivity and activity or potentiality and actuality. It stands to reason, however, that if the "secret sense" is within language then it is never simply revealed or concealed, it is neither simply potential nor simply actual.

4. It is nonetheless perplexing that, for instance, Roberto González Echevarría's *Myth and Archive*, which is devoted to the anthropological and archival origins of Latin American literature, makes no mention of "The Ethnographer," despite González Echevarría's explicit concern with the secret both *of* and *as* the archive (30–37).

5. I will not take up Mahlke's reading in what follows, but it is worth noting that she makes an explicit connection between "La biblioteca de Babel" and "El etnógrafo" when she reads the Professor's advice to Fred Murdock to go to the "reserva" as being fulfilled in his ultimate decision to work in the Yale library: "A nivel antropológico él es el habitante de la biblioteca de Babel, de un mundo que no existe fuera de los libros, y el propio narrador no-narrante. Es uno como Borges que, por azar, nos oculta la historia orientalista, del filólogo, del matemático y del historiador, para mostrar la paradoja del narrar calando en la persona de un etnógrafo que investiga sobre el terreno" (235).

6. Moraña is thus close, right next to, Doris Sommer's reading of Rigoberta Menchú. See Sommer 115–37, 308–14.

7. It should be obvious that I am not following recent discussions of mourning in the context of Latin American literature and culture. Mourning is not the effect of a failure of representation or of the perpetual retreat of the real: "Lo real está en su retirada, se manifiesta en su modo de pérdida" (Moreiras 1999, 125), as if the real were something that eluded the subject. Nor do I agree that "A mournful kind of representation admits that there is much that it cannot say, that the past cannot be recuperated fully into the present" (Jenckes 133). It is certainly the case that the past, which is no longer, cannot "be recuperated fully into the present," but this is because the present is not either. The traces of what is no longer (and what never will have been) are left for the future; they are never recovered in the present. Jenckes's description of mourning makes it seem inadequate, at a loss, but mourning, which is another name for experience, nevertheless is the condition of possibility that anything happen. It is not that there is some past that

was once present and fully in itself which was then destroyed. It never was: it will have been mourned in anticipation of its loss, because it will never have been in the first place. Finally, in *The Castrophe of Modernity*, Patrick Dove also inscribes mourning in the present: "The topos of mourning in *Trilce* is frequently accompanied by images that speak of untimeliness and disjointure. Mourning finds its proper tone in the sense that, in one way or another, things are 'out of joint.' It thus takes shape as a belated confrontation with the real, passing over an event whose moment has already come and gone, but whose traces continue to haunt the present. To mourn is to grapple with an event that has already occurred without ever taking place" (175). If the event never took place, it will be impossible to say that it occurred. If its traces haunt the present, they do so from the future, for if the traces haunted the present in the present, they would simply be present, neither no longer nor to come.

8. The long history of encounter and conversion bears this out; more recently, however, there is a remarkable (and damning) moment in Barbara Tedlock's *The Beautiful and the Dangerous* (208–209) in which she denies that anthropology has ever been about the other's secrets. It would be easy enough to demonstrate, however, that what is at stake in *The Beautiful and the Dangerous* (and by extension perhaps all of anthropology) is the desire to keep the secrets of the other thus preserving the other's alterity *for us, for anthropology*.

# Bibliography


Agamben, Giorgio. 2005. *The Time That Remains: A Commentary on the Letter to the Romans.* Trans. Patricia Dailey. Stanford: Stanford University Press.

———. 1999. *Potentialities: Collected Essays in Philosophy.* Trans. Daniel Heller-Roazen. Stanford: Stanford University Press.

Ahmed, Hasanuddin. 1996. *An Introduction to the Science of the Qur'an.* www.netnavigate.com/hasan/studyquran/ch13.html. Accessed 15 November 2005.

Almeida, Ivan. 2004. "De Borges a Schopenhauer." *Variaciones Borges* 17: 103–41.

Anidjar, Gil. 2002. *"Our Place in al-Andalus": Kabbalah, Philosophy, Literature in Arab Jewish Letters.* Stanford: Stanford University Press.

Arendt, Hannah. 1971. *The Life of the Mind.* New York: Harcourt.

Aristotle. 1991. *On Rhetoric.* Trans. George Kennedy. Oxford: Oxford University Press.

———. 1984. *The Complete Works of Aristotle: The Revised Oxford Translation.* Ed. Jonathan Barnes. Princeton: Princeton University Press.

———. 1957. *Physics.* 2 volumes. Trans. P. H. Wicksteed and F. M. Cornford. Cambridge, MA: Harvard University Press.

———. 1941. *The Basic Works of Aristotle.* Ed. Richard McKeon. New York: Random House.

———. 1938. *Categories, On Interpretation, Prior Analytics.* Trans. H. P. Cooke and Hugh Tredennick. Cambridge, MA: Harvard University Press.

———. 1933. *Metaphysics.* 2 volumes. Trans. Hugh Tredennick. Cambridge, MA: Harvard University Press.

Aubenque, Pierre. 1963. "Sur l'amitié chez Aristote." *La prudence chez Aristote.* Paris: Presses Universitaires de France. 179–83.

Augustine. 2003. *City of God.* Trans. Henry Bettenson. New York, Penguin Classics.

———. 2000. *Confessions.* 2 volumes. Trans. William Watts. Cambridge, MA: Harvard University Press.

———. 1991. *Confessions*. Trans. Henry Chadwick. Oxford: Oxford University Press.

Avelar, Idelber. 2004. *The Letter of Violence: Essays on Narrative, Ethics, and Politics*. New York: Palgrave MacMillan.

Averroës. 1954. *Tahafut al-Tahafut*. Volume 1. Trans. Simon van den Bergh. Oxford: Oxford University Press.

Balderston, Daniel. 2000. *Borges: Realidad y simulacros*. Buenos Aires: Editorial Biblos.

———. 1993. *Out of Context: Historical Reference and the Representation of Reality in Borges*. Durham, NC: Duke University Press.

Benjamin, Walter. 1996. "The Task of the Translator." *Selected Writings, Volume 1: 1913–1926*. Ed. Marcus Bullock and Michael W. Jennings. Cambridge, MA: Harvard University Press.

Bennington, Geoffrey. 1994. "The Perfect Cheat: Locke and Empiricism's Rhetoric." *Legislations*. London: Verso. 119–36.

Benveniste, Émile. 1971. *Problems in General Linguistics*. Trans. Mary Elizabeth Meek. Coral Gables, FL: University of Miami Press.

———. 1969. *Le vocabulaire des institutions indo-européennes, 1. Économie, parenté, société*. Paris: Éditions de Minuit.

Bioy Casares, Adolfo. 2006. *Borges*. Ed. Daniel Martino. Barcelona: Ediciones Destino.

Blanchot, Maurice. 2003. *The Book To Come*. Trans. Charlotte Mandell. Stanford: Stanford University Press.

———. 1959. *Le Livre à venir*. Paris: Éditions Gallimard.

Block de Behar, Lisa. 1987. *Al margen de Borges*. Mexico City: Siglo Veintiuno Editores.

Borges, Jorge Luis. 2000. *Selected Non-Fictions* [SNF]. Ed. Eliot Weinberger. New York: Penguin.

———. 2000. *Selected Poems* [SP]. Ed. Alexander Coleman. New York: Penguin.

———. 1999a. *Autobiografía*. Trans. Marcial Souto and Norman Thomas Di Giovanni. Buenos Aires: Ateneo.

———. 1999b. *Borges en* Sur*: 1931–1980*. Buenos Aires: Emecé Editores.

———. 1998. *Collected Fictions* [CF]. Trans. Andrew Hurley. New York: Penguin.

———. 1996. *Obras completas*. 4 volumes. Buenos Aires: Emecé Editores.

———. 1994. *Inquisiciones*. Barcelona: Editorial Seix Barral.

———. 1981. *Borges: A Reader*. Ed. Emir Rodgríquez Monegal and Alastair Reid. New York: Dutton.

———. 1964. *Other Inquisitions* [OI]. Trans. Ruth L. C. Simms. Austin, TX: University of Texas Press.

———. 1921. "La metáfora." *Cosmópolis* XI, number 35 (27 August): 395–402.

Borges, Jorge Luis, and José Edmundo Clemente. 1998. *El lenguaje de Buenos Aires*. Buenos Aires: Emecé Editores.

Borges, Jorge Luis, and Osvaldo Ferrari. 1998. *En diálogo I.* Buenos Aires: Editorial Sudamericana.

Brogan, Walter. 2005. *Heidegger and Aristotle: The Twofoldness of Being.* Albany, NY: SUNY Press.

Cámpora, Magdalena. 2011. "*The Providential Apotheosis of His Industry*: Display of Causal Systems in Borges." *CR: The New Centennial Review* 11.1: 125–41.

Cascardi, Anthony J. 2002. "Mimesis and Modernism: The Case of Jorge Luis Borges." In Gracia, et al. 109–27.

Cassirer, Ernst. 1981. *Kant's Life and Thought.* Trans. James Haden. New Haven: Yale University.

Cervantes, Miguel de. 1985. *Don Quijote de la Mancha.* 2 volumes. Ed. Martín de Riquer. Barcelona: Editorial Juventud.

———. 1999. *Don Quijote.* Trans. Burton Raffel. New York: Norton.

Christ, Ronald. 1974. "Borges at NYU." In *Prose for Borges.* Ed. Charles Newman and Mary Kinzie. Evanston, IL: Northwestern University Press. 396–411.

Clark, David L. 2001. "Kant's Aliens: The *Anthropology* and Its Others." *CR: The New Centennial Review* 1.2: 201–89.

Claro, Andrés. 2009a. "Broken Vessels: Philosophical Implications of Poetic Translation (*the limits, hospitality, afterlife and marranism of languages*)." *CR: The New Centennial Review* 9.3: 95–136.

———. 2009b. *La inquisición y la cábala: Un capítulo de la diferencia entre ontología y exilio.* 2 volumes. Santiago, Chile: LOM Ediciones.

Cordua, Carla. 1997. *Luces oblicuas.* Santiago, Chile: Ediciones Universidad Nacional Andrés Bello.

———. 1988. "Borges y la metafísica." *La Torre* (new series) 2.8: 629–38.

Dan, Joseph. 2006. *Kabbalah: A Very Short Introduction.* Oxford: Oxford University Press.

Dawood, N. J. 1999. "Introduction." The Koran. Trans. N. J. Dawood. New York: Penguin.

De Man, Paul. 1979. *Allegories of Reading: Figural Language in Rousseau, Nietzsche, Rilke, and Proust.* New Haven: Yale University Press.

Derrida, Jacques. 2008. *The Gift of Death (2nd Edition) and Literature in Secret*. Trans. David Wills. Chicago: University of Chicago Press.

———. 2007a. "A Certain Impossible Possibility of Saying the Event." Trans. Gila Walker. *Critical Inquiry* 33.2: 441–61.

———. 2007b. *Learning to Live Finally: The Last Interview*. Trans. Pascale-Anne Brault and Michael Naas. Hoboken, NJ: Melville House Publishing.

———. 2005a. *Paper Machine*. Trans. Rachel Bowlby. Stanford: Stanford University Press.

———. 2005b. *Rogues: Two Essays on Reason*. Trans. Pascale-Anne Brault and Michael Naas. Stanford: Stanford University Press.

———. 2002a. *Acts of Religion*. Ed. Gil Anidjar. London: Routledge.

———. 2002b. *Negotiations: Interventions and Interviews, 1971–2001*. Ed. and Trans. Elizabeth Rottenberg. Stanford: Stanford University Press.

———. 2001a. *On Cosmopolitanism and Forgiveness*. Trans. Mark Dooley and Michael Hughes. London: Routledge.

———. 2001b. *Without Alibi*. Ed. and Trans. Peggy Kamuf. Stanford: Stanford University Press.

———. 2001c. *The Work of Mourning*. Ed. Pascale-Anne Brault and Michael Naas. Chicago: University of Chicago Press.

———. 2000a. *Demeure: Fiction and Testimony*. Trans. Elizabeth Rottenberg. Stanford: Stanford University Press.

———. 2000b. *Of Hospitality*. Trans. Rachel Bowlby. Stanford: Stanford University Press.

———. 1998. *Monolingualism of the Other; Or, the Prosthesis of Origin*. Trans. Patrick Mensah. Stanford: Stanford University Press.

———. 1997. *Politics of Friendship*. Trans. George Collins. London: Verso.

———. 1995a. *Moscou aller-retour*. La Tour d'Aigues: Éditions de l'aube.

———. 1995b. "Passions: 'An Oblique Offering.'" Trans. David Wood. *On the Name*. Ed. Thomas Dutoit. Stanford: Stanford University Press. 3–31.

———. 1994. *Specters of Marx: The State of the Debt, the Work of Mourning, & the New International*. Trans. Peggy Kamuf. London: Routledge.

———. 1993. *Aporias*. Trans. Thomas Dutoit. Stanford: Stanford University Press.

———. 1991. *Given Time: I. Counterfeit Money*. Trans. Peggy Kamuf. Chicago: University of Chicago Press.

———. 1989. *Mémoires: For Paul de Man*. Revised Edition. Trans. Cecile Lindsay, Jonathan Culler, Eduardo Cadava, Peggy Kamuf. New York: Columbia University Press.

———. 1988. *Limited, Inc.* Ed. Gerald Graff. Evanston, IL: Northwestern University Press.

———. 1985a. "Des Tours de Babel." Trans. Joseph F. Graham. In Graham. 165–207.

———. 1985b. *The Ear of the Other: Otobiography, Transference, Translation.* Ed. Christie V. McDonald. New York: Schocken Books.

———. 1982. *Margins of Philosophy.* Trans. Alan Bass. Chicago: University of Chicago Press.

———. 1981. *Dissemination.* Trans. Barbara Johnson. Chicago: University of Chicago Press.

———. 1978. *Writing and Difference.* Trans. Alan Bass. Chicago: University of Chicago Press.

———. 1974. *Of Grammatology.* Trans. Gayatri Chakravorty Spivak. Baltimore, MD: The Johns Hopkins University Press.

———. 1973. *Speech and Phenomena.* Trans. David B. Allison. Evanston, IL: Northwestern University Press.

Derrida, Jacques, et al. 1985. "Roundtable on Autobiography." Trans. Peggy Kamuf. In Derrida 1985b.

Derrida, Jacques, and Maurizio Ferraris. 2001. *A Taste for the Secret.* Ed. Giacomo Donis and David Webb. London: Polity.

Derrida, Jacques, and Bernard Stiegler. 2002. *Echographies of Television.* Trans. Jennifer Bajorek. London: Polity Press.

Descartes, René. 1991. *The Philosophical Writings of Descartes: The Corresponence.* Volume 3. Trans. John Cottingham, et al. Cambridge: Cambridge University Press.

———. 1985. *The Philosophical Writings of Descartes.* Volume 1. Trans. John Cottingham, et al. Cambridge: University of Cambridge Press.

Dove, Patrick. 2004. *The Catastrophe of Modernity: Tragedy and the Nation in Latin American Literature.* Lewisburg, PA: Bucknell University Press.

Egginton, William. 2007. *The Philosopher's Desire: Psychoanalysis, Interpretation, and Truth.* Stanford: Stanford University Press.

Egginton, William, and David E. Johnson, Eds. 2009. *Thinking with Borges.* Aurora, CO: Davies Group Publishers.

*Five Books of Moses, The.* 2004. Trans. Robert Alter. New York: W. W. Norton & Co.

Gasché, Rodolphe. 2010. *Un arte muy frágil: Sobre la retórica de Aristóteles.* Trans. Rogelio González. Santiago, Chile: Metales Pesados.

———. 2009. *Europe, or the Infinite Task: A Study of a Philosophical Concept.* Stanford: Stanford University Press.

———. 2006. *Views and Interviews: On "Deconstruction" in America*. Aurora, CO: The Davies Group Publishers.

———. 1994a. "Leaps of Imagination." *The Path of Archaic Thinking: Unfolding the Work of John Sallis*. Ed. K. Maly. Albany: SUNY Press. 35–47, 280–81.

———. 1994b. *The Invention of Difference: On Jacques Derrida*. Cambridge, MA: Harvard University Press.

———. 1986. *The Tain of the Mirror: Derrida and the Philosophy of Reflection*. Cambridge, MA: Harvard University Press.

———. 1985. "The Operator of Differance." In Derrida, et al.

———. 1981. "Autobiography as *Gestalt*: Nietzsche's *Ecce Homo*." *Boundary* 2, 9.3–10.1: 271–90.

Gingerich, Stephen D. 2009. "Nothing and Everything: Theoretical and Practical Nihilism in Borges." In Egginton and Johnson. 21–40.

Gómez López-Quiñones, Antonio. 2004. *Borges y el nazismo, 1937–1945:* Sur. Granada: Servicio de Publicaciones de la Universidad de Granada.

González Echevarría, Roberto. 1990. *Myth and Archive: A Theory of Latin American Narrative*. Cambridge: Cambridge University Press.

Gracia, Jorge J. E. 2002. "Borges's 'Pierre Menard': Philosophy or Literature?" In Gracia, et al. 85–107.

Gracia, Jorge J. E., Carolyn Korsmeyer, Rodolphe Gasché, Eds. 2002. *Literary Philosophers: Borges, Calvino, Eco*. New York and London: Routledge.

Graham, Joseph F., Ed. 1985. *Difference in Translation*. Ithaca, NY: Cornell University Press.

Guthrie, W. K. C. 1981. *A History of Greek Philosophy, Vol. VI: Aristotle: An Encounter*. Cambridge: Cambridge University Press.

Gutiérrez Berner, Virginia. 2009. "Mystical Laws: Borges and Kaballah." *CR: The New Centennial Review* 9.3: 137–64.

Hägglund, Martin. 2011. "The Radical Evil of Deconstruction: A Reply to John Caputo." *Journal for Cultural and Religious Theory* 11.2: 125–50.

———. 2009. "Chronolibidinal Reading: Deconstruction and Psychoanalysis." *CR: The New Centennial Review* 9.1: 1–43.

———. 2008. *Radical Atheism: Derrida and the Time of Life*. Stanford: Stanford University Press.

Hegel, G. W. F. 1998. *Science of Logic*. Trans. A. V. Miller. Amherst, NY: Humanity Books.

Heidegger, Martin. 1997. *Kant and the Problem of Metaphysics*. 5th Edition. Trans. Richard Taft. Bloomington, IN: Indiana University Press.

———. 1996a. *Being and Time*. Trans. Joan Stambaugh. Albany, NY: SUNY Press.

———. 1996b. *Hölderlin's Hymn "Der Ister."* Trans. William McNeill and Julia Davis. Bloomington, IN: Indiana University Press.

———. 1995. *Aristotle's* Metaphysics Θ *1–3: On the Essence and Actuality of Force*. Trans. Walter Brogan and Peter Warnek. Bloomington, IN: Indiana University Press.

———. 1993a. "'Only a God Can Save Us': *Der Spiegel's* Interview with Martin Heidegger." *The Heidegger Controversy: A Critical Reader*. Ed. Richard Wolin. Cambridge, MA: MIT Press.

———. 1993b. "The Self-Assertion of the German University." *The Heidegger Controversy: A Critical Reader*. Ed. Richard Wolin. Cambridge, MA: The MIT Press.

———. 1992. *Parmenides*. Trans. André Schuwer and Richard Rojcewicz. Bloomington, IN: Indiana University Press.

———. 1988. *The Basic Problems of Phenomenology*. Revised Edition. Trans. Albert Hofstadter. Bloomington, IN: Indiana University Press.

———. 1975. *Early Greek Thinking*. Trans. David Farrell Krell and Frank A. Capuzzi. New York: Harper & Row.

Heller-Roazen, Daniel. 2007. *The Inner Touch: Archaeology of a Sensation*. New York: Zone Books.

Hobbes, Thomas. 1996. *Leviathan*. Ed. Richard Tuck. Cambridge: Cambridge University Press.

Hume, David. 1978. *A Treatise of Human Nature*. Ed. P. H. Nidditch. Oxford: Oxford University Press.

Husserl, Edmund. 1988. *Cartesian Meditations*. Trans. Dorion Cairns. Boston: Kluwer Academic Publishers.

Irby, James, Napoleón Murat, and Carlos Peralta. 1968. *Encuentro con Borges*. Buenos Aires: Editorial Galerna.

Japaridze, Tamar. 2000. *The Kantian Subject:* Sensus Communis, *Mimesis, Work of Mourning*. Albany, NY: SUNY Press.

Jenckes, Kate. 2007. *Reading Borges after Benjamin: Allegory, Afterlife, and the Writing of History*. Albany, NY: SUNY Press.

Johnson, Barbara. 1985. "Taking Fidelity Philosophically." In Graham. 142–48.

Johnson, David E. 2007. "*As If* the Time Were Now: Deconstructing Agamben." *South Atlantic Quarterly*, Special Issue: *Late Derrida* 106.2: 265–90.

———. 2004. "Marking (Out) Ethics, In Other Words: On a Single Line in Kant and Juan García Ponce." *Interdisciplinary Literary Studies* 5.1: 50–72.

Kant, Immanuel. 2006. *Anthropology from a Pragmatic Point of View*. Trans. Robert B. Louden. Cambridge: Cambridge University Press.

———. 2000. *Critique of the Power of Judgment*. Trans. Paul Guyer and Eric Matthews. Cambridge: Cambridge University Press.

———. 1998. *Critique of Pure Reason*. Trans. Paul Guyer and Allen W. Wood. Cambridge: Cambridge University Press.

———. 1996. *The Metaphysics of Morals*. Trans. Mary Gregor. Cambridge: Cambridge University Press.

Korsmeyer, Carolyn. 2002. "Literary Philosophers: Introductory Remarks." In Gracia, et al.

Kronick, Joseph G. 1999. *Derrida and the Future of Literature*. Albany, NY: SUNY Press.

Lambert, Gregg. 2002. *The Non-Philosophy of Gilles Deleuze*. New York: Continuum.

Locke, John. 1975. *An Essay Concerning Human Understanding*. Ed. Peter H. Nidditch. Oxford: Oxford University Press.

Mahlke, Kirsten. 2006. "La reserva del etnógrafo (J. L. Borges: 'El etnógrafo')." *Variaciones Borges* 22: 217–36.

Maimonides, Moses. 1956. *Guide for the Perplexed*. Trans. M. Friedländer. New York: Dover Publications.

Marchant, Patricio. 2000. *Escritura y temblor*. Ed. Pablo Oyarzún and Willy Thayer. Santiago, Chile: Editorial Cuarto Propio.

Martín, Marina. 2002. "Borges: Perplejo defensor del idealismo." *Variaciones Borges* 13: 7–21.

———. 2000. "Borges Via the Dialectics of Berkeley and Hume." *Variaciones Borges* 9: 147–62.

Meeks, Wayne A., Ed. 1972. *The Writings of St. Paul*. New York: W. W. Norton & Co.

Menninghaus, Winfried. 1999. *In Praise of Nonsense: Kant and Bluebeard*. Trans. Henry Pickford. Stanford: Stanford University Press.

Menocal, María Rosa. 2002. *The Ornament of the World: How Muslims, Jews, and Christians Created a Culture of Tolerance in Medieval Spain*. Boston: Little, Brown, and Company.

Merrell, Floyd. 1998. "J. L. Borges, C. S. Peirce y un tiro de dados: signos de nuestros tiempos." *Variaciones Borges* 5: 67–85.

———. 1991. *Unthinking Thinking: Jorge Luis Borges, Mathematics, and the New Physics*. West Lafayette, IN: Purdue University Press.

Mitchell, Andrew J. 2008. "Contamination, Essence, and Decomposition: Heidegger and Derrida." *French Interpretations of Heidegger*. Ed. David Pettigrew and Francoise Raffoul. Albany, NY: SUNY. 131–50.

Molloy, Sylvia. 1994. *Signs of Borges*. Trans. Oscar Montero. Durham, NC: Duke University Press.

Moraña, Mabel. 2003. "Borges y yo. Primera reflexión sobre 'El etnógrafo.' " *Heterotropías: Narrativas de identidad y alteridad latinoamericana*. Ed. Carlos A. Jáuregui and Juan Pablo Dabove. Pittsburgh, PA: Biblioteca de America. 263–86.

Moreiras, Alberto. 2001. *The Exhaustion of Difference: The Politics of Latin American Cultural Studies*. Durham, NC: Duke University Press.

———. 1999. *Tercer espacio: Literatura y duelo en América Latina*. Santiago, Chile: Lom Ediciones/Universidad Arcis.

Naas, Michael. 2008. *Derrida From Now On*. New York: Fordham University Press.

*New Oxford Annotated Bible, The*. 2001. New Revised Standard Version. Ed. Coogan, et al. Oxford: Oxford Univesity Press

*Noble Qur'an, The*. 1993. Trans. M. Taqi-ud-Din Al-Hilâlî and Muhammad Muhsin Khân. Riyadh, Saudi Arabia: Maktaba Dar-us-Salam.

Oyarzún R., Pablo. 2010. "Secreto y Poder." *Alcances: Revista de filosofía*, vol. 1, número 1. www.alcances.cl (accessed 10 March 2011)

———. 2009. *La letra volada: Ensayos sobre literatura*. Santiago, Chile: Ediciones Universidad Diego Portales.

Peláez, Sol. 2009. "On the World: 'My Desperation as a Writer.' " *CR: The New Centennial Review* 9.3: 165–203.

Pereira G., Francisco. 2009. *David Hume: Naturaleza, conocimiento y metafísica*. Santiago, Chile: Ediciones Universidad Alberto Hurtado.

Petrilli, Susan. 2002. "Text Metempsychosis and the Racing Tortoise: Borges and Translation." *Semiotica* 140.1: 153–67.

Piglia, Ricardo. 1997. "Los usos de Borges." *Variaciones Borges* 3: 17–27.

Ponzio, Augusto. 2002. "Reading and Translation in Borges's *Autobiographical Essay*." *Semiotica* 140: 169–79.

Ricoeur, Paul. 1977. *The Rule of Metaphor*. Trans. Robert Czerny, et al. Toronto: University of Toronto Press.

Rodríguez Monegal, Emir. 1978. *Jorge Luis Borges: A Literary Biography*. New York: Dutton.

Rosman, Silvia. 2002. "Politics of the Name: Borges's 'El Aleph.' " *Variaciones Borges* 14: 7–21.

Rosenzweig, Franz. 1955. *On Jewish Learning*. Ed. N. N. Glatzer. New York: Schocken Books.

Sarlo, Beatriz. 1993. *Jorge Luis Borges: A Writer on the Edge*. Ed. John King. London: Verso.

Shell, Marc. 2005. *Stutter*. Cambridge: Harvard University Press.

Schmitt, Carl. 1975. *The Concept of the Political*. Trans. George Schwab. Cambridge, MA: MIT Press.

Scholem, Gershom. 1965. *On the Kabbalah and Its Symbolism*. Trans. Ralph Mannheim. New York: Schocken Books.

———. 1941. *Major Trends in Jewish Mysticism*. New York: Schocken Books.

Schopenhauer, Arthur. 1969. *The World as Will and Representation*. Volume 1. Trans. E. F. J. Payne. New York: Dover Publications.

Sommer, Doris. 1999. *Proceed With Caution, When Engaged by Minority Writing in the Americas*. Cambridge: Harvard University Press.

Steiner, George. 1975. *After Babel: Aspects of Language and Translation*. Oxford: Oxford University Press.

Strauss, Leo. 1995. *Liberalism Ancient and Modern*. Chicago: University of Chicago Press.

Sussman, Henry. 2002. "The Writing of the System: Borges's Library and Calvino's Traffic." In Gracia, et al.

Tedlock, Barbara. 1992. *The Beautiful and the Dangerous: Encounters with the Zuni Indians*. New York: Viking.

Vázquez, María Esther. 1984. *Borges, sus días y su tiempo*. Buenos Aires: Javier Vergara Editor.

———. 1977. *Borges: Imágenes, memorias, diálogos*. Caracas: Monte Ávila Editores.

Waisman, Sergio. 2005. *Borges and Translation: The Irreverence of the Periphery*. Lewisburg, PA: Bucknell University Press.

Wicks, Robert. 2003. "Literary Truth as Dreamlike Expression in Foucault's and Borges's 'Chinese Encyclopedia.'" *Philosophy and Literature* 27.1: 80–97.

Zahavi, Dan. 2003. *Husserl's Phenomenology*. Stanford: Stanford University Press.

Ziarek, Krzysztof. 2009. "The 'Fiction' of Possibility." In Egginton and Johnson. 73–91.

*Zohar: The Book of Enlightenment*. 1983. Ed. and Trans. Daniel Chanan Matt. Mahway, NJ: Paulist Press.

# Index